# STRESSES IN SPECIAL EDUCATIONAL NEEDS TEACHERS

# Stresses in Special Educational Needs Teachers

*Edited by*
Graham Upton
Ved Varma

Published by
Arena
Ashgate Publishing Limited
Gower House
Croft Road
Aldershot
Hants GU11 3HR
England

Ashgate Publishing Company
Old Post Road
Brookfield
Vermont 05036
USA

**British Library Cataloguing in Publication Data**

Stresses in special educational needs teachers
  1. Special education teachers – Job stress
  I. Upton, Graham, 1944–  II. Varma, Ved P. (Ved Prakash),
  1931–
  371.9'019

**Library of Congress Catalog Card Number:** 96-85818

ISBN 1 85742 272 4

Typeset in Palatino by Raven Typesetters, Chester
Printed in Great Britain by Hartnolls Ltd, Bodmin

# Contents

**Part II   General considerations**

**Part III   Effective provision**

# Notes on contributors

**Rob Ashdown** is Headteacher of St Luke's School, Scunthorpe, which is a day special school for pupils with severe/profound and multiple learning difficulties. He is a graduate of University College, Cardiff, and received his PhD for research into teaching language skills to young children with severe learning difficulties. After completing his training as a teacher at Bristol Polytechnic, he has worked exclusively in special schools in England for pupils with severe learning difficulties, apart from two years teaching mainstreamed children with language disorders in Vancouver, British Columbia.

**Martin Brown** was a primary teacher in Inner London for twenty-five years, and has worked in a variety of positions, including two headships. He is currently involved in special educational needs support and Traveller education in an Outer London borough. He is Assistant Editor of the journal *Education for Tomorrow*.

**Elizabeth Chapman** is an Honorary Research Fellow in the School of Education at the University of Birmingham, where she formerly taught on courses on the education of visually-impaired pupils. Her international work has included the professional development of teachers through short courses, consultancy and seminars, and she has published widely in the field. She received an OBE in 1985 for services to education.

**Harry Daniels** is Professor of Special Education and Educational Psychology at the University of Birmingham. Together with Brahm Norwich, he has been involved in studies of the impact of teacher support teams in primary and secondary schools over the last four years. He is also involved with research on the processes of gender differentiation in mainstream primary school special needs practice. He has published widely on many aspects of special educational needs.

**Brian Fraser** is a Lecturer in Education at the University of Birmingham. He established a training course for teachers of the deaf at that university in 1976, after working in schools for the deaf in New Zealand and the United Kingdom and as a headteacher responsible for a local authority service for hearing-impaired children in the English Midlands.

**Neil Hall** is Consultant Psychologist at TEAM Health Care, Knowle, and Honorary Lecturer in the School of Education, the University of Birmingham. He regularly provides expert testimony on behalf of children and their families in court proceedings, and publishes and teaches on matters relating to child protection and forensic child psychology.

**David Jones** is a Senior Lecturer in Psychology at Birkbeck College, University of London. He is also a clinical psychologist. He has worked with and carried out research on children with learning disabilities over a period of thirty years. His other interests include the psychological assessment of children, and family therapy.

**Ann Locke** is a qualified teacher, a speech and language therapist and an educational psychologist. She has spent most of her professional life promoting the educational needs of children with speech and language impairments, through in-service training and the publication of teaching materials. She currently runs a postgraduate distance learning course in the area of language and communication impairments and education at the University of Sheffield.

**Derek May** is Senior Lecturer in Educational Psychology and a member of the Psychology and Special Needs Group at the University of London, Institute of Education. He is Course Leader for masters degrees in the Psychology of Education at the Institute. As well as carrying out research on teacher stress, he has recently participated in the European Youth and History research project. He also has a special interest in psychological counselling.

**Brahm Norwich** has worked as a teacher and an educational psychologist. He is currently Professor of Special Needs Education and Head of the Psychology and Special Needs Group at the Institute of Education, London University. His interests include organisational and support systems for special educational needs.

**Christopher Robertson** has had extensive experience in teaching pupils with physical disabilities but has also worked with pupils with severe learning difficulties and profound and multiple learning difficulties. He was formerly a lecturer with a specialism in the area of physical disability at the London Institute of Education, and is now Senior Lecturer in the Special Needs Research Development Centre at Canterbury Christ Church College.

**Dev Sharma** is an Educational Psychologist with the London Borough of Newham. He has wide teaching experience, which includes working with children with learning disabilities. He also has extensive experience in school psychological services and of working with children from ethnic minorities.

**Juliet Stone** is a tutor to courses for teachers of children and young people with visual impairments at the University of Birmingham. She was previously a Senior Advisory Teacher for special educational needs in Gloucestershire. She has worked extensively abroad, and is also a qualified teacher of mobility.

**Graham Upton** is Professor of Special Education and Educational Psychology at the University of Birmingham, where he is also Pro-Vice Chancellor. He has taught in ordinary and special schools, and has been involved in teacher education for over twenty years. In addition, he has conducted individual and large-scale funded research and written widely on many aspects of special education.

**Ved Varma** was formerly a teacher in London and Middlesex and an educational psychologist with the Institute of Education, University of London, the Tavistock Clinic and the London Boroughs of Richmond and Brent. He has edited or co-edited more than thirty books in education, psychology, psychiatry, psychotherapy and social work, and is an international figure in the area of special needs.

**Jean Ware** is Lecturer in the Psychology of Education and Special Educational Needs at the University of Wales, Cardiff. She has been engaged in research on the education of pupils with severe and profound learning difficulties, and in-service training for teachers working with these pupils, for the past twelve years, and has written a number of books and articles. Previously, she taught pupils with profound learning difficulties.

**Cecile Wright** is a Senior Lecturer in Sociology at the Nottingham Trent University, having previously been a Lecturer in Education at the University of Leicester. She has carried out research and written extensively in the field of race, ethnicity and education, and her book *Race Relations in the Primary School* (David Fulton, 1992) is based on an ethnographic study carried out in an inner-city primary school.

# 1 Stress in teachers of children with special needs: Past, present and future

*Derek May*

## The changing scene: A case to answer

Changes in educational legislation in England and Wales which have affected teachers of children with special educational needs have been manifold and profound during the past twenty-five years. The 1981 Education Act, the 1988 Education Reform Act and Part III of the 1993 Education Act, which reaffirms the right of as many children as possible to be educated in the mainstream school context and sets out an associated *Code of Practice on the Identification and Assessment of Special Educational Needs* (DfE, 1994), have each carried implications for change and innovation. The challenge entailed for schools in the implementation of these changes represents an intensification of developments which have origins that antedate the Warnock Report (DES, 1978) and which, in their post-Warnock phase, are extensive in their demands (Wedell, 1993, reviews these points in some detail).

Such developments have also to be viewed in a wider context of change. For Local Management of Schools (LMS), a climate of competition between schools and the operation of market forces through public presentation of league tables of results, increased parental rights and the redefinition of conditions of employment of public sector teachers in fundamental ways have all furnished additional sources of turbulence.

There thus seems to be a genuine possibility that in such a climate of change and uncertainty, special needs teachers will have paid a price by way of stress at some level of severity. Apart from new demands inherent in the legislation, a case may also be made that the process of prolonged change is, of itself, stressful. Within the research literature on stress, it has been argued that change, especially imposed change, is stressful no matter whether the events surrounding it are perceived as welcome or threatening (Holmes and Rahe, 1967; Rahe and Arthur, 1978).

1

Not all special needs staff will have been continuously exposed to all these changes, of course, since they have been spread over a period of years. The case outlined is only a prima-facie one. In recent times, however, pressures arising from change do seem to have intensified, and it is necessary to recognise that change and uncertainty are, for many people, both threatening and fearful.

This chapter will attempt to investigate the possibility that special needs teachers are subject to heightened stress by first exploring in greater detail possible effects of the legislation which make their situation potentially stressful, and then by examining some available empirical evidence.

## Goals, resources and stress

For Norwich (1992), changes in legislation have carried tensions in their wake, due to an essential incompatibility in the underlying principles of the various Acts. The market forces implication of the 1988 Education Reform Act demands that mainstream schools pursue high academic standards in an absolute sense. Simultaneously, the same Act requires these schools to fulfil an entitlement for *all* pupils, including those with Statements of Special Educational Needs, to be educated according to the National Curriculum.

The tension between these requirements, it can be reasoned, all too easily leads to conflicts over resources, time and funding among staff with differing aims and concerns. A climate of low concern with special needs easily follows from a perceived necessity to enhance school rolls and to go with the culture of the marketplace. The following example, perhaps extreme, may serve to illustrate the point. It is taken from a qualitative 'audit' of teacher stress within one secondary comprehensive school (May et al., 1991) and shows how a sense of diminished status, low influence, stress and demoralisation may be subjective consequences for special needs staff.

The school (Earlsbridge) had been subject to considerable pressure to maintain its pupil numbers under open enrolment in the face of competition from a rival school which had a reputation for achieving superior GCSE examination results. Within the previous year, a new headteacher had been appointed, and with the aid of the senior management team, was imposing changes in the style and public presentation of the school with some sense of urgency. The possibility of grant-maintained status was being mooted with staff.

In an extended interview, the head of special needs rated 'going public' in expressing opinions about grant-maintained status in front of colleagues and her experience of an in-depth school inspection as only low stressors compared with the stress of 'feeling manipulated' by the senior management team and the 'new broom' activities of the head. She complained that promises of consultation over the restructuring of her department had failed to materialise, and expressed feelings of 'frustration, low self-esteem, manipulation and being undervalued'.

She further complained that she had discovered that money intended for the benefit of pupils with Statements had been diverted for more general use, and that '*my* department is being dismantled by the senior management team'. The intense texture of the resentment she felt was evident in the tone of her responses throughout the interview, as she talked of 'feeling betrayed, jiggery-pokery, unfairness, frustration at how to secure these pupils' rights'. Other stresses were also described, arising from having to 'cultivate non-specialist staff to secure their co-operation in applying the Curriculum appropriately...'.

Understandably, the headteacher and senior management team held a different view. They saw priorities for allocation of resources in terms of market forces and school survival. The salient feature of the contrast of perspectives revealed by interviews in the audit, however, lay not so much in any simple lack of acknowledgement by the head and senior management of the issues involved for special needs so much as in an apparent failure to appreciate the texture of feelings and the sense of personal affront engendered in special needs staff. The stress experienced by the headteacher and senior management team at Earlsbridge was of a different quality. Work overload was much in evidence in their lives, but the texture of stress they reported was of a more self-actualising kind. They felt in control of their situation, and experienced more what has been termed *eustress* ('the pleasant stress of fulfilment ... without the harmful consequences of damaging stress, that is, distress' – Selye, 1974, 1991).

A single case example can but offer illustration. It would be unfair to suggest that all schools are like the instance described, and it must be recognised that, by now, many mainstream schools have begun to adapt and settle down under LMS. The extent to which further examples comparable to our illustration currently exist is an empirical issue, and as we shall see, poses a question not adequately answerable from currently available research. Further survey and monitoring is much needed, but our example can serve to sensitise us to possibilities.

What is certain, however, is that legislation on Local Management of Schools has led school governors to pay close attention to school budgets. In many schools, balancing the budget in times of budgetary exigency has meant reductions in staffing. Special needs staffing has not been exempt.

# Staffing resources and stress

As early as 1991, a study of 81 local education authorities (LEAs) carried out by the National Foundation for Educational Research revealed that 15 per cent of them reported that schools in their area had made cuts in special needs co-ordinator posts and learning support provision (Fletcher-Campbell and Hall, 1993). It remains to be seen how far the requirement from 1994 for schools to identify in their budgets their use of delegated special needs funding will improve staffing and other resources. Likewise, we wait to see how far the requirements, from 1995, to have in place special needs policies which have regard to the Code of Practice, including a member of staff nominated as special needs co-ordinator (SENCO), will effectively serve to redress the position.

It cannot safely be assumed that the situation will necessarily improve. Concern that identified delegated special needs funds in school budgets will prove insufficient for necessary staffing and other resources to be achieved has already begun to be expressed. This concern derives from attempts to assess the overall cost to a school of implementation of the Code of Practice. In particular, there are anxieties about the workload likely to fall on special needs co-ordinators at stages 1 and 2 of the Code (Johnson, 1995).

Unmanageable workloads will prove stressful for special needs co-ordinators and will defeat the effectiveness of the Code of Practice. It is therefore not surprising to learn that the Department for Education and Employment (DfEE) has recently commissioned research into pressures on the role of the special needs co-ordinator.

Contiguous with staffing reductions in their own ranks and diminished LEA support services, teachers with special needs expertise in mainstream schools have in many instances faced an increased demand to provide specialist support for colleagues unused to teaching growing numbers of pupils with special educational needs as integration has progressed. UK government statistics indicate that by January 1995, some 57 per cent of children with Statements of Special Educational Needs are now accommodated within mainstream provision.

A corollary of this may well be a change in the population of special schools in the direction of greater concentration of pupils with severe or complex needs. Monitoring the levels of stress in both mainstream and special schools which may potentially result is again a matter of urgent empirical enquiry, as precise research evidence is not currently readily available.

Problems of resourcing for special needs provision and attendant potential stress risks are not limited to mainstream schools. Within further education (FE), Corbett and Barton (1993) investigated the fears and expectations of special needs co-ordinators. They described the struggles of co-ordinators in that context to reconceptualise their definitions of special needs within a low-priority climate.

Interestingly, Corbett and Barton traced the tensions experienced by FE co-ordinators to 'the culture of their previous professional identity' as teachers in special schools, which still informed their definitions of appropriate provision. There is little reason to suppose it will be different for special needs staff who have moved into mainstream schools from special schools, and it is doubtful whether previous expectations about appropriate provision will command a sympathetic hearing in the context of hard-pressed school budgets.

## Stress, discourse and the process of defining special educational needs

Dyson (1993) has argued that the role of the special needs co-ordinator is full of tensions and contradictions, as occupants of these posts find themselves unclear about the boundaries of their responsibilities, what they should expect from colleagues, and their distinctive contribution to the school as a whole. He offers a helpful analysis of the origins of this perceived role ambiguity.

Dyson describes special needs practice and provision in mainstream schools as caught between two patterns of discourse which are fundamentally at odds. The first is predicated upon a discourse of *specialness* – a discourse which divides needs into the special and the ordinary, and which seeks to meet special needs through special provision and teaching. The second entails a discourse of *commonality* which emphasises 'what it is that all children – and by implication the techniques of teaching all children – have in common'.

Transposing role ambiguity into discourse deserves serious attention, for discourse is not just about how people talk about special needs and consciously conceptualise them; it takes us also to the realm of 'common knowledge' (Edwards and Mercer, 1987). Through discourse and communication, participants come to develop 'shared' understandings which are not necessarily conscious agreements so much as assumptions and tacit meanings. Ground rules which are sensitive to particular contexts and issues develop and serve to legitimise participants' perceptions as normal, as well as proscribing alternative expectations.

When the tacit meanings and ground rules are unclear, or at least not agreed, social interaction itself is likely to become stressful. From a social psychological perspective, Potter and Wetherell (1987) have shown how attitudes are embedded within discourse, and Billig (1988, 1996) demonstrates how attitudes, discourse and context interrelate when arguments and rhetoric rear themselves up over controversial issues. Financial exigencies and resource allocation in schools are invariably controversial and often involve participants taking up contrary attitudes. If the ground rules for the discussion of issues are not rooted in common knowledge and discourse, then here is a seed bed for stressful modes of interpersonal relationship as well as enduring conflict and failure of negotiated resolution.

Carefully conducted studies from within a framework of discourse analysis could prove a fruitful way forward for exploring stress in special needs teachers, especially those working in mainstream contexts. It could well provide an alternative to quantitative studies, and would present a level of sophistication beyond the present simple interview and qualitative data which is available. Unfortunately, it is at the moment virgin soil, as yet untilled.

## Empirical research in the UK: Burnout?

Although much teacher stress research has been carried out since the late 1970s, British studies of stress in teachers of children with special educational needs occupy no prominent status in the general teacher stress literature. Available empirical evidence remains disappointingly sparse and fragmentary. Published studies have mostly been small-scale and reliant on simple scales and checklists. Some interesting qualitative material does exist but is mostly illustrative in kind, and criteria of 'usefulness beyond the parochial example' (Youngman, 1995) are rarely met.

These studies which have been carried out are spread over a considerable time span, but there has been little or no longitudinal investigation or systematic use of normative measures which might enable the impact of legislative change during this time to be monitored or assessed from a systematic baseline. Few studies have linked directly to the impact of legislative change at all.

A study which did seek to address this impact was that carried out by Abbotts et al. in 1991. They used questionnaires and supporting interviews to try to establish the extent to which headteachers perceived themselves and their teacher colleagues as experiencing a significant increase in stress as a consequence of being required to deliver the National Curriculum to their pupils. The schools compared included those for pupils with emotional and behavioural difficulties (EBD), severe learning difficulties (SLD) and moderate learning difficulties (MLD).

Most headteachers reported that they and their staff were experiencing greatly or moderately increased stress, and more EBD schools than other types of school reported greatly increased stress. Increased workload (paper-work and monitoring of pupils), inadequate facilities and personal resources/expertise, time pressures and pupil factors (anxiety, motivation, attitudes) were perceived as underlying causes.

A much earlier study which revealed signs of the initial impact of change on special needs teachers is that carried out by Dunham (1983). He investigated stress within a sample of 220 teachers and care staff working with children with special educational needs in day schools, children's homes, residential EBD settings and secondary schools. Within this rather heterogeneous sample, the most frequently reported signs of stress were feelings of exhaustion (55 per cent of sample), frustration (55 per cent), sleep disturbances (45 per cent), withdrawal from contact with other staff (40 per cent) and tension headaches (35 per cent).

Dunham's findings led him to conceptualise stress in his study as arousal and 'burnout'. He characterised burnout in terms of impairment of teacher performance. Performance was seen to decline from an optimal level as burnout progressed in the face of increasing job demands; anxiety, over-reacting, agitation, poor concentration and faulty decisions, not to mention panic and fatigue, seemed to Dunham to be markers along the way (Dunham, 1983, 1984).

'Burnout' has a ring of such severity that it is not a term to be used lightly or casually. Baron (1986), for example, defines it as an 'erosion of the human spirit' resulting from prolonged, chronic exposure to high levels of occupational stress. It is thus differentiated from stress by its long-term rather than episodic quality, and there is a suggestion of almost clinical severity, such that the sufferer will not recover without help. Similarly, Cunningham (1983), in a review of the teacher burnout studies up to that time, defined teacher burnout as 'the syndrome resulting from prolonged teacher stress, primarily characterised by physical, emotional and attitudinal exhaustion'.

Pines (1993), in a detailed theoretical review of the nature of burnout, observes that 'individuals who enter a profession with a cynical attitude are unlikely to experience burnout: but those with strong desire to give of themselves and who feel helpful, excited and idealistic are susceptible to the most severe burnout.' For Pines, burnout is related to motivation in a way that usual job stress, and even alienation and depression more generally, are not.

It must be questioned whether 'burnout' is a term justifiably applied to teachers of children with special educational needs. Claims about burnout seem altogether too extreme for a number of reasons.

First, in Dunham's study itself, a proportion of teachers made no claim to stressful experience at all. Second, his claims for burnout have to be set against Lawrenson and McKinnon's (1982) finding in a study of 33 teachers of emotionally disturbed children, that being aware of the stressful nature of the job in itself is protective in helping prevent burnout. Surely, special needs teachers, especially those working in the EBD setting, do have such an awareness.

Again, Pont and Reid (1985) presented data on 21 teachers and 24 social workers in four Scottish residential schools for behaviour-disordered children, and found that while some staff in the residential EBD setting showed signs of heightened anxiety and reported the occurrence of almost twice as many potential stressful events as a comparison group of 20 non-special needs staff in a comprehensive school, neither they nor their secondary school counterparts rated their work as extremely, or even very, stressful.

Claims about burnout may also be judged too extreme for another reason. They may simply offer too global a label by which to describe stress in special needs teachers. The Maslach Burnout Inventory (Maslach and Jackson, 1986) interprets burnout in terms of three discrete, not necessarily correlated, normative subscales: sense of depersonalisation (an unfeeling and impersonal response towards recipients of one's care), feelings of emotional exhaustion, and low sense of personal accomplishment. Global references to burnout are not precise enough to be helpful, and at worst, can be misleading.

# Emotional exhaustion in special needs teachers

Male and May (1995) employed the Education form of the Maslach Burnout Inventory (albeit with American standardisation) in a preliminary attempt to monitor stress in special needs teachers. Data was obtained from 57 SLD teachers and 82 mainstream special needs teachers. Schools were selected so as to reflect local education authority variations in size and response to changes in UK legislation.

For SLD teachers, there was evidence of emotional exhaustion at 'high' levels relative to the norms for the scale, and some (less pronounced) evidence for low sense of personal accomplishment. The data furnished no evidence of heightened feelings of depersonalisation. For the mainstream special needs teachers, emotional exhaustion and sense of personal accomplishment were at moderate levels, again with no suggestion of feelings of depersonalisation.

In a parallel study, Cohen (1995) obtained data from 78 teachers working in schools for emotionally disturbed children (42 in EBD day schools, 20 in EBD boarding schools and 16 in EBD combined day/boarding). Moderate to high levels of emotional exhaustion were evident, which were highest among teachers working in combined day/boarding schools. There were only low to middle levels of depersonalisation and medium levels of sense of low personal accomplishment in the sample, though in the latter case, feelings were of high intensity for some individuals in the day and combined day/boarding schools.

The Male and May and the Cohen studies provide some support for feelings of emotional exhaustion being present in special needs teachers; both studies provide evidence of a differentiated pattern of results according to the Maslach subscales and according to type of work context; neither study justifies any exaggerated, global claim about burnout as the fate of special needs staff. Accusations of 'crying wolf' may be risked by those who make such a claim.

Findings about emotional exhaustion from the Male and May and the Cohen data do fit in with Dunham's early study (1981), in that he observed that while teachers and carers valued team support, they appeared to be too exhausted to benefit from after-school discussion groups organised for support. This requires to be set alongside the findings of Trendall's (1989) report that teachers in special schools find it difficult to forget the children's problems at the end of the day, and express a need for access to others to whom they can express their feelings.

There are implications here which reinforce current trends towards developing teacher support groups. However, the findings also suggest issues about the nature and scheduling of the support required, and about the skills needed for facilitating such support.

# Stress and health

Sometimes, reference to 'burnout' carries an implied suggestion about ill health of a more organic physical nature which might be attendant upon prolonged stress. In Trendall's (1989) study, teachers in the 30–39 age group appeared vulnerable to health stress, especially males. The findings for this subgroup in the sample agree with Chakraverty's fears that teachers in special schools and remedial classes may be particularly prone to stress-related illnesses (Chakraverty, 1989). However, in their studies, Male and May (1995) and Cohen (1995) used a stress and health scale, but could find no evidence to corroborate marked vulnerability to illness.

It is perhaps important to keep in mind Kyriacou's cautionary comment (Kyriacou, 1989) that while there is evidence that stress at work appears to be implicated in the ill health of many teachers, the relationship between occupational stress and subsequent ill health is not a simple one. Thus, for example, school holidays may intervene to enable teachers to recover physically and mentally, thereby mitigating ill health (or indeed burnout) in a way that is not open to most professions.

# Intensity of feelings at a given moment

Rebuttal of extreme claims about ill health and burnout should not be confused with questions about whether special needs teachers experience moments, or even particular days, of what may be intense stress. In Male and May's (1995) study, teachers were asked to respond to an open-ended question inviting them to describe their feelings when they do judge themselves to be experiencing stress. The qualitative data obtained was of a texture and intensity more severe than that suggested as the enduring level by the Maslach quantitative data.

Two assessors not connected with the research were independently given the task of rating individual responses by sorting them into four piles according to perceived severity of stress. They were then asked to describe the criteria which seemed to them to differentiate the piles.

One rater described a sense of panic along with physical and mental symptoms, including sleep disturbance, which characterised the two most severe piles. The other assessor characterised her two most severe piles in terms of respondents being 'almost out of control/over the edge, serious physical or emotional symptoms, sometimes close to or actual panic, a feeling of not being able to cope or function any longer'. She was also aware of feelings of anger and anxiety expressed by teachers. A similar procedure was followed in Cohen's (1995) study, which again produced evidence of powerful feelings.

The following examples, which avoid the most dramatic statements, illustrate the texture of some of the data in the two most severe categories:

I feel not on top of everything, not sleeping – things keep churning over in my mind; as if anything else comes my way I'll explode! Ratty with my own children in the evenings; depressed, withdrawn – not wishing to discuss, inadequate. (SENCO, age 33, 11 years in post)

... angry, despondent, difficult to concentrate, shallow breathing, near to tears. Sudden unexpected pains in my chest, like a metal band squeezing my ribs. (SLD, age 34, four years in post)

... a huge effort, wanting to cry all the time, frightened to go to work. (SLD, age 27, one year in post)

... Close to tears, pins and needles in my face walking up and down, not really knowing what to do. (SLD, age 44, eight years in post)

... depressed, low self esteem, incredibly tired, reluctance to socialise, quiet and withdrawn. (EBD, day school, age 48, 8 years in post).

It would be incorrect to characterise these descriptions as being of clinical severity unless they were persistent and not retrievable by ordinary means of coping. Nevertheless, they do represent powerful, passing feelings in the individuals concerned, and it should be noted that approximately 40 per cent of teachers' responses in each study were judged by the assessors as being of such severity. It is questionable whether it is acceptable for professional teachers to be subject to such intense feelings in their work.

# Workload and sources of stress

Earlier in this chapter, reference was made to concerns about workload in special needs teachers. Male and May (1995), and Cohen (1995) also sought to address this. Teachers of children with special educational needs in the mainstream setting reported a mean of 46.3 hours worked in a typical week, while the corresponding figure for teachers in SLD schools was 50.9 hours. In all three EBD settings, mean working hours of around 50 hours per week were reported, with staff in residential schools highest at 54.85 hours per week. (The working week is defined as the total number of hours spent on work-related activities, both at home and at school, during a period of seven days. Personal leisure time, family time and breaks during the school day when the teacher is not involved in school related activity are excluded.)

There were considerable differences between individual teachers within each group, and it is worth noting that in all groups approximately 1 in 5 teachers reported working in excess of 60 hours. The results must be accepted with caution, since the estimates are obtained only from self-report questionnaires, not validated by direct activity sampling or even occupational work diary checks. Nevertheless, they offer pointers about stress and workload.

Workloads are higher than those reported on a similar basis in a recent study of 570 mainstream teachers in Scotland carried out by Johnstone (1993). She found that at a correspondingly early stage of the school year, the mean number of hours worked was 42.5, and she similarly identified a proportion of teachers working over 60 hours per week. These totals are also higher than other studies conducted through the teachers' unions have indicated (AMMA, 1991; Travers, 1992).

The studies reported here included a scale intended to give an additional indication of the extent to which *perceived* work overload constitutes a source of stress. Ratings obtained from the special needs teachers working in the mainstream setting and those from the SLD setting were again similar, and both fell in the 'high' category of the scale. Cohen (1995) found similarly high perceived work overload ratings in her EBD sample.

A further open-ended question used in these studies invited teachers to identify the most intense sources of stress in their jobs. Work overload was the most frequently cited stressor, in particular, demands for completion of paperwork, including documentation relating to the National Curriculum, report writing, annual reviews and the implementation of the Code of Practice, as well as preparation of Individual Education Programmes (IEPs). Pressure for paperwork completion was evident for both SLD and mainstream special educational needs teachers, but was significantly more pronounced for the latter group, with over half the mainstream sample reporting this as a source of stress. There was evidence of similar pressure in about one-third of the EBD teachers.

Among EBD teachers, the main source of stress reported, however, was the challenging, sometimes violent or even dangerous behaviour of pupils, with two-thirds of the sample citing this. This finding is in agreement with Dunham's report about an EBD school twenty-five years ago (Dunham, 1981). There, the stressors indicated by staff lay chiefly in irrational behaviour of pupils and in teachers' feelings of being personally, rather than professionally, the target of pupil anger or malice. In Cohen's data, one-fifth of the teachers cited stress arising from difficulties in the implementation of the National Curriculum with their pupils, but the second most frequently cited stressor after pupils' challenging behaviour referred to the politics of management in the schools (e.g. headteachers implementing changes without consultation or discussion).

The emergent picture described in the foregoing paragraphs is not too different from that obtained by Trendall (1989). In her study, too, workload and lack of time featured among the most salient sources of stress, but she also found that large classes, too much teaching and pupil misbehaviour were cited as sources of stress. A sense of work overload, characterised by high peaks and troughs for teachers in special schools, was linked with changes in education policy. Surprisingly, though, none of this meant that any overwhelming proportion of teachers in the study expressed dissatisfaction with their jobs.

Trendall's study sought to make direct comparisons of stress in teaching across mainstream and special education. Her sample of 237 teachers, 70 of whom took part in more detailed follow-ups, was drawn from primary, secondary and special schools within one LEA. Results showed that while primary and secondary teachers did not differ greatly in the extent to which they felt stressed at school, there were overall differences between mainstream and special school teachers. Special school teachers reported feeling significantly less stressed by their school situation than their mainstream counterparts, though both found teaching to be a stressful occupation. Kyriacou (1987), on the other hand, identified almost twice as many potential stressors for staff in special schools compared with mainstream schools, but reported that the mean stress rating did not vary.

# Comparisons with North American research

Research on teachers in special education in the USA since 1980 is more extensive than in the UK. A major review of this is beyond the scope of this chapter, and only certain themes can be outlined. Although caution needs to be exercised due to the different cultural and educational contexts involved, instructive comparisons can be made between research in the two countries.

Some similarities in levels of stress reported among special needs teachers in the UK and USA are evident. As in Britain, research in America reveals special needs teachers to have been subject to stress at moderate to high levels which fall short of burnout. Thus Presley (1982) reported that 91 per cent of special needs educators in his study were not experiencing burnout, but also estimated that between 30 and 50 per cent might be approaching it, while Beasley et al. (1983), Klas (1984) and Fimian and Blanton (1986) reported moderate stress levels in special education teachers.

Bradfield and Phones (1985) found that 85 per cent of special education teachers in their sample experienced moderate to high stress as a result of their jobs, but also noted that for some staff, job-related stress was compounded by stress arising from broader life events. The latter finding is in some disagreement with what Trendall (1989) discovered in the UK, where stressful life events in the wider life space of individual teachers seemed not to be correlated with stress experienced at school. This appears to be an important area for future research, including investigations to determine the risk, if it exists, that stress generated in the school context may fuel stress in the home setting.

Using the Maslach Burnout Inventory, Crane and Iwanicki (1986) reported moderate levels of emotional exhaustion and depersonalisation in special needs teachers, and discovered these to be associated with role conflict and role ambiguity. Earlier research by these authors had demonstrated low sense of personal accomplishment in special needs teachers to be associated with role ambiguity, but not role conflict.

The American research tends to place greater reliance on standardised scales, such as the Maslach and other useful alternative scales, than does research in the UK. One alternative scale which might profitably be considered for future UK use, with appropriate re-pilot preparation, is known as the Teacher Stress Inventory (TSI), standardised and well validated by Fimian (see Fimian, 1986; Fimian and Blanton, 1986). This scale is intended to monitor more immediate outcomes than burnout, and has subscales to investigate present personal and professional stressors, sense of personal distress, motivation, time management and emotional/physiological fatigue in special needs teachers.

Interestingly, as early as 1982, use of this inventory suggested that while special education teachers did not differ from their mainstream counterparts in their perceptions of frequency of stressful events in school, they did suffer greater professional distress (Cherkes and Fimian, 1982). This result is somewhat in the reverse direction to Kyriacou's (1987) UK finding, and is also not in agreement with Trendall (1989), who found special needs teachers to be less stressed by their school situation than their mainstream colleagues.

These differences perhaps suggest that it is the context rather than the inherent nature of special needs teaching itself which engenders stress in special needs teachers. This would also account for the variation which has been noted in findings comparing special needs and mainstream teachers in different places in the USA, with some researchers reporting higher levels of stress in special needs teachers, others reporting the reverse, while some report no differences (Billingsley and Cross, 1992). Differences in measurement instruments and investigative methods may be an alternative explanation for the variation in results, of course.

American research on special needs teachers often has a more applied tone about it than research in the UK. Thus, for example, Style et al. (1987), in a study of stress in early childhood special educators, focused on their perceptions of 25 characteristics of the environment and working conditions. Results indicated that highest stress levels were associated with problems of salaries and benefits, time management, having to face multiple job responsibilities, negative attitudes towards required teaching programmes, support available from outside agencies and family support.

Similarly, in a study carried out by Pullis (1992), a survey of 244 teachers of behaviourally disturbed students revealed (perhaps surprisingly, given the potentially demanding teaching involved) that factors to do with the school as a workplace, career concerns and workload variables came before direct contact with the students in teachers' perceptions of sources of stress. Exhaustion, frustration and negative carry-over to life outside the classroom were frequently described.

In part, the applied tone of the American research reflects worries in the USA about attrition from the teaching profession. Thus, Billingsley and Cross (1992), noting that a declared intention to leave the profession within five years had been found among 34 per cent of teachers, sought to identify predictors of commitment and job satisfaction as prognostic of intention to stay in the profession. Their study was based on some 1,100 teachers.

Level of stress was one among other closely job-related variables, such as supervisory/leadership support received from senior staff, work involvement, role conflict and role ambiguity, which were found to be more effective predictors of job satisfaction and commitment than were demographic indicators such as age, gender or ethnicity.

The investigators drew attention to possibilities for reducing attrition rates, since job-related rather than demographic variables are more alterable and within the immediate power of education agencies to change. Except in matters of job description and teacher appraisal, changes which have taken place in teachers' conditions of service in the UK have arisen more as outcomes of legislative demand or simple appraisal, rather than as outcomes of positive possibilities offered by an informed occupational psychology. This is true even of the increased emphasis on in-service training. Systematic consideration given to work study, job analysis and conditions for optimal professional performance appears to be less part of the UK's education culture than in the USA, as does the belief that employment conditions for staff can be improved through this.

Billingsley and Cross note that within the school, principals (headteachers) can adopt deliberate strategies to increase feedback, encouragement and acknowledgement. They can use consultation and participatory decision-making, as well as clarifying staff roles. All these strategies for supervisory support will in themselves have consequences for stress reduction, thereby increasing job satisfaction and job commitment.

However, Cherniss (1988), in a smaller-scale SLD study, found a supportive but more directive work problem approach by the principal to be effective in reducing teacher stress. It may be the case that the consultation and participatory decisionmaking suggested by Billingsley and Cross needs to be tempered with the creation of an unambiguous, well-ordered, task-focused climate in school. This is consistent with the findings about role ambiguity and stress referred to earlier.

Fimian (1986) demonstrated lower stress levels in special education teachers who received supervisory support compared with those who did not. In addition, he found peer support from colleagues to be important in promoting low levels of stress. Further studies have found conflicts with other staff members and lack of support from colleagues to relate to high stress and losses from the teaching profession.

The type of support most helpful to teachers of children with special educational needs, and how it can best be managed, is undoubtedly an area which will repay further research, both in the USA and, as earlier noted, in the UK.

There are numerous sources of stress for special needs teachers in the USA which have been identified in the American literature. Some will be rather familiar to British readers. Among the main sources of stress identified are the following: administration and paperwork, discipline, contacts with parents (Faas, 1984; Klas, 1984; Karr and Landerholm, 1991), working with other teachers (Hudson and Meagher, 1983; Klas, 1984) and last week of school, disruptive pupils and overcrowded classrooms (Welch, 1983).

# Transactional models of stress

One difficulty with both the British and American research literature is the varying and often not very precise definitions of stress which are used. The special needs teacher stress literature in both countries hardly seems to try to develop adequate models of stress processes either. Perhaps this is not surprising, although it is regrettable, for it is widely acknowledged that stress is not necessarily susceptible to simple, comprehensive, formal definition.

Some writers have focused mainly on the environmental features of stress, and effectively equate the term with pressures, or stressors, in the environment. Other writers emphasise the individual's response, either psychological or physical/physiological. Some equate longer-term stress with strain. Kyriacou (1989), in a helpful account of the nature of teacher stress, sets out his preferred definition as:

> teacher stress refers to the experience by teachers of unpleasant emotions such as anger, tension, frustration, anxiety, depression and nervousness resulting from aspects of their work as teachers. (p.27)

Kyriacou rightly draws attention to the experiential and *affective* nature of stress in his definition. Some authors in the general literature on stress use 'anxiety', 'depression', 'guilt' or even 'embarrassment' as synonymous with stress. Certainly, the feeling tone conveyed by such terms is a key component in stress, and helps us not to become inured to the potential seriousness of what has become a cliché in routine conversation. We need to be able to recognise stress in others in all its guises. Somatic disturbances (tension, sweating, headaches, etc.) play an important part, along with more behavioural qualities, like edginess and loss of spontaneity.

A basic aspect of stress, however, lies in its *cognitive* referent. Worry, indecision and fixedness of thought, for example, are characteristic features. Many psychologists have been concerned to underline the cognitive basis of stress, and see the prior restructuring of individual perceptions and cognitions as fundamental to alleviating feelings of stress.

Attention is often drawn to how stress may arise from a discrepancy between the perceived requirements of a person's (working) situation and his/her perceptions of personal resources and capacities for satisfying such requirements. Thus, Sarafino (1994) defines stress as:

> the condition that results when person/environment transactions lead the individual to perceive a discrepancy – whether real or not – between the demands of a situation and the resources of the person's biological, psychological or social systems. (p.77)

The cognitive appraisal theory of Lazarus and Folkman (1984) has been highly influential among stress researchers. An account of the model involved is beyond the space allowed here, but its distinction between *problem-focused coping* (attempts to overcome the problem at source) and *emotion-focused coping* (attempts to come to terms with, or rework, powerful, fearful or angry feelings of frustration) can be noted. The interested reader is referred to Sarafino (1994) for a short account.

Sarafino's definition of stress as involving person–environment *transactions* reflects current trends in attempts to model stress processes. Transactions are understood to occur as a continuous process between environmental stressors and intrapersonal tensions/strains, with each affecting and being affected by the other. The continuous nature of this interactional process is fundamental to understanding stress. Pont and Reid (1985), alone among those researching stress in special needs teachers in the UK, have given explicit recognition to the transactional nature of stress.

## Stress and the interpersonal encounter

Although it is possible to identify stressors such as administration and paperwork as sources of stress in special needs teachers, it can be argued forcefully that it is their interpersonal consequences which give such stressors their power. Worrall and May (1989) have linked the texture of stress to a 'person-within-situation' process, in which interpersonal encounters are the key.

Their model proposes that the teacher's immediately prior prevailing emotional state is the crucial determinant of whether an episode is experienced as stressful. The affective component of stress is thus paramount, and may, at any given time, be more or less volatile. The model distinguishes between three sorts of influence likely to determine this volatility.

First, there is *anticipatory stress*. Imagine, as an example, a special needs teacher on Sunday evening experiencing growing trepidation at the prospect of school on Monday morning, possibly with some urgent administrative task left unfinished over the weekend, or the looming prospect of an argument with a non-special needs colleague in the morning, or a co-ordinator facing a meeting over resources. Fantasy and defence may be needed to ward off the slowly cumulating tension about the day to come.

Second, there is *ambient stress* – the 'noise' of concurrent pressures and issues which contribute to volatility. These may or may not lie within the school itself; there may be painful relationships at home with the teacher's spouse or children; there may be worries about sick/elderly relatives who need a visit for which there is no time. Problems in the broader zones of the teacher's life space are not necessarily in abeyance when he/she is at school.

Third, and critically, there is *core stress*. This refers to memory residues of unresolved experiences from both early and more recent times in the teacher's personal history. The originating experiences may be traumatic incidents, often linked with loss or deprivation of regard (e.g. death of a parent, loss of a previous job, insult, injury or personal disappointment). The incidents may be chronic or an accumulating burden of life stresses, minor hassles, or recurring scenarios (including relationships and memories from the teacher's own schooldays). Core stress may be latent, unconscious, or manifest in consciousness.

Core stress has a peculiar sense of activity within itself, of autonomous processes which may sometimes obtrude into consciousness without any obvious external trigger. An unexplained tenseness, shifting of mood, even worry in search of a cause, may be the subjective tone.

Core, ambient and anticipatory stress together combine to yield *volatility*, which interacts with any incident or encounter at a moment in time in a dynamic way to determine its stress potential. A clash with an ill-mannered pupil, an argument with a colleague, or a summons to meet an irate parent are all encounters which are more or less stressful depending upon prior volatility within the individual teacher.

If volatility is high, then there may be loss of 'strategic flexibility' in relating to others. The teacher who usually displays a variable, subtle blend of ways of relating to other staff – as a colleague, in the role of a teacher with a particular expertise in special needs, or sometimes simply as a fellow indi- vidual – can be driven to a rigid pattern of overreaction. In the face of some issue or incident, they become inappropriately locked into just one of these modes of relating. When this happens, stress through heightened volatility leads to a rigid self-presentation likely to provoke a similar rigid, tense response from a colleague in the moment of encounter. This then becomes a cyclic process, such that stress is fairly described as an interpersonal trans- actional phenomenon.

Understanding stress within the terms of transactional models means trying to focus both on situational variables as perceived stressors and on cognitive and affective processes within individuals. It entails trying to capture the flux wherein psychological processes within the individual inter- act with processes in the environment or situation of the individual. The activity of others in situational encounters, and what their activity means and feels like to the individual, is an essential part of this. The locus of stress is not just the response within the individual, it is transpersonal.

If future research on stress in teachers of children with special educational needs is to progress beyond its present rather limited boundaries, it seems essential that it take on board a more sophisticated definition or psycho- logical conceptualisation of the multifaceted nature of the processes involved. To understand how stress works, or why events are stressful to the individual, might offer better ways into stress control than simply monitoring stress levels through questionnaires or constructing lists of things teachers find stressful.

Even making comparisons of stress levels across different contexts of special needs teaching seems a rather sterile pursuit unless it can, through more sophisticated statistical procedures, help us understand how underlying variables combine together in different special needs contexts to produce differential stress outcomes. On the qualitative front, something more than simple interviews is needed: a more truly ethnographic flavour to research, or perhaps discourse analysis, might better serve to advance our understanding of stress processes among special needs teachers in their various working situations.

## Teachers coping with stress

Understanding coping is surely a part of analysing stress processes within the transactional approach. Compared with other contexts in which stress research has been carried out, the British special needs teacher stress literature seems to have paid relatively less attention to how teachers cope with the stress they experience.

An exception to this is the contribution of Freeman (1989). In her attempt to model individual variability in teachers' coping patterns, she notes that children with special educational needs may be particularly challenging to their teachers because the latter may have an idealistic commitment to their choice of occupation. Their choice is likely to reflect a wish to improve the lot of the child with special needs within a schooling system that fails the pupil.

Freeman believes that such children often challenge their teachers' confidence that they understand how children learn. For the teachers, there is then a 'divide between their professional idealism and the reality of the classroom, where they can become frustrated and unable to use their expertise'. That is what needs to be coped with.

The American literature is full of suggestions for stress management strategies by special educators to help them take control of their own life. Rasshke et al. (1988), for example, identify diet and exercise, relaxation techniques, making full use of social support systems, time management, goal setting, use of social networks, compartmentalisation of job and personal life, use of leisure time and hobbies, self-talk and self-encouragement, catching pupils being good and the use of humour as ways of coping with stress.

Some of these are recognisable, commonsense ways of coping, often likely to be employed by teachers whichever side of the Atlantic they are on. Others, however, are strategies of a less obvious nature. Possibilities of supporting coping through improved time management, in-service training and shared stress support groups, even residential courses such as those described by Woodhouse et al. (1985), or teacher counselling may nowadays be added to the list. Evaluation of the effectiveness of all the suggestions for coping would seem to be another useful way forward in research on special needs teacher stress.

Beyond specific coping devices, the 'therapeutic' advice on coping offered by Brent Slife in a keynote address to special educators in America in 1988 is worth heeding on both sides of the Atlantic. His advice may be summarised under the following five points:

1   Adopt a consultative attitude to work (by this he means that the special educators should not be so self-effacing that they fail to recognise the depth of specialised knowledge they have to offer a school, and that in their own sphere, they do know what is best and have power to act as 'experts').
2   Take a systems perspective on the school and its context. Avoid feeling responsible for only the small part of the system where special education is entailed. Come to understand its contribution to the whole, and avoid feeling a victim trapped by the system.
3   Look for ways and opportunities, small and large, in which to communicate to others in the system rather than blaming and taking sides against the administration or senior management. Try to see the acts of others in context, and recognise the circumstances from which they act.
4   Underpin a sense of professional identity by having some intellectual understanding or theoretical orientation towards the work you do.
5   Recognise the limits of what is possible in the special needs role, what can and cannot be changed in others, and know your own limits as a professional. (Slife, 1988)

'Good advice, but rather abstract for coping with stress,' the reader may say. True – not so easy in practice! Nevertheless, this advice does seem to address fundamental issues about status and empowerment which seem to the author germane to teachers of children with special educational needs in British, especially mainstream, schools today.

# Conclusion

The research literature on stress in teachers of children with special educational needs does not seem to point up crisis levels, and the prima-facie case with which this chapter began may be something of an overstatement.

Nevertheless, the studies referred to, albeit limited in scope in Britain, together with the qualitative data described, do point to peaks of stressful feeling which need continued monitoring.

Evidence has been presented which points to workload, especially paper-work, as an ingredient of the stress and emotional exhaustion special needs teachers experience. For EBD schoolteachers, the challenging behaviour of pupils is paramount. All this needs to be understood within a transpersonal, interactional model of stress. The stress of the present moment has as its dynamic the stress of the past as well as the anticipated fear of the future. Greater sophistication in modelling stress processes is needed to guide research if it is to contribute more effectively to stress reduction.

Rather than dissecting out stress as a phenomenon on its own, it is necessary to see it within the full context of special needs teachers' jobs. Partly, this will mean continued attention to the legislative, budgetary and resource conditions in which their work is set. However, it may also mean a greater focus on studying the jobs themselves, developing a more thorough occupational psychology of teaching. The different contexts in which special needs teachers work will need a specific focus, rather than considering special needs teacher stress in general. Effective supervisory support, train-ing and organisational development to moderate stress may be enhanced in this way.

Understanding stress in special needs teachers may also require adopting fresh approaches to research in the future, such as the analysis of discourse, or more ethnographic methods, if the job in the round is to be understood and stress processes sufficiently interpreted.

# References

Abbotts, P., Clift, S. and Norris, P. (1991) 'Implementing the 1988 Education Reform Act: A study of stress levels generated in teachers and headteachers of special schools', *Maladjustment and Therapeutic Education*, 9, 1, 16–27.

AMMA (1991) *Workload in Schools*, London: Assistant Masters' and Mistresses' Association.

Baron, R.A. (1986) *Behavior in Organisations: Understanding and Managing the Human Side of Work* (2nd edn), Boston, MA: Allyn and Bacon.

Beasley, C.R., Myette, B.M. and Serna, B. (1983) 'On-the-job stress and burnout: Contributing factors and environmental alternatives in educational settings', paper presented at the Annual Meeting of AERA (American Educational Research Association), Montreal.

Billig, M. (1988) 'Rhetorical and historical aspects of attitudes: The case of the British Monarchy', *Philosophical Psychology*, 1, 83–103.

Billig, M. (1996) *Arguing and Thinking* (2nd edn), Cambridge: Cambridge University Press.

Billingsley, B.S. and Cross, L.H. (1992) 'Predictors of job satisfaction, and intent to stay in teaching: A comparison of general and special educators', *Journal of Special Education*, 25, 453–71.

Bradfield, R.H. and Phones, D.M. (1985) 'Stress and the special teacher: How bad is it?', *Academic Therapy*, 20, 571–7.

Chakraverty, B. (1989) 'Mental health among school teachers', in Cole, M. and Walker, S. (eds) *Teaching and Stress*, Milton Keynes: Open University Press.

Cherkes, M. and Fimian, M.J. (1982) 'An analysis of the relationship among personal and professional variables and perceived stress of maintstream teachers and special education teachers', unpublished report, Storrs, CT: Connecticut University.

Cherniss, C. (1988) 'Observed supervisory behavior and teacher burnout in special education', *Exceptional Children*, 54, 5, 449–54.

Cohen, S. (1995) 'Is there more stress in teachers of children with emotional and behavioural difficulties? A comparison of SEN teachers working in three types of EBD schools and mainstream and SLD schools', unpublished MA dissertation, London: Institute of Education, University of London.

Corbett, J. and Barton, L. (1993) 'The changing context of further educational provision: Fears and expectations of special needs co-ordinators', *International Studies in Sociology of Education*, 3, 2, 271–84.

Crane, S.J. and Iwanicki, E.F. (1986) 'Perceived role conflict, role ambiguity and burnout among special education teachers', *Remedial and Special Education*, 7, 24–31.

Cunningham, W.G. (1983) 'Teacher burnout – solution for the 1980's: A review of the literature', *Urban Review*, 15, 37–51.

DES (1978) *Special Educational Needs* (The Warnock Report), London: HMSO.

DfE (1994) *The Code of Practice on the Identification and Assessment of Special Educational Needs*, London: HMSO.

Dunham, J. (1981) 'Disruptive pupils and teacher stress', *Education Research*, 23, 3, 205–13.

Dunham, J. (1983) 'Coping with stress in school', *Special Education*, 10, 2, 6–9.

Dunham, J. (1984) *Stress in Teaching* (1st edn), London: Croom Helm.

Dyson, A. (1993) 'Do we need special needs coordinators?', in Visser, J. and Upton, G. (eds) *Special Education in Britain after Warnock*, London: David Fulton.

Edwards, D. and Mercer, N. (1987) *Common Knowledge: The Development of Understanding in the Classroom*, London: Routledge.

Faas, L.A. (1984) 'Stress producing factors among regular educators and various types of special educators', paper presented at the Arizona Federation of the Council for Exceptional Children, Tuscon.

Fimian, M.J. (1986) 'Social support and occupational stress in special education', *Exceptional Children*, 52, 436–42.

Fimian, M.J. and Blanton L.P. (1986) 'Variables related to stress and burnout in special education trainees and first year teachers', *Teacher Education and Special Education*, 9, 9–21.

Fletcher-Campbell, F. with Hall, C. (1993) *LEA Support for Special Needs*, London: NFER-Nelson.

Freeman, A. (1989) 'Coping and SEN: Challenging idealism', in Cole, M. and Walker, S. (eds) *Teaching and Stress*, Milton Keynes: Open University Press.

Holmes, T.H. and Rahe, R.H. (1967) 'The social readjustment rating scale', *Journal of Psychosomatic Research*, 11, 213–18.

Hudson, F. and Meagher, K. (1983) 'Variables associated with stress and burnout of regular and special education teachers', unpublished report, Kansas University, Department of Special Education.

Johnson, P.J. (1995) 'Costing the Code of Practice', *Headlines: Journal of the Secondary Headteachers Association*, 18 September, 2–6.

Johnstone, M. (1993) *Teachers' Workload and Associated Stress*, Edinburgh: Scottish Council for Research in Education.

Karr, J. and Landerholm, E. (1991) 'Reducing staff stress and burnout by changing staff expectations in dealing with parents', unpublished position paper.

Klas, L.D. (1984) 'Factors which stress the special teacher: A comparison to other educational specialists and regular classroom teachers', *Canadian Journal of Special Education*, 1, 166–71.

Kyriacou, C. (1987) 'Teacher stress and burnout: An international review', *Education Research*, 29, 146–52.

Kyriacou, C. (1989) 'The nature and prevalence of teacher stress', in Cole, M. and Walker, S. (eds) *Teaching and Stress*, Milton Keynes: Open University Press.

Lawrenson, G.M. and McKinnon, A.F. (1982) 'A survey of classroom teachers of the emotionally disturbed: Attrition and burnout factors', *Behavioral Disorders*, 8, 41–9.

Lazarus, R.S. and Folkman, S. (1984) *Stress, Appraisal and Coping*, New York: Springer.

Male, D. and May, D.S. (1995) 'Burnout and workload in teachers of children with special educational needs: A comparison of teachers working in mainstream and special schools', unpublished report, Department of Educational Psychology and Special Educational Needs, University of London Institute of Education.

Maslach, C. and Jackson, S.E. (1986) *Maslach Burnout Inventory Manual* (2nd edn), Palo Alto, CA: Consulting Psychologists Press.

May, D.S., Worrall, N. and Halil, T. (1991) 'Auditing teacher stress: A psychological approach', unpublished report, London: Nuffield Foundation.

Norwich, B. (1992) *Time to Change the 1981 Act*, London: Tufnell Press.

Pines, A.M. (1993) 'Burnout', in Goldberger, L. and Breznitz, S. (eds), *Handbook of Stress: Theoretical and Clinical Aspects* (2nd edn), New York: Free Press.

Pont, H. and Reid, G. (1985) 'Stress in special education: The need for transactional data', *Scottish Educational Review*, 30, 3–14.

Potter, J. and Wetherell, M. (1987) *Discourse and Social Psychology: Beyond Attitudes and Behaviour*, London: Sage.

Presley, P.H. (1982) 'Teacher burnout in special education: Myth or reality?', unpublished paper presented at the 60th Annual International Convention for the Council for Exceptional Children, Houston, Texas.

Pullis, M. (1992) 'An analysis of the occupational stress of teachers of the behaviorally disordered: Sources, effects and strategies for coping', *Behavioral Disorders*, 17, 3, 191–201.

Rahe, R.H. and Arthur, R.J. (1978) 'Life change and illness studies: Post history and future directions', *Journal of Human Stress*, 4, 3–15.

Rasshke, D., Dedrick, C. and De Vries, A. (1988) 'Coping with stress: The special educator's perspective', *Teaching Exceptional Children*, 21, 10–14.

Sarafino, E.P. (1994) *Health Psychology: Biosocial Interactions* (2nd edn), New York: John Wiley.

Selye, H. (1974) *Stress Without Distress*, Philadelphia: Lippincott.

Selye, H. (1991) 'History and present status of the stress concept', in Monat, A. and Lazarus, R.S. (eds), *Stress and Coping* (3rd edn), New York: Columbia University Press.

Slife, B.D. (1988) 'Coping strategies for teachers', *Academic Therapy*, 24, 9–15.

Style, S.W., Wright, R.E., Davis, D., Moore, B., Templeman, T.P., Toews, J. and Wilson, T. (1987) 'Stress: Perceptions of environmental characteristics and events', *Journal of the Division for Early Childhood*, 12, 77–83.

Travers, C. (1992) 'Teacher stress in the UK: A nationwide survey', *BPS Education Section Review*, 16, 2, 78–82.

Trendall, C. (1989) 'Stress in teaching and teacher effectiveness: A study of teachers across mainstream and special education', *Educational Research*, 1, 1, 52–8.

Wedell, K. (1993) *Special Needs Education: The Next 25 Years*, NCE Briefing No. 14, London: National Commission on Education.

Welch, F.C. (1983) 'Research based answers to questions about stress and burnout', paper presented at the 61st Annual International Convention of the Council for Exceptional Children, Detroit.

Woodhouse, D., Hall, E. and Wooster, A. (1985) 'Taking control of stress in teaching', *British Journal of Educational Psychology*, 55, 2, 119–23.

Worrall, N. and May, D.S. (1989) 'Towards a person-in-situation model of teacher stress', *British Journal of Educational Psychology*, 59, 2, 174–86.

Youngman, M. (1995) Editorial, *British Journal of Educational Psychology*, 65, 1, 1–2.

# Part I

## The impact of handicapping conditions

# 2 Learning difficulties

*David Jones and Dev Sharma*

Few would dispute that teaching is a challenging profession. The task of providing an environment and a system of instruction which allows children to attain their maximum potential is complex and demanding. Often, the dedication and efforts of teachers are directly rewarded by perception of the manifest academic success of pupils. For many teachers, work satisfaction has to come from recognition that they have done the best possible job under difficult circumstances.

As was noted in Chapter 1, education has been the subject of enormous changes in policy and reorganisation in recent years. Teachers themselves have had surprisingly little influence or control over these changes, and many teachers report dismay over feeling undervalued and ignored while still struggling to fulfil their responsibilities to their pupils and to society. Teachers are not alone in the caring professions in feeling undervalued. The highly emotive term 'burnout' has come to be applied to professionals who are experiencing difficulty in continuing at work because their perception of self-worth in the job situation has been driven down to unacceptable levels by external factors. The definition of burnout given by Edelwich and Brodsky (1980) refers to a progressive loss of idealism, purpose and energy in members of the helping professions who are perceiving a deterioration in their conditions of work.

Sadly, there is nothing new in the widespread concern about the level of stress among teachers, although reasons given for the causes of stress vary. Over the past two decades, numerous reports of teachers being under severe stress have appeared in the literature. For example, Dunham (1976), on the basis of a survey of schoolteachers, concluded that both the incidence and the level of stress had increased. Hunter (1977) made comparisons between different occupational groups and claimed that the level of stress experienced by teachers was nearly the same as that faced by air traffic controllers and surgeons. Andrews (1977) also argued that stress among teachers appeared to be on the increase. It is clear that concern about stress in teachers has been expressed over many years, and not just in one country.

Our particular concern in this chapter is to describe the specific stresses experienced by teachers of children with learning disabilities. It can be argued forcefully that helping these children attain their potential is one of the most difficult tasks in teaching. One of the greatest differences between teaching children with learning difficulties and teaching most other groups of children is that the goals of education have to be modest. Teachers will rarely bask in the glory of the academic successes of their pupils who have learning difficulties. They will get frequent satisfaction from facilitating the development of life skills and competence, but most gains will have involved considerable effort. Professionalism helps protect against disappointments, but not from the sadness which comes from caring about the progress of vulnerable children.

## Changes in definition and pattern of provision

A major problem for teachers in recent years, particularly those involved with children with learning difficulties, has been the need to react to a sequence of changes in educational policy and the subsequent changes in the expectations of what education should provide and how it should be provided. The rapid move towards integration of special needs provision within mainstream classrooms means that many more teachers are now involved, albeit on an occasional basis, with children with learning difficulties. A brief account of the changes in educational practice for children with learning disabilities over the last half century will hopefully set the scene for a meaningful attempt to evaluate the stresses confronting their teachers.

The 1944 Education Act defined as 'educationally subnormal' (ESN) children who were educationally retarded by more than 20 per cent for their age. A further group of children with more severe disabilities in intellectual and cognitive functioning were deemed 'severely educationally subnormal' (SSN) and were considered to be ineducable in the school system. The care and training of SSN children was made the responsibility of health authorities.

It was not until after the 1970 Education Act (Handicapped Children) that a serious attempt was made towards integrating children with more severe learning disabilities into the school system administered by local educational authorities. There were changes in terminology, and a greater emphasis was placed on categorising children with learning difficulties in terms of scores obtained on standardised tests of intelligence. Children with IQ levels below about 50 were labelled as 'severely educationally subnormal' and placed in ESN(S) special schools. Those with IQs in the range 50–70 were identified as 'moderately educationally subnormal' and tended to be placed in different special schools, referred to as ESN(M) schools.

The teaching of children with learning disabilities in special schools in the 1970s came to be regarded almost as a sub-profession. To a large extent, teachers in these schools had freedom in their approach to the curriculum. Many of the special schools were quite well resourced, and the class sizes were considerably smaller than those in mainstream schools. Nevertheless, despite the original good intentions, the attempt to create protective environments for vulnerable children resulted in an uncomfortable pattern of segregation. Increasingly, there was dissatisfaction with the criteria used to identify children thought unsuitable for education in mainstream schools, given the considerable influences of social and cultural factors on children's performance on IQ tests. Only rarely did children return to mainstream schools following placement in ESN(M) schools.

Many teachers who used to work in these special schools feel that the system was made unworkable by the ever-increasing tendency to use ESN(M) schools for children with behavioural difficulties who had been failing to make satisfactory progress in mainstream schools. There was also concern at a political level that in some areas, disproportionally large numbers of ethnic minority children were being placed in ESN(M) schools on the grounds of difficulties in adjusting to the requirements of mainstream schools. Even though children with learning difficulties frequently also exhibit behaviour difficulties, they have different educational needs from children whose learning difficulties are a direct consequence of behavioural problems or social and cultural disadvantage. The containment of disruptive behaviour is a very different challenge, and it presented teachers in the ESN(M) schools with a range of additional stresses.

The Warnock Report (DES, 1978) brought the term 'learning difficulties' into general use and signalled the changes to follow in the 1981 Education Act, which finally came into force in 1983. Although Warnock was against the idea of categorising children, the report suggested that learning difficulties may be usefully described as mild, moderate or severe, depending on the degree of the individual needs. It was suggested that moderate learning difficulties may arise from a variety of causes, often including limited general ability, mild and multiple sensory difficulties, and adverse social and emotional experiences.

More than anything else, the Warnock Report influenced the move towards integration of special education into mainstream schools. Distinctions were made between three forms of integration: locational, social and functional. 'Locational integration' refers to the physical siting of the special unit within mainstream schools. 'Social integration' refers to positive action to achieve mixing between children with special needs and main-stream children during break-times and a limited range of lessons. In contrast, 'functional integration' refers to the process of children with different needs learning together in the mainstream classroom. The 1981 Education Act defined a child as having 'special educational needs' if 'he has a learning difficulty which calls for special educational provision to be made for him'. With the 1988 Education Reform Act and the adoption of the National Curriculum, the move towards functional integration for as many children as possible was underway.

More recently, the Code of Practice (DfE, 1994) introduced following the 1993 Education Act has summarised the present position. It is assumed that about 20 per cent of children may have some form of special educational needs at some time, and that most such needs will be met at their school, with outside help if necessary. It is estimated that only about 2 per cent of children will need a statutory Statement of Special Educational Needs. School governing bodies have statutory duties towards pupils with special needs, and to formulate a policy for the school. It is clearly stated that provision for pupils with special educational needs is a matter for the school as a whole. The SEN co-ordinator for the school has responsibility for the operation of the policy, working closely with teachers and non-teaching support staff.

# Who are the children with learning difficulties?

By far the largest group of children currently identified as having special educational needs consists of children with learning difficulties (Gulliford, 1985). It is a diverse group, both in terms of range as well as complexity, particularly towards the severe end of the learning difficulties continuum, because of the interacting effects of usually multiple causative factors. Jones and Barrett (1990) suggested that differences within the group of children with learning difficulties are at least as numerous as the differences between them and other children. The largest single subgroup is those children who would have been described as having 'mild learning difficulties' by the Warnock Report. The appropriate support often includes 'remedial teaching' and also teaching that takes into account their difficulty in mastering complex tasks. Many of these children require constant personal support and encouragement in order to make progress in their learning. The expectation is that they will follow the National Curriculum, although this may have to be at a slower pace than their peer group. Apart from learning difficulties, these children will often have unmet and continuing social and emotional needs.

Those with more severe problems may have a 'Statement of Special

Educational Needs'. Some with severe and multiple problems will continue to be educated in special units with varying degrees of integration. For children in this category, the focus of their education is often on developing independence, social skills, communication skills and other aspects of their development by means of precisely analysed and small, incremental objectives.

Children with learning difficulties are thus to be found at all levels of the education system. As such, all teachers are potentially teachers of children with learning difficulties, and thus vulnerable to the stress inherent in working with children with these particular needs. The degree of stress experienced by a teacher responsible for the education of one or two children with mild learning difficulties in a large mainstream class may be no less than that faced by a teacher responsible for a small group of children with severe learning difficulties in a special school.

# Sources of stress

Stress results from a complex interaction between personal and environmental variables. One might ask why some people choose to work in the caring professions. In this chapter, only the environmental factors responsible for stress among teachers of children with learning difficulties will be examined. Our database is in part a series of informal interviews with teachers currently working in nine different local educational authorities in Greater London and the Home Counties. Some of these teachers are working in special units for children with learning difficulties, others are employed as support teachers, and some are mainstream classroom teachers who have recent experience of working with children with learning difficulties in their classes. We also interviewed several SEN co-ordinators, educational psychologists and school governors. It is a sign of the times that a more formal survey of teachers' opinions would have been almost impossible to arrange.

## General organisational and systemic factors

The most frequently voiced complaint was that the present system expects mainstream schools to meet the needs of children with learning difficulties with little or no extra resources made available. It seems unproductive that irrespective of the facts, so many professionals should be feeling irritated by budgets and costings. Generally, teachers welcomed what they perceived as parental participation in decisionmaking, but there was a distinct sense of unease that parental powers have increased, with corresponding increases in teachers' obligations and accountability. There was a feeling of unease that teachers' responsibilities have been left unclear. The National Curriculum provisions of the 1988 Education Reform Act and the Code of Practice (DfE, 1994) issued under the 1993 Education Act have further increased the pressures on teachers. Many teachers of children with learning difficulties find the National Curriculum provisions too prescriptive, even irrelevant in the case of children with severe learning difficulties (Rieser, 1994).

At a more general level, we encountered concern that the recent changes that have occurred in education, as in health and other areas, are fundamental in nature, with far-reaching implications for working practices. There are suggestions in the recent literature that some teachers feel out of sympathy with the radical shift in values from those of dependency culture to those determined by market forces. In the dependency culture, as Halton (1995) argues, 'there is a primary concern for the welfare of the person in the dependent position, which has been an inspirational element in the work of teachers, health practitioners and others' (p.188). Halton goes on to suggest that with the ascendancy of market forces, education has become entangled with two contradictory value systems, creating a great deal of uncertainty, confusion and stress among teachers.

## Low morale

While so much more is demanded of teachers of children with learning difficulties, many perceive that the rewards and opportunities have, in fact, diminished. Many special schools have been closed, and with many more under the threat of closure, the sense of job insecurity has become acute. Some teachers formerly working in special schools accepted, out of necessity and with a measure of reluctance, the move to work as support teachers in the mainstream schools.

A teacher who made such a move remarked:

> It was a choice between having a job or no job and being able pay your mortgage. I was quite happy teaching in the special school with my own classroom and doing a good job for the children. But having to travel to so many different schools in the course of one week is something I find tiring and unsettling.

## Lack of adequate support

Teaching children with learning difficulties requires a good deal of effort in terms of organisation, curriculum planning and methods of teaching. A mainstream class teacher who may have several children with learning difficulties in her/his class will therefore need a great deal of extra help to support these children. The perception is that this support is too often meagre, or non-existent. One of the most contentious aspects of integration of children with learning difficulties in mainstream schools is the feeling of lack of adequate support. One of the teachers we interviewed remarked:

> I have at least four children in my class, if not more, who have substantial learning difficulties, two of them on Statements. In addition, I have several other children whose behaviour is very difficult, and so often I end up spending much of my time in just containing them. All I get is three sessions of support by a learning support teacher, that is very little really. Where can you find time to liaise with the support teacher and with parents, attend meetings and prepare individual educational plans? I so often feel I am not getting very far with these children. It is so frustrating!

Moreover, teachers feel increasingly burdened with rapidly escalating administrative tasks and paperwork. With the introduction of the Code of Practice, paperwork for teachers of children with learning difficulties has increased further. Many teachers resent these demands as unnecessarily bureaucratic. There is some irritation that the presentational aspects of school life have assumed greater importance. There is a strong feeling among teachers that the time spent by them on producing glossy reports could better be used to carry out what they perceive as their real job. Also, a lot more time is now being spent on meetings, usually outside school hours. Rees (1989) found that the 'vast majority of teachers saw meetings as a growing source of stress' (p.27). But senior managements in schools regard meetings as an important means of planning, organising and effectively running a school. There is thus a real conflict of priorities, leading to resentment among teachers.

## Role ambiguity and role conflict

The role of teachers, particularly during the second half of the twentieth century, has increasingly widened. The range of duties expected of teachers of children with learning difficulties is even wider. In special units for children with severe learning difficulties, the teacher often has to function as a counsellor, carer, cleaner, nurse, social worker, liaison officer and more. These many, varied and sometimes ambiguous and conflicting demands can be a major source of stress (Dunham, 1984). A teacher with several years' experience in a school for severe learning difficulties children commented:

> When I decided on the move to work with special needs children a few years ago, it was meant to be a positive move, but now I sometimes wonder if what I am doing is teaching, really. I was trained as a teacher, but I find myself being expected to be doing things I never imagined I would have to be doing. I do sometimes wonder if what I am doing is teaching. It is confusing, even disheartening.

# Characteristics of the children as sources of stress

Children with learning difficulties sometimes exhibit a variety of behaviours which are likely to produce negative effects among their carers and teachers. Research shows that children with learning difficulties themselves experience significantly more stress relative to other children, and have fewer resources to deal with it (Siperstein and Wenz-Gross, 1991). This, in turn, can be a source of stress for people who come into contact with them.

## Lack of perceived success

One of the greatest differences between teaching children with learning difficulties and teaching most other children is the lack of usual success perceived by teachers. The focus is so often on the child's problems that their teachers sometimes fail to appreciate success in improved life skills and social behaviour. Teachers, as a group, are geared to measuring success in academic terms. However, examination grades and other measures of attainment leading to league tables for schools are far from clear-cut measures of job success. Teachers of children with learning difficulties rarely experience the satisfaction of helping their pupils to pass examinations and go on to university. They will thus have little opportunity to share in their pupils' achievements. One such teacher working with children with severe learning difficulties remarked:

> The most frustrating thing is the despair that comes with not being able to make a real and tangible impact on the situation of these children. You want to change things for the better. So you try this or try that. You consult with specialists. But so often you do not see much of a change.

Lack of perceived success may lead to low self-esteem and eventually to burnout (Collins, 1977). It is not so much the reality of the situation but its perception by the individual that contributes to poor self-esteem and eventual stress.

Working with children with learning difficulties is a very intensive experience. The demands made by the children can seem unending, and the need for direct contact may appear excessive. The children may require constant adult supervision. In the case of children with severe learning difficulties (see Chapter 8), their safety, security and welfare is a matter of constant concern each minute of the day. The risks of accidents and injury are constantly present, as well as the potential dangers of children intentionally or unintentionally injuring others. Stories of hepatitis infection from bites may sound alarmist, but even such slight risks add to the overall stresses of a difficult job. Many children have serious medical conditions, and their health has to be monitored constantly. Some teachers live in dread of having to cope with a medical emergency.

There is a high incidence of poor health prognosis among children with severe learning difficulties. Not infrequently, a child will die, which causes a great deal of distress among staff as well as pupils. Commenting upon the death of a child in her class, a teacher said:

> We have lost three children during the past year, including one in my group. We knew it was likely to happen, and in a way we were all prepared for it. But when it came it was so upsetting for everybody. A sort of constant reminder of your own mortality.

## Challenging and difficult behaviour

Many children with learning difficulties exhibit difficult, unpredictable and challenging behaviour. The behaviour of some children, particularly those with severe learning difficulties, can be confounding and perplexing for teachers. One teacher referred to never being able to adjust to unpredictable, loud shrieks. Tolerating a high noise level from the children seemed a particular problem for those still working in special units. There is a strong correlation between learning difficulties and behavioural difficulties at all levels. Also, as a group, children with learning difficulties are more likely than other children to show restless and hyperactive behaviour and other aspects of attention deficit disorder (Barkley, 1990).

Children with learning difficulties often show a reduced awareness and appreciation of their difficulties, which makes it more difficult for them to learn from their own experiences. These characteristics can become a barrier against teachers' attempts to bring about positive change, producing further frustrating and disheartening experiences, both for teachers as well as pupils.

In the mainstream classroom, there can be problems when children with learning difficulties are unaware of the effects their behaviour may be having on other children. Teachers feel the need for constant vigilance to prevent misunderstandings. The constant worry about the safety of all the children in the class can create a great deal of stress among teachers. A teacher of children with severe learning difficulties who had three children with very aggressive behaviour remarked:

> I have three children in my group who need constant watching in case they hurt others. Peter constantly bites anyone, anywhere he can. He has actually drawn blood several times this term. I have to make sure he does not get too close to any-one. I have to hold him half the time. Ged's behaviour can be so unpredictable. He nearly strangled a girl with her own hair. He can appear to be so lovable one

minute, but what he could do a minute later you couldn't tell. He keeps you on your toes. It kind of wears you out.

Teachers working with older children with severe learning difficulties have to deal with sexualised behaviour by children, which they may find quite uncomfortable and anxiety-provoking. This may range from having to inhibit exposure, masturbation and other forms of self-stimulation in children, to more extreme cases of female teachers having to resist sexual advances. Male teachers constantly need to take care that their own actions are not misinterpreted as sexual advances. There is evidence that children with learning difficulties are more likely to be victims of physical and sexual abuse. Teachers, along with carers, are responsible for their protection. Such responsibility for vulnerable children can be stressful for teachers. A teacher responsible for an older group of children with severe learning difficulties thus expressed his concerns:

> Most of the children in my group require constant and close physical contact. Two or three children are rather too sexually aware, sometimes even provocative. One is never sure of the implications of a close physical contact with these children. But so often it is not really avoidable. Recently a parent got really upset about her child being inappropriately 'handled'. But the result of not providing the physical boundaries could have been potentially dangerous for the child.

Teachers have to be vigilant for the safety of their pupils, but will not lightly take on the stresses of asking for a formal inquiry when they have uncertainty about their suspicions. In this area, as in so many others, teachers of children with learning disabilities have to take very difficult decisions.

### Lack of stimulation and feedback for teachers

Teaching in mainstream schools can be a stimulating experience for teachers, because of the variety of intellectual challenges provided by the curriculum and the quality of feedback received from pupils. But the opportunities for positive feedback for teachers working with children of learning disabilities are few and far between. Kadushin (1974), in his research with carers of people with learning disabilities, identified the lack of such feedback as a significant source of stress. He argues that the flow of emotion is, by and large, a one-way process, leading to the emotional depletion of the worker.

## Stresses in relating to parents

The intricacies of parent–teacher relationships and their impact on children, parents, and indeed on teachers, are not well researched or understood. But it is obvious that for all teachers, there are sometimes stresses associated with interactions with the parents of the children they are working with. In many cases, the nature of the interactions with the parents of children with learning difficulties is qualitatively different from other teacher–parent exchanges. Not infrequently, parents have not come to terms with their child's difficulties. Research shows that children with learning disabilities have a negative impact on parental health, which in turn is likely to affect the attitudes of the parents to the outside world (Siperstein and Wenz-Gross, 1991). Mothers of children with learning disabilities have been found to show greater depression and more preoccupation with their children. They have also been observed to show more possessiveness, but less enjoyment and less of a sense of maternal competence (Cummings et al., 1966). Similarly, fathers have been shown to be more likely to exhibit depressed behaviour, to have lower self-esteem and less interpersonal satisfaction (Cummings, 1976).

Siperstein and Wenz-Gross (1991) argue that the stressful family climate created by the presence of a child with learning difficulties in a family may, in turn, become a stressor for the child. It may also adversely affect parents' interaction with the outside world, particularly with professionals and agencies involved with their child's education and care. There is evidence that teachers are sometimes inappropriately blamed by parents for the arrangements for their children's education. They may also be blamed for the unavoidable difficulties created by other children. Teachers may thus feel abused by the very people they have worked very hard to help. In these circumstances, teachers need to be able to understand the context of such negative feelings coming from parents. They will sometimes have to confront parents with the realities which other professionals have failed to explain. Those teachers who do not receive enough support and supervision for this complex work may find these demands stressful.

A teacher of a child with a learning disability commented:

> I know it is not easy bringing up a child with such needs for any parents, but they should also try to understand how difficult things can be for teachers. I do feel they could be a bit more helpful. I can understand their frustrations with the system. But I do feel as if they are taking it out on me. It can be so annoying and frustrating sometimes.

## Management of stress

While on the one hand, stress may take a heavy toll on the physical and mental wellbeing of the individual teacher, it is also likely to affect his/her work with children. According to Freudenberger (1977), stress may lead to general fatigue, irritability, boredom and even depression. Unless appropriate steps are taken to relieve stress, its effects càn be persistent. The teacher may become less flexible and resistant to change, and may respond to children and other professionals with cynicism and negativism (Maslach, 1976). The teacher under stress may also withdraw from people and activities and become isolated from the general life of the school (Mattingly, 1977). It may affect classwork with children adversely, and it is therefore imperative, both in the interest of the wellbeing of teachers as well as their work with children, that appropriate measures to combat stress are taken.

Management of stress has to be tackled at the organisational and systemic level as well as at the level of help for the individual teacher. Teachers of children with learning disabilities need, and deserve, adequate support from the school system as well as from parents. They need enhanced opportunities for in-service training to improve their skills in working with children with learning disabilities.

Just as the reasons for stress among teachers of children of learning disabilities, and the consequences of it, are many and varied, so are its remedies and prevention (Weiskopf, 1980). Individual teachers have little power to influence organisational changes. They deserve to be given the opportunity to see that they play an important part in the wider care system.

## Awareness

The early effects of stress may be quite subtle. If it goes unrecognised for some time, more serious consequences may emerge. It is therefore important to be able to recognise stress as early as possible. In recent years, individual teachers, as well as schools as a whole, have sought more training in the area of early recognition and management of stress. But there is some evidence that the quality of these training courses has been found wanting. Improved in-service training opportunities in this area are called for.

A number of strategies to manage stress are believed to be useful, though there is little empirical evidence in support of these claims. Commonly suggested strategies can be divided in two broad categories. One is the effective management of personal resources, energies and time in the work setting. The other is adapting and maintaining a healthy lifestyle, including various methods of relaxation. For teachers of children with learning disabilities, it is important to tackle some of the specific issues which have an impact on their life.

Teachers of children with learning disabilities need to protect themselves from becoming overinvolved in their work. They need to be able to delegate responsibility for some of the more routine tasks to relieve pressure on themselves. They need to manage their time more effectively and guard against committing themselves beyond their resources and energies.

Weiskopf (1980) suggests that staying mentally alert and being involved in intellectually stimulating pursuits is a very useful way of reducing stress. She suggests that teachers will benefit from attending workshops or field trips involving both recreation and intellectual challenges, and also providing opportunities to share concerns and ideas with colleagues. Freudenberger (1977) also suggests that it can be very useful for teachers to share their experiences and feelings through group participation activities, which can help them to relax and to decelerate the process of burnout.

Taking a regular 'mental break' from the hard daily routine has also been recommended as a helpful way of reducing stress. In his study, Stanton (1989), examined a number of strategies in which subjects were encouraged to either just 'switch off' or turn attention to something pleasant for some time regularly each day. He found that subjects who regularly used these strategies reported fewer symptoms of stress. Some other techniques, such as meditation and other relaxation methods, are believed to be similarly helpful.

At the organisational level, it is important to recognise that systems which go through periods of major change are frequently vulnerable to stress. Education now needs a period of stability with an emphasis on creating a climate which will allow individual class teachers to rediscover their sense of self-esteem. This is particularly true for teachers of children with learning difficulties, whether they be class teachers, support teachers or teachers in special units.

# References

Andrews, A.G. (1977) 'Ground rules for the great debate', *Cambridge Journal of Education*, 7, 90–4.

Barkley, R.A. (1990) *Attention-Deficit Hyperactivity Disorder: A Handbook for Diagnosis and Treatment*, New York: Guilford Press.

Benz, W.K., Hollister, W.G. and Edgerton, J.W. (1971) 'An assessment of the mental health of teachers: A comparative analysis', *Psychology in the Schools*, 8, 72–6.

Collins, G.R. (1977) 'The hazard of professional people-helpers', *Christianity Today*, 21, 740–2.

Cummings, S.T. (1976) 'Impact of child's deficiency on the father: A study of fathers of mentally retarded and chronically ill children', *American Journal of Orthopsychiatry*, 46, 246–55.

Cummings, S.T., Bayley, H. and Rie, H. (1966) 'Effects of child's deficiency on the mother: A study of mothers of mentally retarded, chronically ill and neurotic children', *American Journal of Orthopsychiatry*, 36, 596–608.

DES (1978) *Special Educational Needs* (The Warnock Report), London: HMSO.

DES (1989) *Discipline in Schools* (The Elton Report), London: HMSO.

DfE (1994) *The Code of Practice on the Identification and Assessment of Special Educational Needs*, London: HMSO.

Dunham, J. (1976) 'Stress situations and responses', in National Association of Schoolmasters (ed.) *Stress in Schools*, Hemel Hempstead: National Association of Schoolmasters.

Dunham, J. (1984) *Stress in Teaching* (1st edn), Beckenham: Croom Helm.

Edelwich, J. and Brodsky, A. (1980) *Burnout: Stages of Disillusionment in the Helping Professions*, New York: Basic Books.

Freudenberger, J.J. (1977) 'Burn-out: Occupational hazard of the child care worker', *Child Care Quarterly*, 6, 90–8.

Gulliford, R. (1985) *Teaching of Children with Learning Difficulties*, Windsor: NFER-Nelson.

Halton, W. (1995) 'Institutional stress on providers in health and education', *Psychodynamic Counselling*, 1, 187–98.

Health and Safety Executive (1990) *Managing Occupational Stress: A Guide for Managers and Teachers in the School Sector*, London: HMSO.

Hunter, M. (1977) 'Counter irritants to teaching', *Instructor*, 87, 122–5.

Jones, D. and Barrett, H. (1990) 'Coping with unhappy children who have learning difficulties', in Varma, V. (ed.) *Coping with Unhappy Children*, London: Cassell.

Kadushin, A. (1974) *Child Welfare Services*, New York: Macmillan.

Maslach, C. (1976) 'Burned-out', *Human Behaviour*, 5, 16–22.

Mattingly, M. (1977) 'Sources of stress and burn-out in professional child care work', *Child Care Quarterly*, 6, 127–37.

McCormick, B. (1991) 'Thinking, discourse and the denial of history: Psychodynamic aspects of mental handicap', *Irish Journal of Psychological Medicine*, 8, 59–64.

Rees, F. (1989) *Teacher Stress: An Exploratory Study*, Windsor: NFER-Nelson.

Rieser, R. (1994) 'Making sense and nonsense of the Code of Practice', *New Learning Together Magazine*, 2, 4–9.

Siperstein, G.N. and Wenz-Gross, M. (1991) 'Stress in mentally retarded children and adolescents', in Colten, E.C. and Gore, S. (eds) *Adolescent Stress: Causes and Consequences*, New York: Aldine de Gruyter.

Stanton, H.E. (1989) 'Teachers under stress: The mental holiday procedure', in Waxman, D. (ed.) *Hypnosis: 4th European Congress at Oxford*, London: Whurr.

Weiskopf, P.E. (1980) 'Burnout among teachers of exceptional children', *Exceptional Children*, 47, 18–23.

# 3 Hearing impairment

*Brian Fraser*

## Introduction

For many teachers of the deaf now coming towards the end of their career, there have been changes in practice and attitudes that few would have foreseen as they entered the profession. In the middle decades of this century, it was assumed that deaf children should be educated in schools for the deaf, that the predominant educational approach should be oral, and that the curriculum should be dominated by language development programmes and by articulation work.

The received wisdom was that deaf young people would have little difficulty finding employment when they left school, and that they required little more than practical craft ability and some language. If they had problems with integration into the complex of responsibilities of adulthood, then there would be the missioner for the deaf – a clergyman attached to the local deaf club – and the developing specialist social work services to take over the protective umbrella which had been provided by the schools.

These schools were, for the most part, long established, and provided a residential education for most children. In some urban areas, like London, Birmingham, Manchester and Sheffield, there were day schools, but the old, established, independent and non-maintained schools dominated the practice and preserved the traditions. It was a closed and apparently comfortable world, with a patronising view of the deaf adults that the children within it grew up to be. The teachers were trained within the system, apart from those who were certificated by the Department for the Education of the Deaf at the University of Manchester, and many of these gained a postgraduate certificate in the education of the deaf and went directly into the schools without significant mainstream experience. The system was even preserved within families, and it was not uncommon for headmasters of

41

schools for the deaf to be succeeded by their sons!

In the past forty years, this comfortable microcosm has disappeared. The majority of deaf children are now educated within mainstream schools, with only 18 per cent remaining in schools for the deaf (BATOD, 1989). Most of the schools for the deaf which were operating forty years ago have been closed, and those that remain have taken on a very specialised role and work in very different ways to those which prevailed in the first half of the century. There are many reasons for this, and it is difficult to tell which are the most important. Certainly, there were three major catalysts for change. One was the recognition in the late 1950s that there were significant numbers of children with hearing loss within mainstream schools whose special educational needs were not being met. Another was the development of techniques for the early detection of hearing loss in babies and subsequent early intervention programmes of parent guidance. Both of these developments led to the establishment of non-school-based services for hearing-impaired children in all local educational authorities (LEAs) and changed radically the practice of teachers of the deaf. The third reason for change was the recognition of the use of residual hearing in deaf children, and the developments in electronics which allowed this to be capitalised upon by the effective use of hearing aids. Coupled with these developments were greater understandings of the way in which children developed and learned, and particularly an understanding of the processes underpinning the acquisition of language.

These factors all resulted in a change in the nature of the education of deaf children and placed greater intellectual and knowledge demands upon their teachers, which were met by an increase in higher education training courses and a decrease and eventual disappearance of the on-the-job training provided within schools and examined by the professional body for teachers of the deaf. The study of education of the deaf and of deaf people within society became academically respectable and led to an awareness of the needs and aspirations of deaf people and of the language which had been used in deaf communities for generations. Curious experiments were tried, and language systems were developed, applied, and after a year or two, dropped. Systems like the contrived Paget-Gorman Sign Language and Cued Speech were experimented with, responded to with enthusiasm by some teachers of the deaf, and then discarded.

The last forty years have been a period of extensive change and confusion in the education of the deaf, with new challenges in professional practice creating major demands on teachers. The certainty of practice which had dominated education of the deaf, with its structured approaches to language work, its drills in speech and its narrow curricular base, has been replaced by a need to respond to a constituency of children, young people and their parents in a wide variety of placements and with a range of understandings and practices which are continually developing and which require a professional commitment not previously demanded.

In many ways, the development of understanding of deafness in children and the opportunities to apply new developmental knowledge and electronic technology to their needs makes this a very exciting and promising time in the education of deaf children. The achievements of many deaf children now leaving education far outstrip those of their predecessors. Notwithstanding these developments, the stress associated with the rapidity of change is increased by factors external to the perceived practice of teachers of the deaf, which are seen by many of them to conflict with their practice and with the needs of the children with whom they work. These external factors relate to the impact of new educo-political thinking and its reflection in educational legislation and policy, and to relationships with other professional services. There is also the whole question of the mode of communication to be used and the responses to different special interest groups of deaf people and their friends.

# Changes in provision

Local education authority non-school-based services for hearing-impaired children grew in an unplanned and uncoordinated way from the late 1950s until they were the largest employers of teachers of the deaf. Such teachers perform a variety of roles, with some attached to mainstream schools in facilities loosely described as 'units for hearing-impaired children'. Others provide support for hearing-impaired children integrated into mainstream classes, and advice and guidance for their teachers. Other roles of such services relate to early parent guidance and counselling and to educational audiology. Educational audiology is the educational application of audiology, the science of hearing, which integrates the assessment of auditory functioning with the efficient and effective management of residual hearing. The specialisation in educational audiology has grown as an academic discipline over the past forty years, with many teachers of the deaf having taken additional postgraduate specialist courses in this field.

Guidance and counselling of parents of deaf babies and young children is regarded as the priority provision of most services for hearing-impaired children. Early intervention from as young as 3 months has resulted in a major change in the nature of the special needs which confront teachers of the deaf in the early school years, with many deaf children having made important strides in early language development. If we look at this particular role of services for hearing-impaired children, we can see the way in which educo-political thinking, associated legislation and changes in the administration of education pose a potential threat to existing practice, resulting in what many would see as the de-skilling of some teachers of the deaf and a reduction in the provision for very young deaf children and their families.

## Pre-school services

The delivery of pre-school services has been dependent upon two main factors: the early detection of hearing loss, and the goodwill of the local education authority, which needed to be convinced of the developmental value of such provision. Changes in health service provision and practice and a managerial rather than educational focus in LEAs imperil the continuance of pre-school services, and as such, contribute to the anxiety and stress of teachers of the deaf.

Early detection has depended upon health visitors, who have received training and whose skills are monitored and regularly updated. McCormick (1988) demonstrated the importance of these latter two points, and also demonstrated that without adequate monitoring and updating, health visitors were likely to pass as normal 90 per cent of deaf babies in screening programmes. The money available for health visitor training has shrunk in recent years in most district health authorities, and many such workers are now dependent upon a 'sitting-with-Nellie' training programme, with few opportunities for regular updating or for the monitoring of their work. Fundholding general medical practitioners may wish to take on this screening work for themselves, but on the basis of no, or very little, specialist training.

Recent reports (e.g. *Independent*, 8 March 1994) have shown that conventional behavioural screening tests of hearing are not particularly successful at identifying severe and profound hearing losses. If the identification of hearing loss in babies is delayed, then valuable developmental time will be lost, thus calling for a change in the future practice of teachers of the deaf, who will be called upon to deal with children who have not had the benefit of early intervention, with all that this implies for the adjustment of parents, early use of residual hearing and the early acquisition of communication skills.

Early detection of hearing loss is of little value if it is not supported by a programme of early developmental intervention with the identified children and their families. This has been a major role of services for hearing-impaired children, and as was noted above, this has depended upon LEAs recognising the value of teachers working with the families of babies as young as a few months of age. In many ways, this particular practice has depended upon the goodwill of the local education authority. There has never been a requirement that teachers of the deaf should provide a guidance programme for such groups, but at a time when the central focus of educational officers seemed to be on children and their development, it was not difficult to develop such practice. This work was pioneered in the 1950s by Watson and Pickles (1957), and has been seen as priority work by all services for deaf children for the past thirty-five years. High levels of skill have been developed by teachers specialising in this work, and the outcomes have been dramatic. The continuance of this area of work is now jeopardised by the changes in educational administration and by responsibilities spelled out in the 1989 Children Act.

## Administrative changes

Local education authorities, like all public bodies in the UK and many other countries, have been influenced by the notions of the market and its management structures and balance sheets. With reduced levels of funding, the work of all LEA services is now, quite rightly, being more carefully scrutinised and audited. It is very likely, in this more austere financial climate, that serious questions will be asked by accountants about continuing the provision of a service which may be seen to be the responsibility of others.

The goodwill upon which services for hearing-impaired children has depended needs to be put into the broader context of educational reforms and the political thinking that underpins these. These reforms are a consequence of the thinking of the 'New Right', and their immediate effect has been to move control of education away from LEAs towards central government, while at the same time shifting responsibility for the management of education to schools, their governors and to parents. Education is now seen as a marketable commodity, in which the individual customer should be liberated from the provision imposed by local government and should have wider options of choice. This 'market liberalism' of the New Right is underpinned by the ethics of a sort of Benthamite utilitarianism, where moral decisions are justified on the basis of their production of the greatest happiness for the majority of people (Codd, 1993). In terms of a perceived marketable commodity such as education, such thinking seeks to maximise average distribution and ignores the production of wide disparities. Efficiency of provision is measured in terms of as many people as possible getting what they want, *even if some end up getting less*. Codd argues that education is seen as a preferred commodity, and 'utility' is the catchword, with the commodity distributed in order to gain optimal average benefits for all, even if the least advantaged become worse off.

This ethical framework of the New Right is very different from that within which most teachers of the deaf have been working. The dominant framework which determined educational thinking and management until recently has been described as social justice as fairness (Codd, 1993). Within this model, equity was given priority over choice as the primary social objective, with a system of redress operating which meant that more could be given to the less advantaged. It was this which fed the goodwill which promoted the development of services for hearing-impaired children and which supported the development of early intervention programmes with very young deaf children. The principles of equity have meant that resources have been allocated, 'so as to improve the long-term expectation of the least favoured' (Rawls, cited in Codd, 1993, p.165). This contrasts with the views which now prevail in many areas of political policy development and which are expressed by some people responsible for educational development. On a recent visit to New Zealand, a country which has enthusiastically embraced a utilitarian market liberal education system, the author was told by an official in the Ministry of Education who was responsible for educational funding that services for children with special educational needs were like 'a mouse in a cheese factory when it comes to funding' and that 'there is a need to stop funding a caviar service for some children'. A principle of economic efficiency seems to have replaced notions of equity. In a just society, primary goods, such as education, are distributed fairly and according to need, and there is a fair distribution of educational benefits without a dominance of economic efficiency or improved consumer choice.

The market liberal system sees education as something which is designed for utilitarian purposes, such as improving overall commercial production capacity, thus achieving a maximum return on the capital invested in the education business. This is likely to involve an unequal distribution of resources upon the basis of perceptions of where they are likely to produce the most satisfactory results in the form of what is deemed to be a quality product, and we can see results of that in the funding of institutions like City Technology Colleges, which may receive as much in funding as all of the other secondary schools together in the same borough.

As we have seen the market liberal philosophy overtake that of social justice, so we have seen a decline in the special educational services that the latter fostered. Major local education authorities with large and well established services for hearing-impaired children have disestablished these and replaced them with much smaller facilities, or have employed a smaller number of teachers of the deaf in generic teams. The new education system is characterised by a greater centralisation of power, with systems of checks and balances such as tests, established national standards, teacher appraisal, curricular audits and regular inspections into which it is difficult to fit some of the work of services for hearing-impaired children, and particularly work with pre-school-age children. The accountant's model of an annual audit is one into which such work fits uncomfortably – at the end of a year, it may be difficult to quantify development in a baby with hearing loss. The outcomes of early intervention may not be apparent for many years.

At the same time as there has been an assumption of educational power by the centre, so there has been a shift of responsibility for the practice and outcomes to the periphery, and this has left a lot less economic flexibility, with the economy of scale of local authorities as they deal with low-incidence problems being severely restricted by budgetary constraints. The shift of responsibility for the process and outcomes of education to schools means that attention does not need to be focused upon the development of a curriculum but upon the distribution and use of resources. Administrators in schools and local education authorities now seem to be more concerned with accounts than with education and development, and seem to be driven more by the managerial skills exemplified by Caldwell and Spinks (1988) and by Walters (1994) than by a professional focus upon need. It is difficult to put a price on individual development, which is hard to measure.

## Recent legislation

Coming into this generally gloomy scenario are the 1989 Children Act and its accompanying Community Care legislation, the 1993 Education Act and the Code of Practice (DfE, 1994). The 1993 Education Act is vague on pre-school support and educational response to need in very young children, although it does say that where it appears that any local authority (meaning social services) could, by taking any specified action, help in the exercise of functions relating to the provision of services for young children, they may be requested to help. The Code of Practice recognises the need for pre-school services for hearing-impaired children, but while the main sections of that document will be monitored by OFSTED, the pre-school component seems to lack a similar scrutiny.

The Children Act is somewhat more explicit. Schedule 2, Part I is concerned with the provision of services for families. Paragraph 6 of Part I says that every local authority (note that it does not say 'local *education* authority') shall provide services designed to minimise the effect on disabled children of their disabilities, and that such children should be given the opportunity to lead lives which are as normal as possible. Paragraph 8 of Part I stipulates that local authorities shall make appropriate provision of advice, guidance and counselling. Part III of the Act (para. 17(11)) says: 'a child is disabled if he [sic] is blind, deaf or dumb or suffers from a mental disorder of any kind or is substantially and permanently handicapped by illness, injury or congenital deformity.' The NHS and Community Care Act, which came into force in April 1993, enjoins social services departments to 'design a package in agreement with users, carers and relevant agencies to meet identified needs within the care resources available and to implement and monitor the agreed packages and review outcomes and service provision' (Russell, 1991).

This all seems to be very explicit, and places a responsibility upon social services departments to make a provision in which services for hearing-impaired children have been developing skills and expertise for nearly forty years. A recent telephone survey of several social services departments showed that there was an awareness that they were required to keep a register of children in need, but few recognised their wider responsibilities. But what of the new breeds of education officers and business managers in locally-managed and grant-maintained schools? They may challenge the role of teachers of the deaf working with pre-school-age children and argue that this is something which is the responsibility of another department. Such services would see the consequences of such thinking resulting in less educational control over the meeting of special educational needs of young hearing-impaired children, and the de-skilling of specialist teachers. Educators and their administrators are only too aware of the world of diminishing resources, and many educational services for hearing-impaired children have faced reorganisation and disestablishment. Education managers in local education authorities are on the look-out for areas in which to economise, and the shifting of the responsibility for the guidance of parents of pre-school-age hearing-impaired children onto another agency could effectively save between 8 and 10 per cent of the hearing-impaired service budget. Such services could negotiate with social services departments to sell their skills, but social services departments are not exactly over-resourced.

The anxieties of teachers of the deaf – related to the future of pre-school, and therefore *all* educational services for hearing-impaired children – are that if local education authorities cease to recognise this work as part of their role, then there would appear to be only three options, none of which would be seen by such teachers as very satisfactory, and which would be unlikely to meet the needs of all deaf children. The first is the development of some lesser provision by social services departments, which would use a structured programme not unlike Portage. (This is a published programme which was first devised in the US and establishes developmental targets which can be achieved by described strategies. It is designed to be used by workers who do not have in-depth knowledge of child development. These workers are supervised by a team leader who can provide advice and guidance where required.) The second option would see some possible voluntary sector development such as already exists in the provision of specialist social workers by some specialist children's charities. While these are thinly spread, they do provide some measure of support for families and are useful for crisis management. The third option is the development of private services, for which the user would pay. This is hardly an equitable solution, but it is certainly one which fits with the market economy.

It is very unlikely that future provision for pre-school-age deaf children will resemble the practice which has prevailed over the last two or three decades. There are opportunities now for much closer co-operation between education and social services departments, and the resulting service could be considerably better than has been the case so far, but the financial constraints within which both sectors are working means that this is an unlikely development.

## School-age services

As has already been pointed out, the majority of hearing-impaired children are now placed in mainstream schools, and there has been a sharp decrease in the number of schools for the deaf. Twenty years ago, in one region of the UK, the West Midlands, there were six schools for hearing-impaired children, with nearly 600 children being educated in them. A substantial number of children were also placed in schools outside the region. This number of schools has now halved, with only about 150 children on their rolls, and with a small number of children placed in specialist residential schools for the deaf in other parts of the country. The majority of children are in the care of local education authority services for hearing-impaired children. Such services developed a school-like organisation with a headteacher, deputy heads, senior and assistant teachers, but without the governance of maintained schools. This provided a career structure which was professionally attractive to teachers and which provided a degree of permanence and security within the service. It also provided opportunities for a co-ordinated policy to operate within an LEA, where teachers felt that they were members of a corporate team that provided a continuum of special provision for deaf children and their families, and which enabled the efficient development of in-service support and training. Many such services included not only visiting teachers of the deaf, working with pre-school-age children and also working in mainstream schools, but also teachers of the deaf placed in units attached to mainstream schools, and teachers working in tertiary education.

Several large services for hearing-impaired children have been disestablished since the beginning of the 1990s and have been reconstructed as smaller entities, either as part of generic special needs provisions or in their own right, but without the structure and team hierarchy that had previously existed. In many instances, the units and their teachers of the deaf have come directly under the management structure of their host schools, but often with funding from the central authority. This has produced a service structure which no longer has the same opportunities for leadership and co-ordination, and which provides less support for those teachers working within it. At the same time, it has opened the possibility for individual responses to deaf children to be developed by teachers, which may not relate to what had occurred earlier in a child's programme, and which take little account of what may follow.

The changes which have been and are being implemented have created fewer opportunities for professional development and promotion, and have, as in all areas of education, reduced the levels of security of employment of teachers. What is different to most other areas of education is the profile of the teachers who are recruited into it. As will be shown below, where we discuss issues related to the training of teachers of the deaf, the average age at which teachers qualify to work with deaf children is now 38–39. With fewer opportunities for a developing career structure and for security, it is likely that it will become difficult to attract teachers into this field.

Of the schools for hearing-impaired children operating in England and Wales, 24 are local authority schools, and 15 are independent. A survey of these conducted recently by the author shows that there are twice as many children in local authority provision as there are in the independent sector, the majority of whom are supported by local education authorities. As all local educational authorities have some provision for hearing-impaired children, there is a reluctance on their part to buy places in out-authority provision that they feel that they are able to provide within their own resources. For some children with multiple special needs the most prominent of which is deafness, it may be easier to make a case for such placement, but for children who appear to have straightforward hearing losses, it may be more difficult to make a case that such provision is in the child's best interests, and that within-authority placement is incompatible with the efficient use of resources. Schools for the deaf in the independent sector are finding it more difficult to recruit and retain children, and numbers are falling, with a consequent effect upon the number of teachers who can be employed.

## Training of teachers of the deaf

Since 1909, there has been a mandatory requirement that teachers working with deaf children in schools and classes should have a specialist qualification. In 1919, it was agreed that specialist training could be funded by government grants or by local education authority bursaries, and in 1948, secondments on full salary to training courses became available to qualified and experienced teachers. Until 1988, teachers on specialist training courses were either seconded or were direct-entry teachers, either qualifying via a postgraduate certificate in education, taking the qualification immediately on completion of initial teacher training, or pursuing a combined honours course in the education of the deaf at the University of Manchester. A significant number of teachers qualified through in-service programmes, which were examined by the British Association for Teachers of the Deaf and its predecessor, the National College for Teachers of the Deaf.

In 1988, Department of Education and Science regulations changed, and it was no longer possible for direct-entry initial training recruitment into this specialist area. From then on, only qualified and experienced teachers could undertake training. The reality of this is that fewer young teachers are entering education of the deaf, and there are fewer opportunities for deaf people themselves to train as teachers of the deaf, as they may have difficulties in obtaining relevant mainstream teaching experience. The average age of all entrants to specialist training courses for the past few years has been in the late thirties, and while there are some entrants still in their twenties, there are many in their forties or even fifties. A consequence of this is that few teachers of the deaf can build up the range of experiences and practice which, in the past, informed the rounded development of those people who later went on to take positions of responsibility in the profession. Education of deaf children is likely to work within a narrower range of experiences than has been the case in the past.

In recent years, the amount of money available for secondments has been adjusted by the Department for Education, with local education authorities being expected to find 40 per cent of the cost. It is much more attractive for such authorities to use this money to train teachers of the deaf on a part-time basis, either by developing campus-based, part-time programmes, or through the distance learning programme developed at the University of Birmingham. Such programmes generally last two years, and will allow trainees to remain in post for at least four days per week. These courses are not cheap, but they do offer an economy, in that the 40 per cent of the overall cost of secondment and the recruitment of replacement teachers can be used in a way which appears more effective to the administrator. The emotional cost to the student is enormous, with an expectation that they will complete all coursework, assignments and visits largely in their own time, while at the same time preparing and teaching in a field where they have limited experience, and often, restricted support. The author and a colleague recently conducted a survey of teachers who had qualified as teachers of the deaf via a distance learning course, where it was found that nearly three-quarters of the teachers commented on the very heavy workload imposed by this form of professional development. Comments on the course suggested that there was an overpowering workload, which imposed a terrible strain. Many people found the process of study very stressful, and this was added to by difficulties in combining the course, teaching and family commitments. Many people commented on how lonely they felt while following a course of training by this approach.

The opportunities for full-time courses have diminished greatly, with very few students now receiving secondments. The demand for such training is still there, and there are a significant number of people who are prepared to sacrifice their salary for a year and to draw upon their savings to support themselves. When they return to teaching, they often face an accumulated financial penalty from which it may take years to recover.

# Modes of communication

There are currently three modes of communication in use in the education of deaf children: auditory/oral, bilingual and total communication. These are practised as part of the philosophy of different schools, units and services for hearing-impaired children and seemingly, should not be a source of stress in the work of specialist teachers of the deaf. It might be assumed that decisions will have been made on the needs of the child, and that child will then be placed in a provision which uses the appropriate communication mode – in other words, that there is a nice straightforward and objective educational response to need. Nothing could be further from the truth. Let us first look very briefly at each of these modes of communication, and then at some of the issues that underpin their use.

## Auditory/oral

Underpinning this approach are two principles. The first is that it is very unusual for a deaf child to have a total hearing loss, and with early, consistent and appropriate amplification, residual hearing can be used to maximum effect in the development of interpersonal communication skills. The second principle relates to the way in which children acquire language. It is argued that deaf children do not differ from any other children, and if the linguistic input is correct – if it is contingent upon the developmental need of the child – then that child will acquire language. There is no doubt that many children have developed very high levels of verbal language skills using this approach, but it places rigorous technological and psycholinguistic demands upon teachers of the deaf and on the families of the children.

## Bilingual mode

This is a relative newcomer on the education of the deaf scene, and is a consequence of the recognition of the sign language used among some deaf people in social communities. This has been analysed and studied by linguistic scientists, and is recognised as a rich and complex language, but not one which relates to the spoken language of the wider society. It is argued that Sign is the natural language of deaf people, and is central to the culture of deaf communities, and as such it should be the preferred language for teaching. It is also argued that it is much easier for deaf children to acquire, that the acquisition process is the same as for children learning any language, and depends, like the auditory/oral approach, upon an input which will promote natural development.

Practice in this approach is dependent upon deaf children having exposure to contingent language models, and it does require high levels of Sign skills in teachers and parents. Generally, heavy use is made of deaf Sign users as educational ancillaries. There are few deaf teachers of the deaf who use Sign. Its rapid growth as a practice over the past five or six years is a consequence of two main factors. One is the demand of some deaf people and social workers for the deaf that Sign should be taught so that deaf children can take their place in the deaf community. The second is the increasing recognition that the third mode, total communication, has not met its promise, and that the outcomes for children who have passed through all of their schooling in this approach are not substantially different to their predecessors (Lynas, 1994).

## Total communication

Although this mode has been left to the end, it is probably the oldest of the current approaches. The term 'total communication' has been in use for a relatively short time, since the late 1960s. The approach itself has been in use for much longer than those described above. Many older teachers of the deaf can remember using a 'combined approach' in schools for the deaf in their youth, thirty or forty years ago. This approach utilises a mixed input, using normal spoken language with auditory input together with signs to support the spoken word and fingerspelling where necessary. In some practices, Signed Exact English is used, where the signs, taken from British Sign Language, are modified and are used in English word order, with appropriate signed prefixes and suffixes. Total communication replaced the old oral method used in schools for the deaf – probably because it reflected what was actually happening, but also because studies, such as that by Conrad (1979), showed how woefully inadequate were the outcomes of educating deaf children. Such workers saw the reasons for this as lying in the communication mode, which was heavily dependent upon lipreading, and felt that this should be supplemented with some element of manual input to facilitate language reception.

The issues underpinning the choice of mode of communication are, to some extent, in conflict and this conflict can cause dissension among teachers of the deaf. Lynas (1994) sees these issues as relating to the orthofunctional outcomes of the educational process and to the sociocultural position that some deaf people and their friends see worthy of developing and preserving. The issues relate to what is possible in terms of educational outcomes and what is morally desirable.

Lynas shows that it is possible for some deaf children to develop efficient verbal language skills and to take their place in the wider community. Some people feel that such development may deny these children their identity as deaf people, and deny access to Sign and to the community of some other deaf people. There are disagreements among educationalists and deaf people about the issues of educational outcome and moral desirability, and it is clear that what is morally desirable in the development of a deaf child depends upon the source of the morality. The diversity of this is such that there are several clearly-focused and incompatible moral standpoints, which makes the development and schooling of deaf children a field of much contention. The needs of deaf children are defined not necessarily upon the basis of the characteristics of the child, but often upon the ideas and opinions of adults, generally professionals, about the education of deaf children. The advocates of each of the three approaches argue about the perceived needs and interests of deaf children from a distinct viewpoint, and the result is that how the child will be educated will depend upon the particular view of the professional who is in the position to make decisions – this person could be responsible for establishing the policy of the local education authority, or could be an independent consultant.

Lynas (1994) sees the question of ownership of the right to make decisions on behalf of young deaf children about how they are to be educated as central to the whole debate on the modes of communication to be used. She argues that decisions should be made which will enable deaf children to make the widest possible choice of how they will lead their adult lives in deaf and hearing communities. Teachers of the deaf may find themselves working in situations where their professional judgement and their considered appreciation of the needs of the child are in conflict with the declared policy of a particular school or service for hearing-impaired children. This can be a source of much stress.

# Conclusion

Teachers of the deaf are faced by all the anxieties and confusions that face all teachers as a consequence of the educo-political changes that have been initiated over the past decade or so in the UK and in other countries. These have come at a time when knowledge of language development and of the learning and audiological needs of deaf children has increased considerably as the result of researches by people such as Wood et al. (1986), Wells (1981) and Tucker and Nolan (1984). These changes have placed greater intellectual and knowledge demands upon teachers of the deaf, and new challenges to their professional practice. The management and financial changes which have had an impact upon the educational scene have allowed fewer opportunities for both personal and corporate development, particularly with the fragmentation of previously cohesive local education authority services for hearing-impaired children.

Management-focused education authorities have been changing the structure of their provision for hearing-impaired children. Educational services for such children have been 'rationalised' and dismantled, with the result that there is less security for individual teachers and more uncertainty about who is responsible for what. The financial restraints under which local education authorities are working mean that the out-authority placement of deaf children, which, in the past, added to the range of provision available, is now very difficult to obtain. A consequence of this is that pressure is being placed upon independent special schools for the deaf, with uncertainties about their continued viability. Teachers of the deaf working in local authorities are often now expected to cater for a child for whom they know that more appropriate provision would be available outside the authority. The resources available for meeting the needs of such a child within the authority may be limited, and the teacher may be placed in the stressful position of having to condone inappropriate provision.

There are positive stresses to be seen in the development of broader recognition of different approaches to the education of the deaf. These stresses are part of the expected development of any professional practice. The pity is that they are often overlaid by emotive and political dimensions which create contentions between and within a number of special interest groups associated with deaf people and their education.

Perhaps the greatest source of stress for teachers of the deaf as a body is the sheer rapidity and breadth of change. Most of the change that is being experienced is positive, but those elements which are negative and threatening have the potential to divert energy from those which should result in developed professional practice.

# References

BATOD (1989) 'Report on staffing and salary structure in schools', *Journal of the British Association for Teachers of the Deaf*, May, 2–3.

Caldwell, B.J. and Spinks, J.M. (1988) *The Self Managing School*, London: Falmer Press.

Codd, J. (1993) 'Managerialism, Market Liberalism and the move to self-managing schools in New Zealand', in Smyth, J. (ed.) *A Socially Critical View of the Self-Managing School*, London: Falmer Press.

Conrad, R. (1979) *The Deaf School Child*, London: Harper and Rowe.

DfE (1994) *The Code of Practice on the Identification and Assessment of Special Educational Needs*, London: HMSO.

Lynas, W. (1994) *Communication Options in the Education of Deaf Children*, London: Whurr Publishers.

McCormick, B. (1988) *Paediatric Audiology: 0–5*, London: Taylor and Francis.

Russell, P. (1991) 'The Children Act: A challenge for all', *British Journal of Special Education*, 18, 3, 115–18.

Tucker, I. and Nolan, M. (1984) *Educational Audiology*, London: Croom Helm.

Walters, B. (1994) *Management for Special Needs*, London: Cassell.

Watson, D. and Pickles, A. (1957) 'Guidance for parents', in Ewing, A.W.G. (ed.) *Educational Guidance and the Deaf Child*, Manchester: Manchester University Press.

Wells, G. (1981) *Learning Through Interaction: The Study of Language Development*, Cambridge: Cambridge University Press.

Wood, D., Wood, H., Griffiths, A. and Howarth, I. (1986) *Teaching and Talking with Deaf Children*, Chichester: John Wiley.

# 4 Visual impairment

*Elizabeth Chapman and Juliet Stone*

Teachers of children and young people with visual impairments need a specific expertise if they are to meet their pupils' needs. Some of these needs arise directly from the visual impairment. As Lowenfeld (1971) has pointed out, a severe visual impairment restricts both the quality and quantity of children's experiences, and also affects their ability to move around independently. All of this can lead to a marked delay in all aspects of children's development, including motor, language, cognitive and social-emotional aspects.

Although many of these children and young people have additional impairments, some are very able, and there can be a particular stress for teachers in the tension between ability and current level of functioning. This and the stresses experienced by teachers in different sectors of provision for visually-impaired pupils are discussed in this chapter.

## Educational provision

In the UK, there is a long tradition of special school provision for children who are visually impaired, dating back to 1790, when the Royal School for the Blind in Liverpool was established. The fact that in a country where there is a low incidence of blindness in children (Walker et al., 1992) some children attend special schools indicates that these schools continue to be the educational placement of choice for a significant number of visually-impaired children and their families. Besides the special schools in the voluntary sector, there are a few local education authorities which maintain special day school provision for children with little or no sight. These placements are a part of the continuum of educational provision, ranging from total

57

integration in mainstream schools to daily or residential attendance in special schools for visually-impaired pupils. Nursery provision for children from 2 years of age, often with day 'drop-in' facilities, outreach services fitting into mainstream provision and further education opportunities combine to provide a vital element in the continuum of special educational provision for pupils with visual impairment that is current national policy.

# Stresses for teachers in special schools

For teachers working within the special school sector, there are some specific challenges and stresses. These schools are generally very well furnished, with advanced technical equipment, and provide resources for braille production, print enlargement and methods for making tactile diagrams and maps. Some of the advantages of special school placements are described by Gale (1991):

> A priceless asset is the amount of stimulus and support given with academic subjects. In each subject group there are never more than seven people and often fewer; also there is plenty of scope and time for receiving extra individual attention from members of the staff, wherever this would be helpful.

This must sound like an almost idyllic situation, especially to a teacher with large classes in an inner-city comprehensive school. Teachers in such schools must obtain a specialist qualification in the education of visually-impaired children within three years of appointment, and a teacher newly appointed to a special school for visually-impaired children can expect to join a staff of experienced and specially-qualified staff within a school with an established reputation for expertise in the education of such children. However, this can be an initial cause of stress, especially if the teacher concerned has had no experience of working with children with little or no sight.

Some comfort can be derived from the realisation that all schools must benefit from the flow of new ideas and experiences within the staff if they are to retain vitality, and a teacher coming into specialist work should feel confident in offering this, rather than stressed because of inexperience in specific areas. In addition, the mandatory training which must be undertaken can also help to reduce stress by enabling the teacher to have a better understanding of the pupils' needs, and to master specific skills and competencies in order to fulfil them effectively.

## Specialist training for teachers

Undertaking a course of study while still in post brings its own stresses, as does moving into an academic situation for a year if full-time study is chosen as a route to attaining the specialist qualification. This is commonly either a BPhil(Ed) or Diploma in Special Education, although some training bodies confer degrees and diplomas with different nomenclature.

Many teachers choose to qualify through a part-time distance learning mode, such as the course offered by the University of Birmingham. First offered in 1982 (Chapman, 1982), the underlying philosophy involves combining theoretical study with practical work in schools, with the tutors and practical supervisors themselves being experienced teachers of visually-impaired pupils and students. There are economic benefits to undertaking a part-time distance learning course, since a replacement teacher does not have to be found, but it will be readily appreciated that the teacher undertaking training while teaching will have an extremely heavy workload. Stress can be minimised by using interaction with colleagues positively, both in the teacher's own school and in the team of trainers, to discuss problems relating to special learning materials and curriculum access and to proffer solutions. Secondment to a full-time course is an option that many teachers would prefer, but the lack of funding for the secondment and replacement costs in the school render this an increasingly uncommon possibility. Attending a full-time course usually necessitates living away from home, but the stress which this can give rise to is counterbalanced by the refreshing opportunity to stand back from the daily tasks of management, to reflect on past experience, and to concentrate fully on the demands of the course. This is by no means stress-free, but can be stimulating and enjoyable.

Teachers in these schools are for the most part graduates, and always hold initial teaching qualifications, but they need to acquire specific skills. Mastering the special skills involved in teaching pupils with little or no sight can also involve some stresses. Learning braille, for example, is not an intellectually demanding task, but it does involve learning a graphic code with rules and contractions that some people find hard to remember. Regular practice of the code for short periods is usually more effective in achieving competence in this medium than longer, less frequent sessions. Some teachers may question the necessity of learning braille at all, since there are now a variety of methods of transcribing braille to print and vice versa through sophisticated technology. It is, nevertheless, the blind child's means of literacy, and as such, its use needs to be understood and experienced, and it is also an immediate means of communicating with a pupil in a form which is familiar to them. The time and possible stress involved in mastering it diminishes as competence in the medium increases, and pupils tend to respect the fact that those who deal with them have taken the trouble to learn it.

The medical model as a basis for educational categorisation and provision has been abandoned since the recommendations of the Warnock Report

(DES, 1978) influenced subsequent legislation and emphasis was given to the individual development and learning of children with special needs. However, the causes of visual impairment in children can have a direct effect on the way that they function and learn, thus having implications for the way in which learning materials are presented and teaching strategies undertaken. For example, a child who is an albino may want to avoid bright light, a child with a damaged visual field may need to hold work in an unusual position in order to focus on it, another may need enlarged visual material, while braille and tactile diagrams may be needed in the same class by children with no useful sight at all.

Managing such diverse needs in one class, albeit a small one, can be stressful if they are not well understood and provided for so that pupils can work in an efficient and comfortable way. A detailed knowledge of the implications of visual impairments is necessary in order to present appropriate learning materials and methods which give visually-impaired children access to the full curriculum, and while they are acquiring this knowledge, teachers may think of themselves as still being learners.

It is important, in terms of limiting stress among staff, for headteachers, colleagues and school governors to appreciate that the special school is a place where teachers are always learning and in which there needs to be an active and supportive policy of staff development. This can encourage the appreciation and respect of what is involved in extending the skills and knowledge of teachers working in a special school situation, rather than emphasising the negative aspects of stress and anxiety. Currently, teachers undergo assessment as well as being required to obtain a specialist qualification. Both procedures can be viewed positively, but they can also involve some stress, especially in terms of having an assessor in the classroom. However, teachers in special schools are accustomed to the presence of visitors who come to see their work, as well as to the presence of students in training, classroom assistants and therapists, so they may find this situation less unusual than those whose classrooms are less open to other professionals.

Resources in the school itself are also important, in that they can be used to help the teacher to gain confidence in meeting the needs of visually-impaired pupils. A staff library, in particular, can also be enormously helpful within the school if it contains standard texts about visual impairment and its implications in learning as well as current literature on curriculum issues, children's development and learning. There are also useful journals containing articles about specific areas of teaching and research, such as the *British Journal of Visual Impairment* and *New Beacon*, which should be available to staff.

## Stresses in the classroom

Despite small class sizes, pupils in a special school may be in need of considerable individual support because of additional factors such as hearing impairment, physical or intellectual impairments or behaviour problems. These complex needs may have been difficult to meet in a mainstream situation, and put considerable demands on the skill of teachers in special schools. Other pupils may have considerable intellectual ability yet require concentrated academic work in order to fulfil their potential. Equally, the small class is not always a complete benefit to such students, who can be stimulated intellectually by the interchange of ideas from their peers and the debate and discussion of issues with other pupils. In the very small group or with prolonged individual teaching, the interaction between pupil and teacher can become very intense, and requires skilful management if it is not to become stressful.

Good planning and organisation is the key to effective teaching in a group of pupils with diverse needs and complex learning requirements. A knowledge of each pupil's requirements can be built up through the result of formal and informal assessment, observation and previous records. Experienced colleagues will be helpful in advising on the efficient production of tactile diagrams and the scheme that the school operates for replicating and adapting learning materials. There are several relevant texts that are helpful here – for example, Best (1992) gives a useful survey of methods of selecting and adapting material for individual needs – but it is essential to plan ahead, so that adapted materials are available when required for each lesson without the stress of a last-minute rush.

The requirements of the National Curriculum, even in its revised form, put heavy pressure on both teachers and pupils in special schools for visually-impaired children. The staff have generally taken these requirements on board, except in areas where the pupils are perceived to need to follow a developmental curriculum. In fact, this process often reflects a combination of the curriculum areas already in place before the statutory requirements were demanded. Pupils at these schools have been successful over many years in public examinations and in meeting the entrance criteria for university and further education courses. Probably more, rather than less, attention has been given to the individual needs of pupils in terms of access to the full range of the curriculum because of the relatively small class sizes in special schools and the experience of the teachers in managing necessary adaptations in specific curriculum areas. For instance, modern language examinations may contain an illustration which has to be described in the language being studied and mathematical problems may contain a considerable amount of visually-based work. Therefore, stresses for teachers have arisen not from the demands of the curriculum itself, but from the need to deal with, and to make accessible to pupils, specific material that has been designed for fully-sighted pupils.

The way in which this has been achieved has been largely due to the work undertaken by the curriculum committees of the organisation VIEW (Visual Impairment, Education and Welfare), which set up working groups to consider the implications of the requirements of each curricular area in terms of the particular needs of visually-impaired pupils and students. The success of this work has been in large measure due to the energy, commitment and co-operation of the teachers involved. Understandably, the opportunity to work with others who are tackling similar problems and to share in positive initiatives not only brings results but gives individual teachers a chance to solve together some of the stressful problems of meeting new curricular demands. Because special schools for visually-impaired children are small, usually with between 100 and 200 pupils, individual teachers may be either the sole person involved in a particular subject area or one of a very small team. This total, or near total, responsibility for a particular subject area can be an attractive challenge, but also a stressful one.

## The need for teamwork within the special school

The special school which caters for the needs of pupils with visual problems needs to accommodate additional but essential curriculum areas, such as mobility, self-help skills and personal independence. From time to time, all teachers will be called upon to defend their area of the curriculum, for example, in terms of having to bid for finance for specific equipment or for sufficient time in timetable planning to give appropriate attention to the subject. Both practice and research have shown that pupils with little or no sight do need longer than fully-sighted pupils to complete some tasks, and that reading especially can be a slower process (Mason and Tobin, 1986). A team-building approach is essential if the competing demands of each department are to be recognised and priorities agreed.

Possibly one of the most stressful circumstances for teachers occurs when their aspirations for developing their work and the problems they experience in doing so are not understood by those responsible for the management of the school's resources and developing its ethos. There is no evidence that this is a greater cause of stress in the special school than in any other educational establishment, but the staff in a small school may feel that they do not have the support of colleagues, who are defending their own interests. It can be particularly helpful in considering and understanding other's resource priorities for teachers in such situations to meet colleagues through professional associations such as VIEW and to attend conferences organised by such associations. These can be very important in helping to reduce the isolation which the individual teacher can experience in a small special school.

An effective team approach in a special school involves interaction, not only with fellow teachers but with other professionals, including care staff, paramedical staff such as physiotherapists, and classroom assistants. This makes the teachers' work particularly interesting, since aspects of pupils' development and personality which can be gleaned from such colleagues might not be evident in the classroom situation. Of course, views about the way in which a particular child is managed may be perceived differently by the different professionals involved in the process, and open discussion about disciplinary matters can help to build up a shared rather than fragmented approach to many problems.

## The role of parents

In all probability, parents will have played a key role in the placement of a pupil in a special school for children with visual impairments. Although the placement will have been the result of team assessment and subsequent recommendation, the parents must agree to the recommendation, and can appeal if they do not. This inevitably means that parents have invested strong hopes that the child will flourish and succeed in the educational placement which they have endorsed. This is an aim that teachers will share, but the means of attaining it may be perceived differently by parents and teachers. It is not only stressful, but bad for all concerned if such differences develop into conflict. Parents know their child well, and may be aware of strengths and weaknesses that are not always evident in school. They have probably also experienced disappointment, anxiety and stress themselves because of their child's disability, and their hopes for their child's future may not appear to coincide with the approach of the school in every situation. A teacher encountering such a dilemma needs to listen and try to understand the parents' point of view, but should be able to put forward with honesty those of the child's teachers. This requires considerable social skills, since the way in which such issues are addressed may make all the difference between good future co-operation between parents and teachers or seemingly endless misunderstandings. The principles of an effective course in assertiveness can be invaluable for a teacher who feels stressed by encountering different views.

The appointment of a parent governor on the school's management board can do much to help parents to understand the way in which the school works and to give parents the opportunity to be part of it. Special schools frequently have active parent representation in this way, and they can do much to develop mutual respect and common effort between teachers and parents, reducing stressful situations and enhancing positive co-operation.

The work of a teacher in a special school for visually-impaired children shares many of the stresses encountered by all teachers, as well as some that are specific to the particular situation, but the work does have the challenge of making a good deal of difference to the opportunities for development and learning of pupils who have more than most to overcome.

# The development of advisory services

During the past twenty-five years or so, there have been moves to place children and young people with visual impairments within mainstream schools. This was begun by the special schools, which recognised that some of their pupils could, with advantage, work alongside their sighted peers. The Warnock Report (DES, 1978) gave a further impetus to this development, which was confirmed in the 1981 Education Act. It is clear, however, that there have always been pupils with severe visual impairments in mainstream schools. This has either been because, surprising as it may seem, their special needs had not been identified, or because decisions had been made locally to place them within the mainstream sector of provision. The recognition of these pupils and the new policy of integration gave rise to the need for expertise to be made available, both to the pupils themselves and the staff who were teaching them. A new role for teachers of the visually impaired came into being: that of the advisory teacher. This role has brought with it some tremendous challenges and stresses.

Educational advisory services for the visually impaired developed on a rather *ad hoc* basis. Some local education authorities established services in the late 1960s, but there are services which have only been in existence for a few years, and at present there are still authorities which do not have this type of provision.

## Variations in service provision

This variation in the length of time that services have been established means that the range of support they offer differs greatly. Some will have a team of a dozen or more teachers, all offering some particular expertise, while other teams have only two or three teachers. Such differences can produce stress within the smaller teams, which may strive to achieve the same level of service as is provided by the larger teams. There are also other factors which affect the role of teachers within the services; these include: the differences between urban and rural services; the wide range and ability range of pupils who are supported; variations in the numbers of individual teachers' case-loads, and the different expectations of schools and employers, which are usually very demanding, even unrealistic, and a source of much pressure. In addition, a survey undertaken by Stone in 1992 showed that the number of different functions that educational services fulfil is very large. The functions listed by the teachers included: advising other staff, working collaboratively with parents, direct teaching of pupils with visual impairments, providing resources, transcribing braille, making budget proposals, negotiating with education officers, providing in-service training, writing information for Statements of Special Educational Needs, accompanying pupils to eye clinics and negotiating with examination boards. This is not a complete list of all the functions that advisory teachers carry out, but a compilation of what individual teachers felt were their major activities. Therefore, a teacher in one authority may be working in a very different way from a teacher in a neighbouring authority. This can lead to confusion about what the role of an advisory teacher actually is, and this uncertainty can cause a lot of self-doubt and anxiety. Teachers are continually asking themselves: 'Is this what I ought to be doing? Is there any way I can do more, or do what I am already doing better?'

## Placements within mainstream schools

For pupils with visual impairments, there are two main forms of mainstream placement. Some schools will have several pupils who are supported by specialist staff working from a resource centre within the school. Where there are resource bases, relationships between subject or class teachers and the teachers in the resource base can sometimes become strained, and there can be a lack of understanding of what the resource teachers do. Some mainstream teachers may feel that resource staff have an 'easy ride, and this reaction can be very upsetting for the resource teachers.

Other schools will have only one or two pupils who are visually impaired, and these will be supported by specialist staff who visit the school on a regular basis. One of the roles of these staff will be to offer information and advice to the mainstream staff. Teachers who are qualified to teach children with visual impairments are able to advise on how to ensure that the pupils have access the main curriculum and how to provide their special curriculum. The particular stresses for visiting teachers are discussed later.

# Providing for pupils within the mainstream school

An essential factor in the functioning of children with visual impairments is to ensure that the environment does not impede their access to the school and to the curriculum. There are many ways in which this can be achieved, for example through providing the correct levels of illumination and in presenting materials which are suitable for the children's individual needs. In a special school, this is relatively easy to organise. However, in the mainstream school, it may be very difficult. Some children, for example those with cataracts or who have albinism, will function better if the level of lighting is reduced. Other children's vision will be helped if they are provided with additional lighting near to their work. In a mainstream school, it may not be possible to provide for these variations in the children's needs. Specialist teachers may experience a real tension between asking for these adaptations and yet arguing that their pupils can function within the normal school environment. Children and young people will also be helped to function more effectively if adaptations are made to teaching approaches and the curricular materials. It should be realised, however, that the majority of these adaptations will prove beneficial for all the pupils in the class, not just for the visually impaired. The provision of well-produced worksheets and of high-quality blackboards or whiteboards which make any text more visible is good practice for every pupil. None the less, many advisory teachers find negotiating with mainstream teachers a stressful situation.

One of the main responsibilities for advisory teachers who are supporting pupils with visual impairments in mainstream schools is to ensure their access to the full curriculum offered to the sighted pupils. This will involve close collaboration with both class and subject teachers. Ensuring access to the curriculum may involve the specialist teacher in the modification of materials necessary, both for the lessons themselves and also for the attainment tests which are part of the National Curriculum requirements. These modifications will include the provision of large-print, audio and tactile materials. Careful thought will need to go into the preparation of these, as few materials can be enlarged, recorded or brailled without adaptation.

The sheer volume of the full curriculum may also cause problems for the visually impaired. As many of the pupils will require longer to process information, and may also have additional special needs within the curriculum, some priorities may need to be set and some difficult choices made. It may be necessary for one or two subjects to be dropped, or for timetabling arrangements to be altered. It will be the responsibility of the specialist teachers to advise both the pupils and staff, and deciding on the appropriate advice to be given may prove stressful.

## Providing for the special needs of the pupils

As was noted above in relation to special school placement, there are additional aspects of the curriculum needed by pupils with visual impairments which are not part of the curriculum for fully-sighted pupils. These include the learning of braille and independent living skills. There are a number of pupils within mainstream schools who use braille as their medium of communication, but as has already been noted, learning braille can be a source of stress for teachers. For the advisory teacher who is supporting an individual pupil or a group of pupils within a mainstream school, braille may cause additional difficulties. In special schools, all the staff can be expected to have an understanding of the complexities of braille, and the provision of brailled material will be a matter of general policy. In contrast, it is likely that few, if any, mainstream teachers will understand what braille is all about, and the full responsibility for it will fall on the specialist teacher.

Planning for the learning of braille by an individual pupil in a class of print readers requires careful thought. The provision of brailled material may be difficult. Although there are organisations which provide tactile materials, it is necessary to contact them far in advance, which requires a lot of forward planning on the part of all the staff involved. Advisory teachers may find that their colleagues in the mainstream are too involved with the day-to-day teaching situation to be able to do this planning. A possible solution may be to have some volunteer braillists in the locality who will braille material at very short notice but these volunteers need to be located and trained, material will need to be delivered and collected, and this is very time-consuming.

Another aspect of the special curriculum which is accepted in the special school, but is usually not part of mainstream education, is education in mobility and orientation skills. Making arrangements for pupils to receive mobility education may be problematic. To begin with, these skills need one-to-one teaching, which in itself may cause difficulties for the timetabling of mobility lessons. Subject teachers may be reluctant to allow pupils time out from their lessons, especially if they appreciate the amount of additional time that pupils with visual impairments need to access the normal curriculum. As there is a shortfall in the number of mobility specialists available to work in schools on a regular basis, providing the necessary expertise may also not be possible. The specialist teachers themselves may not be able to provide the time from their daily work programmes, and they may therefore feel real concern at failing their pupils.

## The use of technology

Recent advances in technology have had a tremendous impact on the lives of people with visual impairments. Technology can enable pupils to access the curriculum in ways not possible before. However, technology only provides access to the curriculum, it is not a replacement for the curriculum. In addition, any piece of equipment frequently brings with it as many disadvantages as advantages. Unfortunately, this is not always understood by many non-specialists, and it will be necessary for advisory teachers to put considerable effort into increasing the understanding of other teachers and administrators. The possibilities, and limitations, of any item of technology must be fully understood before it is purchased, and the following questions must be considered:

- Will the equipment need to be moved by the pupils or the staff?
- Is there space for it in each of the rooms where it is required?
- Who will be responsible for any software which is needed?
- Are there arrangements in place for maintenance and repair?

In addition to these questions, the advisory teacher will need to ensure that training is made available for other staff and for the pupils.

## Support for individual pupils

The majority of specialist teachers, in addition to their advisory role described above, spend some of their time providing support teaching for individual pupils. This is one of the aspects of their role which they find very satisfying, and it helps to keep them in close contact with the needs of pupils generally, and with individuals in particular. In addition, direct teaching of pupils with visual impairments helps to maintain their credibility with other staff. However, finding time for this important role may be difficult, and fitting in with the timetables of several schools even more so.

# Other issues in advisory work

There are many other functions that are part of the advisory teacher's role which it is not possible to describe in detail here. These would include general administration, managing budgets, negotiation with education officers, preparation of information for Statements, communication with other professionals, negotiation with examination boards and providing in-service training to a wide range of professionals. No one teacher can feel competent in all these areas, and there is almost certainly stress involved in meeting these wide-ranging demands. The peripheral activities to being an advisory teacher are also a source of stress. All teachers whose role is to visit schools will find themselves involved in a certain amount of travelling. For teachers who are working with children with a minority impairment, such as a visual impairment, this travelling may prove excessive. Many people enjoy driving. However, there are those who do not, and in any case, driving under strict time constraints can be stressful. Cars do break down, punctures do occur, and there is not much enjoyment or job satisfaction to be found in changing a wheel on a cold, snowy morning when one is miles from the next school to be visited.

The attitude of mainstream staff to teachers who visit their schools can vary enormously, and can either be a source of support or a source of stress. In the authors' experience, the majority of school staff are welcoming and supportive. Visiting teachers are made to feel a real part of the school, and their expertise is respected. Full and frank co-operation takes place between mainstream and specialist staff, to the benefit of all. At the same time, a few teachers in mainstream schools do have negative attitudes to children with special needs and to the teachers supporting them. This may be due to the personality of the visiting or the mainstream teacher, but it is more likely to be due to the pressures which all teachers experience. However, a negative attitude from a host school can make the role of the advisory teacher very difficult. It can be hard, having travelled many miles, in difficult traffic situations, to be greeted by the comment: 'Oh, you're late – been shopping again?' The visiting teacher needs to learn to swallow hard and smile brightly. It can be equally irritating to have travelled some distance to arrive at a school and be told: 'Oh, Michael's not here, he had a dentist appointment this morning.'

## Professional development

There is, as has been noted, a mandatory qualification for teachers of the visually impaired who work in special schools. Unfortunately, this requirement is not extended to those teachers working in mainstream schools, but it is to the credit of employers that the majority of teachers supporting pupils in mainstream schools do have the additional qualification. However, one aspect of professional development that has never been fully recognised is that very few advisory teachers have had any specific training for this challenging role. Having considered the wide-ranging functions that teachers are expected to fulfil, and the critical nature of many of them (e.g. working with parents), this is not only surprising, but also disturbing. It is certainly a major source of stress for the teachers, who have to train themselves simply through contact with colleagues.

Another aspect of the professional development of these teachers is that promotion prospects may be extremely limited. Within the school system, there is a clear line of promotion. Teachers can apply for posts of special responsibility or to be heads of department. This can lead on to deputy headships and headships. Unfortunately, there is no such progression in support services. Even those services which have comparatively large teams of teachers are unlikely to have more than a dozen or so teachers, who will work under one administrative team leader. Because many services are relatively newly established, promotion in the short term may be non-existent. This is certainly a matter which concerns many teachers.

## The new challenges

In the 1990s, there are many new challenges facing advisory services. Recent government legislation, including arrangements for Local Management of Schools, has brought a feeling of insecurity to many teachers in advisory services. A number of staff have lost their jobs under the new arrangements. In addition, many services are having to give attention to new areas such as marketing, and are having to sell their services to mainstream schools.

The role of the advisory teacher is clearly a very challenging one. There are a number of stresses which are peculiar to the role of the teacher who travels within a locality, visiting many different homes and schools in the space of one day, but the vast majority of teachers who take on this role do so because they find it stimulating, exciting, full of variety and thoroughly worthwhile. There are few who, having experienced the challenges, choose to leave their posts, and the quality of the provision that is provided by these teachers is a tribute to their commitment and enthusiasm.

# Conclusion

The majority of teachers of pupils with visual impairments experience great job satisfaction, whether they work within the special or mainstream sectors of provision. They enjoy the challenges presented, take pride in their additional training and expertise, and offer creative yet structured teaching to their pupils. However, the stresses and pressures which many of them face give rise to fears that not only is their work being undermined, but that the needs of the pupils are also being misunderstood and unmet. It is to be hoped that these fears will prove unfounded.

Further information on schools supported by voluntary organisations can be obtained from the Royal National Institute for the Blind, 224 Great Portland Street, London W1N 6AA.

# References

Best, A.B. (1992) *Teaching Children with Visual Impairments*, Milton Keynes: Open University Press.

Chapman, E.K. (1982) 'A new approach to the training of teachers for children with special educational needs', *Educational Review*, 34, 2, 161–8.

Chapman, E.K. (1993) 'Coping with visually impaired children', in Varma, V.P. (ed.) *Coping with Unhappy Children*, London: Cassell.

Chapman, E.K. and Stone, J.M. (1988) *The Visually Handicapped Child in Your Classroom*, London: Cassell.

DES (1978) *Special Educational Needs* (The Warnock Report), London: HMSO.

Gale, W. (1991) 'RNIB New College Worcester: What kind of school?', *British Journal of Visual Impairment*, 9, 3, 84.

Lowenfeld B. (1971) *Our Blind Children: Growing and Learning with Them*, Springfields IL.: Charles C. Thomas.

Mason, H. and Tobin, M.J. (1986) 'Speed of information processing and the visually handicapped child', *British Journal of Special Education*, 13, 2, 69–70.

Stone, J.M. (1992) 'Educational advisory services – a national provision?', *British Journal of Visual Impairment*, 8, 3, 92–4.

Walker, E.C., McKinnell, R.C. and Tobin, M.J. (1992) *Survey of Needs*, No.2, London: RNIB/HMSO.

# 5 Physical disabilities

*Christopher Robertson*

## Introduction

> The history of the twentieth century for disabled people has been one of exclusion. The twenty-first century will see the struggle of disabled people for inclusion go from strength to strength. In such a struggle, special, segregated education has no role to play. (Oliver, 1995, p.94)

It is difficult to write about stress in teachers of pupils with physical disabilities without, at the same time, considering wider aspects of educational, social and political change. In this chapter, I will attempt to locate what I consider to be real difficulties of stress that teachers are experiencing within this important, broader context. In doing this, I am explicitly acknowledging that teaching is a discursive practice related to educational policies and powerful political ideologies. Individual teachers, particularly those working in marginal areas of education, are likely to be vulnerable to stress that arises from debates and battles that may seem to be distant from their daily lives. For teachers of pupils with physical disabilities, this 'distance' may well be experienced as a sense of 'liminality', or social suspension, as academics move on from discussing the successes and failures of integration to debating and advocating inclusion. This sense is exacerbated when teachers are working in difficult circumstances (in ordinary or special provision), without adequate resources or advice, and without local and national policy guidance.

However, there is no sign that a new coherence at educational policy level is going to bring about positive changes for teachers of pupils with physical disabilities. It is also the case that the views of parents of disabled people themselves, expressed through direct action or as a rigorous theoretical challenge to essentially segregationist educational practice, are here to stay.

This does not mean that difficulties facing these teachers are insuperable.

However, it does mean that suggestions about help and support need to be linked to a consideration of the many constraints and challenges that teachers are facing. Through a discussion of the following themes, I hope to be able to outline some of the specific difficulties teachers encounter, and to highlight good and developing practice that can address the causes and minimise the effects of stress:

- the changing nature of educational provision for physically disabled pupils;
- integration, inclusion and the impact of a social model of disability;
- the curriculum;
- teacher identities and roles;
- working with other professionals and with parents;
- supporting teachers and training needs.

## The changing nature of educational provision for pupils with physical disabilities

In the fifteen years following the 1981 Education Act, a number of changes have taken place which have affected the nature of educational provision for physically disabled children and young people. In general terms, there has been a shift towards more integrated educational provision for *some* physically disabled pupils, though the extent of this development has not been accurately documented. A survey carried out by the Centre for Studies on Inclusive Education (CSIE, 1994) revealed that separate special education provision generally was not in terminal decline, and was in fact thriving. It also revealed that levels of integration varied considerably between local education authorities.

The past decade or so has also witnessed a changing aetiology of physical disability, and this has shaped provision to some extent. While science and technology have brought about advancement in terms of preventive medicine, they have also enabled many babies with complex physical disabilities to survive birth and to thrive. These children clearly have complex educational needs as well as other important medical and therapeutic needs. A picture has emerged, therefore, of the most physically 'able' pupils attending ordinary schools or transferring to them, while those with more complex physical needs have attended separate provision. Some of this discrete provision is on a very small scale, and creates difficulties for educators trying to organise a school within the framework of demands made by the 1988 Education Reform Act.

Teachers working with physically disabled pupils must have to grapple with important moral dilemmas concerning the aforementioned medical 'advancement'. These debates are not simple, but neither are they going to go away. Scientific orthodoxy is questioned by writers like Davis (1987), who has forcefully challenged consensus views that preventive medicine is an intrinsic good. Teachers working with physically disabled pupils may find their own views on these matters and the rationale for their work questioned by others, including members of the teaching profession.

Other changes in special education have led to a re-conceptualisation of specialist teaching. This has had implications for teachers of pupils with physical disabilities. In mapping the dimensions of special education, Fish (1989) has identified an extensive range of possible activities that constitute special educational support and intervention. The implications of this are that teachers working with physically disabled pupils could be working in a wide range of provision, carrying out a broad range of teaching and support activities, some generic and some specialist. For some teachers, this has meant a change of role that they may not always feel at ease with, or trained to undertake.

Educational change in the past decade has been both extensive and continuous, and the structural reforms following the 1988 Education Reform Act have clearly been stress-inducing for all teachers (Dunham, 1992). Change in education is not always rational or about clear, linear progress, as Fullan (1991) has noted. Rather, it is messy, often piecemeal, and not a 'blueprint' for coherent development. Living with and managing change requires teachers at all levels to engage meaningfully with it. For teachers of pupils with physical disabilities, this has been especially difficult, because their work has been so evidently marginal to the main thrust of educational change. Matters of integration and curriculum access have largely been left for teachers to facilitate, but support or guidance to assist in this task has been systematically eroded.

## Integration, inclusion and the impact of a social model of disability

The integration of physically disabled pupils into ordinary schools has operated for many years within the 'transfer' model, whereby students from special schools are gradually moved into ordinary schools, often on an individual basis. A number of teachers, schools and support services have worked hard to develop good practice in this important task, and successful approaches have been highlighted (Gibb and Donkersloot, 1991; Jacklin and Lacey, 1991). The key to this would appear to lie in having a good understanding of individual needs and in systematic forward planning (Halliday, 1989), but intrinsic difficulties exist, as Gibb and Donkersloot note:

> the more people think about mainstream the more likely they are to learn about it. It is sometimes difficult to escape the impression in special schools that mainstream schools, their practices and problems are a total mystery. (1991, p. 33)

The cultures of ordinary and special schools are different, and pupils may have great difficulty in 'bridging' this divide through integration, as Jacklin and Lacey (1991) point out. This difference of culture is something that teachers involved in integration work experience and can find stressful. In many situations, pupils transferring from special to ordinary schools are not doing so in ideal circumstances. Rather, they are being moved in an *ad hoc* way into a local or designated school that may only be minimally prepared for their arrival. Indeed, some teachers in the ordinary school may be at best ambivalent or at worst hostile to the arrival of a physically disabled pupil. These teachers may well be working under duress, teaching large classes in poor accommodation. Their support needs are of great importance (Jacklin and Lacey, 1993) and are not often addressed.

Integrating pupils with physical disabilities, particularly those with more complex needs, is not easy. Beneficial educational outcomes do not necessarily arise from simply 'being there', as Martlew and Cooksey (1989) have noted. It is frequently argued that a significant reason for this is that specialist support and advice have long been tailored to operate in separate special educational settings. This has led to the advocacy of an inclusive model of education, where all specialist work, including that which is interprofessional, is aimed primarily at ordinary schools. Such a model would remove difficulties of transfer or de-segregation at a stroke. However, this approach, as advocated by Ainscow (1995), for example, has both underestimated the complexity of pupil needs and the pedagogy required to meet these. A more open and complex view of inclusive education has been sketched by Wedell (1995); it includes a recognition of the complexity and diversity of pupil needs, and implicit in his perspective is the idea that we should think beyond models of learning that are focused on activity within single educational settings such as the school. Such a framework for inclusion remains a potential one, as Wedell acknowledges. For teachers of physically disabled pupils, neither integration nor inclusion promises to be stress-free. While inclusion appears to be an attractive way forward, it has to be planned for comprehensively at a national level and adequately resourced.

Another key issue in the inclusive education debate that will radically challenge teachers of physically disabled pupils and perhaps cause some of them stress is the redefining of disability by social theorists, and in particular disabled ones. A seminal definition of disability was produced by the Union of the Physically Impaired Against Segregation (UPIAS, 1976). It clearly delineates between impairment and disability, arguing that disability as a phenomenon has been created (Oliver, 1990) by a social organisation that largely ignores the rights and interests of disabled people. The UPIAS definition states that:

> In our view it is society which disables physically impaired people. Disability is something imposed on top of our impairments by the way we are unnecessarily isolated and excluded from full participation. Disabled people are therefore an oppressed group in society. (UPIAS, 1976, cited in Oliver, 1995, p.35)

Understanding and internalising such a perspective can be a transforming and difficult experience for teachers of physically disabled pupils. To adopt such a view of disability involves not only reflection on one's work (Oliver, 1995), but also the development of a new and different kind of commitment. This catharsis might not be an easy experience, as Withers (1986) has indicated; indeed it might serve to accentuate aspects of teaching that involve conflict and struggle, as will the recognition that teaching physically disabled pupils involves working from a position of power and vested interest.

Taking a view of disability that acknowledges developments in social theory will inevitably lead teachers to recognise that it is not generally appropriate to see causes of stress in their working lives as arising from 'within' the children they teach. Rather, stress will be seen as being located in the organisation and structure of schooling at various levels. Of course, this is not to deny that individual pupils will experience problems that will cause teachers stress. The point is that in many circumstances, the causal factors at work, whether they appear to be derived from within a pupil or not, will actually be derived ultimately from matters of organisation that serve to exclude that pupil in some way. Of course, psychological difficulties experienced by pupils will be 'real', and the impact of these on teachers will be authentic. The harder thing for teachers to recognise, however, is that these difficulties that affect their work are not part of an individual pupil's 'pathology', but have been created socially.

# The curriculum

What is taught to children with physical disabilities is often seen as unproblematic. Following the introduction of the National Curriculum in 1988, it has been assumed that such pupils would benefit from entitlement and access to the same curriculum as other children. The modified version of the National Curriculum re-emphasises this view, and subject orders for schools to follow include brief guidance for teachers on the need to ensure access for pupils with physical disabilities. However, there are underlying difficulties in this entitlement perspective that present teachers with significant problems that can be stress-inducing. As well as having to face up to a massive increase in workload since 1988, like teachers generally, those working with physically disabled pupils have also had to face up to major concerns about curriculum priorities, given that the time pupils spend in school is limited. This difficulty is one that confronts teachers working in both ordinary and special schools, and the reforms heralded by the Dearing Report (Dearing, 1993) have only partially assuaged concerns.

The National Curriculum has brought about benefits for physically disabled pupils, and some of these have been described by Lonton and Farooqui (1991) in the context of special school provision. They are worth summarising here:

1   There will be pressures on the school to provide a full and well-structured curriculum for all children.
2   There will be pressures on the local authority to give the school a wide range of subject specialists and appropriate equipment.
3   More emphasis will be placed on disabled children striving for the same goals as able-bodied children.
4   Statutory monitoring of children's progress will take place. (adapted from Lonton and Farooqui, 1991, pp.30–1)

These generally positive benefits can be seen as being particularly valuable, given that the special school curriculum and related aspects of provision have been strongly criticised in recent years (Barnes, 1991). At the same time, teachers of pupils with complex physical disabilities have rightly been concerned to teach pupils relevant material. The problems faced include:

- How to incorporate individual education plans that set targets for things like self-help and therapy into an educational framework that is broad, balanced and meets statutory requirements (DES, 1989);
- how to make the best use of time when pupils may be experiencing difficulties of learning or have non-educational priority needs;
- how to make best use of the school day, which may be short because of transport difficulties.

One response to these problems would be to say that they could be solved by an inclusive model of education. However, this is self-evidently not the case: the complex needs of some pupils, of necessity, make decisions about learning and other priorities imperative. To deny this is possibly to deny some children a right to an education that best meets their needs. The stress for teachers lies in the fact that they work in a *laissez-faire* environment when it comes to receiving guidance about how to prioritise. Advice on whether to modify or disapply parts of the National Curriculum is rarely forthcoming, perhaps because to provide this might been seen as overriding entitlement. This is at best unhelpful to teachers, and for pupils; and as Lonton and Farooqui (1991) observe: 'The highly individual needs of children with severe physical disabilities should never be sacrificed on the altar of ideological uniformity' (p.31).

Another difficulty that teachers of pupils with physical disabilities face is the way that access to the curriculum is sometimes crudely conceptualised for some of their pupils. As Halliday (1989) notes: 'Access to curriculum is more than just access to rooms and equipment and more than just educational experience or opportunity. Teaching methods, expectations of pupil performance and content are all components of the curriculum' (pp.53–4). This more substantial access requires hard work, shared working practices and is time-consuming. Too often, in integrated educational settings, being in a class with a computer is equated with good educational provision. Technology is potentially very liberating for pupils with physical disabilities, but teachers helping them to use it are often faced with difficulties that cause them major concern. First, the technological equipment that pupils may be given to use is frequently either out of date or inappropriate for classroom use (it has been trialled and used in clinical or assessment settings), and technical support for teachers is often lacking. Second, technological innovations are often seen as being inherently good, when in fact they can be dependency-creating, with pupils spending a lot of time following a narrow range of computer-based learning activities to the neglect of more interesting, relevant or social learning. Stereotyping can also arise along the lines of 'she has cerebral palsy and therefore *will* enjoy computer studies', when in fact the pupil is interested in very different subjects. Zola (1982) discusses the way that technology can also deeply 'de-personalise' individuals. Teachers not experienced in working with physically disabled pupils may initially see technology as providing optimum curriculum access, and they may become frustrated when it does not produce the expected outcomes. Its value needs to be assessed in the context of appropriate teaching approaches and adequate resourcing.

The encouragement of self-advocacy, like technology, is also deemed to be an essential good for pupils with physical disabilities, and especially so for older students, where it is linked to ideals of independence and autonomy. This is laudable, but masks some difficulties which teachers may find create tensions in their day-to-day work. There is no point teaching advocacy or decisionmaking skills unless pupils are able to exercise these in practice (Halliday, 1989). Teachers may have to enhance their own understanding of the oppression of disabled people to enable them to fully grasp what self-advocacy might imply for their pupils, and this reflection may involve a questioning of their own educational practice and that of their school. Mittler and Buckingham (1987) have shown how valuable it can be to approach problems of advocacy in formal and structured ways, and to link this work to the 'real world' of life beyond school. However, there are dangers in the mismatch that occurs when teachers try to develop independence and autonomy through curriculum provision that is preparing pupils for a life they will not lead. Such practices can have very negative consequences for pupils with complex physical disabilities, as Corbett (1989) has argued. For teachers, the difficult thing is to acknowledge pupil interests and choices, and to place these in a meaningful (empowering) relationship to post-school/college provision that may not be premised on notions of independence. Achieving this balance will always present difficulties, and teachers will have to acknowledge their own failures as well as successes. Such work is inherently stressful, and teachers need to work with other professionals and the pupils themselves in order to minimise potential difficulties.

A final area of potential concern and stress for teachers of physically disabled pupils in relation to the curriculum is that of inspection. The work of the Office for Standards in Education (OFSTED), in its short life to date, has already had a significant impact on all teachers' lives and the organisation and management of schools. It is interesting to note that Dunham (1992), in a thorough analysis of stress in teaching, does not mention inspection as a cause. Two particular areas of concern are likely to be significant in the context of physical disability. First, that the inspection process, with its rigid framework, may not enable inspectors to adequately inspect the most important aspects of educational provision. Second, that inspectors themselves may not have adequate experience or knowledge of physical disability to make reliable judgements. Such concerns may prove to be unfounded, but that will not prevent teachers from feeling anxious. A recent publication by OFSTED (1995) gives an indication that the inspection process could potentially accommodate limited flexibility, enabling individual schools to provide a rationale for their specialist work. Such a development could be reassuring for teachers of physically disabled pupils.

# Teacher identities and roles

Teachers working with physically disabled pupils are less likely than ever before to be teaching in a traditional role, working with a small, homogeneous group in a special school, unit or designated classroom. If they are working in some kind of discrete provision, as I have noted earlier, it is likely to be with a heterogeneous group of pupils who have complex physical disabilities and possibly some associated difficulties of learning and/or sensory impairments. If they are working in ordinary schools, they are likely to be working in a variety of learning settings, and often providing support and advice rather than direct teaching.

These teaching roles have evolved over a number of years, but not all teachers will have been given systematic training to help them meet the demands of their changing responsibilities. For some teachers, adjusting to working with pupils who have complex disabilities may be a stressful matter, both in terms of emotional adjustment and confidence in their ability to teach an appropriate curriculum. As Fish (1989) notes, the activities that could constitute specialist teaching are numerous, and in relation to physical disability, they are likely to involve tasks that overlap with the work of other professionals from health and social services backgrounds. This overlap with the knowledge and skills of others is important and valuable, but it is also potentially deskilling in the way that it can make a teacher feel that their knowledge is indistinct or underdeveloped in certain areas. It has been suggested that forms of joint training with therapists would be a way of overcoming difficulties of role identity and a way of enhancing professional practice (Norwich, 1990). The most notable example of this approach to training in the area of physical disability is the training of 'conductors' in Hungary, utilising the pedagogy of conductive education. Attempts are being made to replicate this training in the UK, though evaluation of some of this work and its impact on children has suggested that 'transplanting' an eclectic and complex interprofessional educational and therapeutic method is extremely difficult (Bairstow et al., 1993). For most teachers of pupils with physical disabilities, training in conductive education is unlikely to be forthcoming or appropriate.

Conductive education and other therapeutic approaches for physically disabled children would appear to place teachers in a difficult position, and one that can cause great personal stress in relation to parental perspectives on priorities for pupil development and learning. While teaching physically disabled children has been focused on developing better curriculum access in recent years, in the difficult circumstances I have already outlined, some parents have sought 'better' provision, as they perceive it, through the conductive education approach. While conductive education has been roundly condemned as an infringement of human rights (Oliver, 1989), others have seen it as a perfectly logical search for good-quality education and therapy (Beardshaw, 1989). Teachers caught in this crossfire of views must feel very uncomfortable about what is the right stance to take, both in relation to their own work with pupils and in their relationships with parents. What makes this especially stressful for them is that there are no obvious sources of advice and support. Clearly, they might develop a coherent way of grappling with such issues by developing an understanding of, and commitment to, a social model and theory of disability. However, not all teachers will feel that such a model matches their own understanding of physical disability, or that it adequately reflects the realities of the circumstances in which they are working.

The overall effect of these kinds of difficulties, together with poor working conditions has been to lower teacher morale. Poor morale, as Tilstone (1991) has noted, is linked to a lack of confidence, and can lead to high levels of stress among teachers.

## Working with other professionals and with parents

Teaching pupils with physical disabilities is increasingly about managing learning in various settings and working with other professionals to provide effective support. This kind of work is not easy, and teachers involved in it require training and regular advice and guidance. When this is not forthcoming, teaching becomes very stressful. A particular problem for teachers working in integrated settings is that they do not always feel themselves to be full members of a school staff, especially when their teaching role is defined closely in terms of individual pupil support. Dyson (1990) has argued that specialist staff should have other teaching roles too. Such a view is premised on the idea that support should be provided from within the school, not from the outside. This may not always be the most cost-effective or skilful way of meeting the needs of physically disabled pupils in a school, but it would certainly be a way of making specialist work integral to teaching. It would also be a good way of providing natural, symbiotic support between specialist and ordinary teachers.

A key aspect of supporting pupils with physical disabilities in their learning is the co-ordinating and appropriate channelling of advice from various professional perspectives. One way in which teachers are beginning to do this is by using an Individual Education Plan as a means of processing and targeting the priorities of a range of professionals. A number of innovative uses are being made of these plans, legislated for in the Code of Practice (DfE, 1994), but the management of them is already showing signs of becoming oppressively bureaucratic. The consequence for teachers using them is an increase in workload. Good Individual Education Plans for pupils with complex physical disabilities will, of necessity, involve a range of professionals in joint planning, in consultation with pupils and parents. In such an enterprise, there are no short cuts if good practice is to be achieved. Unfortunately, time, resources and interprofessional organisational constraints make this good practice hard to achieve. A consequence for the teachers involved will be that they will feel they are not making optimum use of the skills and knowledge of others.

Working with other professionals is something that teachers tend to learn as they go along, often in the absence of professional development opportunities in this area. This is particularly unfortunate for support work, because it is not the same as teaching either in a special or ordinary classroom (Norwich, 1990), and without training it can become both unfulfilling and stressful.

Working with parents is also a crucial part of teaching physically disabled pupils. As Hornby (1994) notes, teachers 'are [with others] likely to be a main source of guidance and counselling for families who have members with disabilities' (p.194), and as such, are likely to need skills to undertake this work. He identifies four areas where teachers, as well as other professionals, may have particular roles to play in their work with parents:

1   communicating the diagnosis of disability, or the results of assessments, in a sensitive and constructive manner;
2   providing information about the disability, services available and on facilitating the child's development;
3   providing emotional support, and helping parents to understand their feelings and reactions;
4   linking parents with others who are in a similar position to themselves.
    (Hornby, 1994, p.6)

Teachers do assume these roles to some degree, and are often under strain because they do not always feel they have the skills to carry them out. This is particularly the case when they are giving emotional support. In some circumstances, when discussing the needs of a pupil with a deteriorating condition, for example, this support is given without any recognition of their own emotional needs. However, it is easy to overemphasise the counselling role of teachers, to the extent that their work can be perceived as being therapeutic in nature, rather than educational.

This blurring of roles can cause stress for teachers, but can also lead to them assuming roles of unhelpful paternalism and power in their relations with parents. Adopting a 'teacher as counsellor' approach carries with it dangers of this kind. Counselling skills may have some value, but teachers of physically disabled pupils must also recognise that their relationships with parents are inevitably complex and not reducible to models of partnership that see teachers cast in the role of omniscient bestowers of advice and comfort. Instead:

If teachers want to consider partnership with parents in more depth they will have to be prepared to make themselves more aware of what special education is actually offering and why, of the processes they are involved in, whether intentionally or unintentionally, and the consequences for themselves, children and parents. They will have to be prepared to alter structures to make room for parental choice, control and evaluation. They will have to be able to work within more open situations which involve sharing with and supporting other professionals, as well as parents. They will have to be more open about what they are doing and why, to question their own motives, stances and the principles as well as the rhetoric upon which special educational provision is based. (Wood, 1988, pp. 204–5)

This more comprehensive view of working with parents illustrates the need for schools and support services to provide training and support to individual teachers in a systematic way. Without this, teachers will be vulnerable to stress, being caught between the consumer demands of parents and the organisational constraints of their own schools.

# Supporting teachers and training needs

In the preceding sections of this chapter, I have attempted to explore some of the many factors that can cause stress in teachers of pupils with physical disabilities. I have placed particular emphasis on organisational and structural difficulties, rather than on 'within-pupil' factors. In this final section, I will outline in brief some suggestions for enhancing support for these teachers. Inevitably, in attempting to do this, I am presenting a 'listing' of ideas, some of which have been evaluated in practice. However, this listing is not presented as *the* solution to stress, or deemed to be comprehensive. It is offered, instead, in the hope that some of the ideas might encourage teachers to think about issues to do with stress in the context of organisational and staff development.

The suggestions are outlined under two headings, 'Supporting teachers' and 'Training'. They should be of interest to teachers working in ordinary schools, support services, specialist units and special schools.

## Supporting teachers

Schools and support services need to consider providing systematic support for staff. This support should focus on improving organisational resources generally, and need not focus solely on stress. Areas worthy of attention are:

effective selection procedures; induction programmes for all staff; the expansion of staff development and management-training opportunities; support from colleagues; effective management of meetings; teamwork; curricular and organisational change; pupil behaviour, learning and other needs; and stress reduction programmes (adapted from Dunham, 1992, p.142).

Teachers of physically disabled pupils, who might be working in relative isolation in some schools, should consider how they can become more centrally involved in the general current of school life. Similarly, senior managers in schools need to ensure that staff working in specialist areas are involved in organisational decisionmaking and are not seen as marginal to core interests.

Effective school appraisal systems that are linked to whole-school approaches to staff development and are seen as a means of helping teachers in their professional development can also contribute to the reduction of stress. At the same time, a word of caution is appropriate here; appraisal can also heighten stress:

> The appraisal interview has elements both of the confessional and the psychoanalytical encounter, both of which rely upon the dynamics of self-revelation. The appraisees are encouraged to display their shortcomings, to seek out or identify appropriate therapeutic procedures, and to judge themselves and award their own punishment. (Ball, 1990, p.161)

Schools and support services should also consider providing regular and sustained opportunities for staff to participate in short courses that help them to identify the causes of stress in the workplace, and to develop their personal resources for coping with stress (Dunham, 1989). These opportunities could be valuably linked to the development of in-school support systems of the kind described by Tilstone (1991). However, such developments need to be carefully planned if they are to avoid 'medicalising' teachers experiencing difficulties.

Schools and support services might consider adopting, or adapting, a model of support developed by Daniels et al. (1993) and reported in this book in Chapter 12. Key features of this approach are that it is informal, teacher-focused, school-based and non-hierarchical. Although it has been implemented in ordinary schools and in relation to teacher concerns about behavioural or learning difficulties, it would appear to lend itself readily to use in other settings, and there is no reason why it could not be a valuable way of discussing concerns about teaching physically disabled pupils.

Teachers working with pupils who have complex physical disabilities, including those with deteriorating conditions, may often feel isolated, especially if working in ordinary schools. Effective models of support for these pupils, their families and their teachers do exist. Jeffrey (1990) has described good systemic support based on a special school providing a multiprofessional outreach service. Such models need to be replicated – from either ordinary or special school bases. Interestingly, multidimensional support has been a feature of developments in the health service in recent years. An example of this is the research and development of comprehensive systems of care for terminally ill children and their families described by Thornes (1990). Such carefully thought through models could be usefully 'translated' into educational contexts and offer a coherent framework of support for teachers to work within.

## Training

Teachers of pupils with physical disabilities, whatever context they are working in, should have an entitlement to appropriate training. This training may need to operate at different levels in accordance with the needs of teachers. Currently, opportunities for coherent training are limited. However, the efforts of the Special Educational Needs Training Consortium (1996) to place specialist educational training on the political agenda are to be welcomed.

Such training could usefully place emphasis on the following areas:

- working with pupils in a variety of educational settings, including ordinary schools, support services and special schools;
- working with other staff, including classroom assistants (Balshaw, 1991; Fox, 1993);
- collaborative and multidisciplinary work (Lacey and Lomas, 1993);
- developing the social theory of disability and its implications for the planning of inclusive education;
- the use of augmentative communication and associated technology;
- counselling skills (Hornby, 1994), and working with parents (Armstrong, 1995).

Training of this kind ought to be made available to teachers starting specialist careers, but it should also be accessible to teachers already working as experienced practitioners.

## Conclusion

Through looking at issues concerning the changing nature of educational provision, integration and inclusion, the curriculum, teacher roles and identities, working with other professionals and parents, I hope that I have been able to convey some sense of the complexity of factors that, in combination, can cause stress in teachers of pupils with physical disabilities. I have also tried to offer some suggestions for the support of teachers and highlight some training imperatives.

I have avoided projecting the causes of stress onto pupils. This is not to deny individual difficulties experienced by them. Sometimes, these difficulties may be very significant, and have a powerful impact on teachers. However, it is important to see stress in the context of social organisation and the social creation of disability. Like other teachers, those working with physically disabled pupils are working in times of increasing complexity:

> Teachers must not only have regard for the different and sometimes conflicting needs of all children in their classes but respond also to the increasingly centralized systems of control which the state exerts over professional life in schools. Although these different pressures may combine to impose severe constraints on professional action they also present challenges to the homogeneity of professional practice. They highlight the fact that professionals are forced to make choices in their practice which sit uneasily with an ethic of professional service governed solely by the interests of children. (Armstrong, 1995, pp.147–8)

Given this complexity, it is vitally important that teachers receive support at a variety of levels, and that both the causes and symptoms of stress are addressed in ways that avoid simply individualising problems, for a strongly individualising approach will only serve to increase levels of stress.

# References

Ainscow, M. (1995) 'Education for all: Making it happen', *Support for Learning*, 10, 4, 147–55.

Armstrong, D. (1995) *Power and Partnership in Education*, London: Routledge.

Bairstow, P., Cochrane, R. and Hur, J. (1993) *Evaluation of Conductive Education, Parts 1 and 2*, London: HMSO.

Ball, S. (1990) *Foucault and Education: Disciplines and Knowledge*, London: Routledge.

Balshaw, M. (1991) *Help in the Classroom*, London: David Fulton.

Barnes, C. (1991) *Disabled People in Britain and Discrimination*, London: Hurst.

Beardshaw, V. (1989) 'Conductive education: A rejoinder', *Disability, Handicap and Society*, 4, 3, 297–9.

Corbett, J. (1989) 'The quality of life in the "independence" curriculum', *Disability, Handicap and Society*, 4, 2, 145–63.

CSIE (1994) *Segregation and Inclusion: English LEA Statistics 1988–1992*, Bristol: Centre for Studies on Inclusive Education.

Daniels, H., Norwich, B. and Anghileri, N. (1993) 'Teacher support teams: An evaluation of a school-based approach to meeting special educational needs', *Support for Learning*, 8, 4, 169–73.

Davis, A. (1987) 'Women with disabilities: Abortion or liberation', *Disability, Handicap and Society*, 2, 3, 275–84.

Dearing, R. (1993) *The National Curriculum and its Assessment*, London: School Curriculum and Assessment Authority.

DES (1989) *From Policy to Practice*, London: Department of Education and Science.

DfE (1994) *The Code of Practice on the Identification and Assessment of Special Educational Needs*, London: HMSO.

Dunham, J. (1989) 'Stress in teaching', in Jones, N. (ed.) *Special Educational Needs Review 1*, Lewes: Falmer Press.

Dunham, J. (1992) *Stress in Teaching* (2nd edn), London: Routledge.

Dyson, A. (1990) 'Effective learning consultancy: A future role for special needs co-ordinators?', *Support for Learning*, 5, 3, 116–27.

Fish, J. (1989) *What is Special Education?*, Milton Keynes: Open University Press.

Fox, G. (1993) *A Handbook for Special Needs Assistants*, London: David Fulton.

Fullan, M. (1991) *The New Meaning of Educational Change*, London: Cassell.

Fullan, M. (1992) 'We do not have the choice of avoiding change just because it is messy', *The Times Educational Supplement*, 9 October, 2.

Gibb, C. and Donkersloot, P. (1991) 'Planning de-segregation', *British Journal of Special Education*, 18, 1, 33–5.

Halliday, P. (1989) *Children with Physical Disabilities*, London: Cassell.

Hornby, G. (1994) *Counselling in Child Disability: Skills for Working with Parents*, London: Chapman and Hall.

Jacklin, A. and Lacey, J. (1991) 'Assessing integration at Patcham House', *British Journal of Special Education*, 18, 2, 67–70.

Jacklin, A. and Lacey, J. (1993) 'The integration process: A developmental model', *Support for Learning*, 8, 2, 51–7.

Jeffrey, P. (1990) 'Enhancing their lives: A challenge for education', in Dominica, F. et al. (eds) *Listen. My Child has a Lot of Living to do*, Oxford: Oxford University Press.

Lacey, P. and Lomas, J. (1993) *Support Services and the Curriculum: A Practical Guide to Collaboration*, London: David Fulton.

Lonton, T. and Farooqui, A. (1991) 'A disabling curriculum for some?', *British Journal of Special Education*, 18, 1, 29–31.

Martlew, M. and Cooksey, C. (1989) 'The integration of a child with cerebral palsy into a mainstream nursery', *European Journal of Special Needs Education*, 4, 2, 103–15.

Mittler, H. and Buckingham, A. (1987) 'Getting ready to leave', *British Journal of Special Education*, 14, 1, 11–13.

Norwich, B. (1990) *Reappraising Special Needs Education*, London: Cassell.

OFSTED (1995) *Guidance on the Inspection of Special Schools*, London: HMSO.

Oliver, M. (1989) 'Conductive education: If it wasn't so sad it would be funny', *Disability, Handicap and Society*, 4, 2, 197–9.

Oliver, M. (1990) *The Politics of Disablement*, Basingstoke: Macmillan.

Oliver, M. (1995) *Understanding Disability: From Theory to Practice*, Basingstoke: Macmillan.

Special Educational Needs Training Consortium (1996) *Professional Development to Meet Special Educational Needs: Report to the Department for Education and Employment*, Stafford: Flash Ley Resource Centre.

Thornes, R. (1990) 'Towards a comprehensive system of care for dying children and their families: Key issues', in Dominica, F. et al. (eds) *Listen. My Child has a Lot of Living to do*, Oxford: Oxford University Press.

Tilstone, C. (1991) *Teaching Children with Severe Learning Difficulties: Practical Approaches*, London: David Fulton.

UPIAS (1976) *Fundamental Principles of Disability*, London: Union of the Physically Impaired Against Segregation.

Wedell, K. (1995) 'Making inclusive education ordinary', *British Journal of Special Education*, 22, 3, 100–4.

Withers, R. (1986) 'Having sympathies in special education: An argument for the refusal of empathy', *Disability, Handicap and Society*, 1, 2, 197–205.

Wood, S. (1988) 'Parents: Whose partners?', in Barton, L. (ed.) *The Politics of Special Educational Needs*, Lewes: Falmer Press.

Zola, I. (1982) 'Social and cultural disincentives to independent living', *Archives of Physical Medicine and Rehabilitation*, 63, 395–6.

# 6 Speech and language impairments

*Ann Locke*

A significant proportion of children with special educational needs have difficulty establishing spoken language. The problems experienced by most of them can be attributed to more primary problems, such as sensory or physical impairment, generalised learning difficulties or autism. A small group of children, however, 'pose a puzzle. Their language acquisition is abnormal or delayed, yet they appear to have sufficient exposure to language input, normal capacity to perceive language, a brain which is adequate for learning in the non-verbal domain, and intact articulatory structures' (Bishop, 1992, p.2). They are commonly referred to as having a specific language impairment (SLI). The children involved present very disparate patterns of development: some children have difficulty solely with speech, others have difficulty solely with language; language difficulties can involve purely understanding language – making sense of what people say – or purely expressing language – producing words in recognisable sentences – or both; some children have difficulty in understanding and expressing language and producing clear speech.

Impairment in any of these skills – producing clear speech, expressing language and understanding language – occurs on a continuum, ranging from mild to severe, and although all three difficulties can occur in isolation, it is common for children to experience problems in more than one area. A child could have mild difficulties understanding language, moderate difficulties expressing language and severe difficulties producing clear speech. Here, the speech difficulty may well mask a child's poor expressive language. Another child could have little or no difficulty with speech but moderate difficulty both understanding and expressing language. Here, the normal speech may well camouflage the child's difficulty with complex language. Virtually any combination is possible, and no two children are likely to show exactly the same pattern of difficulties.

It is not easy to estimate the incidence of these problems, for the difference between delayed but otherwise normal learning and disordered development can be hard to determine. Although a number of surveys have been carried out over the past forty years, the figures reported are variable. In a long-term study of families in Newcastle upon Tyne in the 1960s (Morley, 1965), 19 per cent of 3-year-old children had speech that was difficult to follow. This had dropped to 5 per cent at 4 years, and around 1 per cent at 6 years. The results of the Isle of Wight survey (Rutter et al., 1970) suggested that only 1 in 1,000 school-age children had severe difficulties. Crystal (1984) argued that around 10 per cent of children have difficulties that may cause problems for themselves and their teachers. Webster and McConnell (1987), reviewing the available evidence, concluded that teachers working in mainstream schools can expect to find two or three children in every class with some degree of speech or language difficulty.

Educational awareness of specific language impairment has been slow to develop. While children with speech difficulties were included in the 1944 Education Act, problems that can occur in children's language development were not understood or even recognised at that time, and language impairment was not included as a category of impairment. In addition, the help offered to speech-impaired children was provided by speech therapists, who were then regularly employed by local education authorities. Government policy throughout the 1950s and early 1960s led to the development of speech therapy through local health services, and the direct employment of speech therapists in schools was withdrawn. It is interesting to speculate on how educational services for children with speech and language impairment might have evolved had speech therapy services become a more integral part of education in the way that psychological services developed.

Although teachers in general are increasingly aware of children with special needs, opportunities for learning more about children with speech and language impairment are still limited. It is now a requirement that all initial teacher training courses include some input to enable teachers to identify and understand the more common learning difficulties. However, the HMI report *Education Observed: Special Needs Issues* (DES, 1990) showed that the quality of this training varied considerably (see also Upton, 1992). Aubrey (1994) describes how drastically the special educational needs component of undergraduate courses has been reduced. In 1981, the course she was concerned with provided $1\frac{1}{2}$ hours' teaching a week to all students in their third year and offered a specialist option in the fourth year. The three-year course offered from 1994 includes a common professional year with postgraduate primary students, during which they receive just one $1\frac{1}{4}$ hour session on special educational needs. It is difficult to imagine how newly-qualified teachers will be able to identify and provide for any category of children with special educational needs with this level of training.

Four part-time post-experience courses are now offered for teachers working with children with speech and language impairment. This may be an effective way of gaining knowledge, but demands considerable time and commitment from teachers, most of whom are likely to be in full-time employment while they are studying.

Although there is broad agreement that the group of speech- and language-impaired children as a whole includes several subtypes of disorder, there is as yet no consensus about what these might be, and Fletcher's (1992) analysis of recent studies suggests that researchers are still some way from providing a comprehensive typology of language impairment. Nor is there as yet any comprehensive explanation of children's underlying impairment, though most have difficulty with auditory discrimination and sequencing skills, and poor auditory memory for sounds and words. The approach taken in this chapter is to provide a behavioural account of specific language impairment, focusing on the three main areas of difficulty: unclear speech, poor expressive language, and comprehension difficulties.

# Children with unclear speech

Although there is considerable variation in the rate at which children learn to speak, most children establish the full range of speech sounds during their third year, and can be easily understood well before they start school. It is not uncommon, however, to find one or two children in a reception class who are still missing out or muddling some sounds, and minor inaccuracies occur quite commonly in children up to the age of around 7. Most of these patterns of difficulty come within the range of normal development, and are unlikely to persist. The most important consideration with children under the age of 4 is that they can be understood by people who know them well, and that they are talking regularly and confidently with familiar adults and children. Where both these conditions are occurring, the clarity of their speech is likely to improve spontaneously.

Nevertheless, children over the age of 3 whose speech is difficult to understand should be considered a cause of concern, for within this group will be some whose problems will be persistent, and any child who is still unintelligible at this age may have long-term difficulties. The group as a whole is divided into three subgroups: phonological difficulties, articulation difficulties and dyspraxic difficulties.

Children with phonological difficulties are slow to establish the rules of how sounds are used in a particular language system. By far the majority of young children with poor speech fall into this category. They usually respond well to intervention, and given regular help in the infant years, should be intelligible and making satisfactory educational progress by the time they move on to the junior years. Articulation difficulties can result from abnormal development of the mouth, such as cleft palate, or weakness and poor co-ordination of the muscles of the speech apparatus. Most of these latter problems are found in children with wider physical impairment, particularly cerebral palsy. Children with dyspraxia experience difficulty imitating and reproducing speech sounds at speed. Most improve with intervention and maturation, though progress can be very slow. The majority do eventually achieve normal articulation, though a small number may have poor speech throughout their life. A useful overview of these disorders is provided by Grunwell (1990).

Difficulty establishing written language, reading, writing and spelling is commonly, though not always, associated with all three categories of speech disorder. The poor auditory discrimination found in children with phonological and dyspraxic difficulties hinders the development of phonic skills necessary for reading and spelling. In addition, dyspraxic children are often clumsy, have poor fine-motor skills, and may also have particular difficulty in the planning and organisation of the fine movements required for writing.

Children with unclear speech commonly experience social difficulties in school. Their most obvious problem is that others do not understand what they say. The fewer the sounds children are able to make or use appropriately, the more unintelligible they will be. In addition, some speech patterns are more liable to distortion than others: a child may be using a range of sounds appropriately at the beginnings of words, but leave off sounds at the ends of words; this produces speech that can be very difficult to follow. Children with speech problems will also inevitably vary in the amount they speak. Some may produce only short sentences and talk infrequently, while others may talk at great length in any situation. Ironically, the more talkative children are usually more difficult to understand than the less talkative, though the latter may have additional difficulties with their underlying language, and need to be encouraged to talk more.

Whatever the degree of children's difficulties, there are bound to be times when they feel frustration and stress at the responses of others. Generally, the younger children are, the less they are likely to be aware of difference in their speech, and children of 4 or even 5 may show no stress at all in their outward behaviour. But once they start school, they are likely to become increasingly aware that they are not always understood by others, even though they do not necessarily know why. And once aware of expressions of uncertainty in others or the inappropriateness of responses to what they say, they are likely to become increasingly tense in any situation when they might have to talk. Tension and stress will add significantly to initial problems of unintelligibility.

Children vary in the ways in which they deal with the difficulties caused by their speech. Some withdraw from contact with others, particularly adults. Others engage in conversation, but simply switch off or change the subject if others falter at what they say. Yet others express their frustration by becoming verbally angry or even physically aggressive. Some children show all these responses in different situations. As children pass through school, they may meet social isolation, teasing or even bullying. Children whose speech is still significantly different from others in the junior years are likely to lack self-confidence and have few established friendships. These difficulties are described in detail by Baker and Cantwell (1992).

The stress felt by teachers working with children who cannot make themselves understood can be considerable. Many infant teachers will have had the experience of a child rushing into the class on a Monday morning, eager to discuss some exciting news about the weekend, but in speech that no one could follow. Trying to respond appropriately to such children, often conscious of the doubt and anxiety in their face, can be most upsetting. Working with children who cannot talk clearly also highlights how much we depend on talk to teach them and evaluate their learning. Monitoring reading, for example, or assessing children's understanding of a science project through their verbal explanation of the results of an experiment, can be difficult and stressful.

There are a number of ways in which teachers can reduce the anxiety and stress felt by the children and themselves. Encouraging personal relationships with adults and other children and building self-esteem can do much to increase children's self-confidence and willingness to communicate. Other strategies can help communication more directly. It is useful to know something of the background to a conversation. This should not be difficult in school, but can be a problem when a child wants to talk about family and home. A home-school book, where teachers and parents make a note of significant events, can be a great aid to this communication. Other children often have less difficulty understanding these children's speech, and are happy to act as interpreters for adults. At the same time, it is important to ensure that these children are not overprotected by their classmates. And although it can be tempting for adults to avoid talking with children who are difficult to understand, it actually helps to listen to them as much as possible: they are likely to be using some sound patterns consistently, and their speech will become more comprehensible with familiarity. Once children and adults trust each other to deal with any difficulties that may arise, the anxiety felt by both tends to lessen.

# Children with poor expressive language

Children vary in the rate at which they acquire language, and in the amount they say. When and how often they talk is governed by many factors, including temperament or personality, their confidence and familiarity with a situation, and their state of physical and mental health. Many young children are reluctant to talk in their first weeks in a nursery or reception class, though they talk readily at home. Most of them are likely to have established expressive language, but do not have the confidence to talk in school. However, a small proportion of children who say little will have delayed development, and an even smaller proportion will have a specific expressive language impairment.

The difference between language delay and language disorder can be difficult to determine, for slow development and paucity of talk is the most characteristic feature of both. Indeed, the length of time it takes children to improve is often the only criterion used to identify an expressive language disorder. All children who have been with a class for more than half a term and have said little to anyone, peer or adult, should be considered in need of additional adult attention to encourage them to talk. Children with delayed language should respond well to this support and increase their use of grammatical sentences spontaneously.

Children who are saying little and are not talking in simple grammatical sentences by 5 years of age are a cause of concern. Some are slow to develop vocabulary and competence with sentence construction, and say little, no matter the context. Others can be quite talkative, but sound like a much younger child, using just phrases or short sentences that are unlike adult forms. As they grow older, their vocabulary may increase, but their sentence construction remains immature. They are particularly slow to develop appropriate use of pronouns, verb endings and auxiliary verbs, often leaving them out of their speech altogether. They frequently have difficulty sequencing words appropriately in sentences, for example to ask questions. Most children with this degree of difficulty with language have unclear speech as well, though a pattern of marked expressive difficulty but clear speech does occasionally occur.

The educational consequences of expressive language are considerable. As children move through the infant classes, those who show reluctance to talk socially or about their work become increasingly problematic. Not only do social relationships build more and more on conversation, there are increasing demands for them to talk to meet specific educational objectives, and their progress in all curriculum areas is monitored by their ability to express ideas through language. Where children have not yet learned to write, the teacher is particularly dependent on talk to evaluate their learning.

Some children with poor expressive skills acquire written language relatively easily, but the majority are likely to be slow learning to read and write, and have difficulty with higher-level language skills even when they have mastered the basic literacy skills. They are poor at interpreting ambiguous sentences, idioms and metaphors; they have difficulty grasping multiple-meaning words, and have problems sequencing and organising their ideas; above all, they are usually slow to develop understanding beyond the literal meaning of both spoken and written ideas. Such difficulties inevitably restrict their progress in all curriculum areas.

Children who have difficulty expressing themselves are at risk of being socially isolated in school, and the older children become, and the less they are talking, the more stressful life in school is likely to be for them. Children's social adjustment depends in considerable part on their ability to form friendships, and this is strongly influenced by their conversational abilities. Many children respond by withdrawing from social contact with others or remaining on the fringe in social groups. Ripley (1986), describing a counselling service in a special school for children with specific language impairment, found that the highest percentage of referrals came from children with deviant articulation and expressive language difficulties. Nevertheless, not all children have difficulty with social relationships, and some, perhaps those with good non-verbal social skills, are readily accepted by their peers.

The immediate stress posed to teachers by children with expressive language difficulties may not be marked; indeed, a quiet child may appear to be a bonus in some classes. The frustration for teachers may come from not understanding the nature of children's difficulties, from not knowing how to help them, or from not being able to provide the conditions that will enable them to make progress.

Encouraging positive relationships through good classroom practice can do much to increase children's self-confidence and self-esteem, for they are likely to lack both. For example, rewarding children's efforts and achievements, no matter how small, can do much to increase their sense of worth. Another objective is to help them to talk more. This should happen spontaneously where a warm relationship with an adult is established, and particularly in situations where children do already talk, even if only occasionally. A useful strategy is to ensure that each child has time, at least once a day, for a relaxed 'social chat' about shared or familiar experiences, and as far as possible, always with the same adult. This not only sets up a positive relationship between the two, it also enables the adult to assess and extend the child's current language. Teachers can also provide support by helping them establish and maintain friendships with other children, through seating arrangements, for example, or by careful grouping of children for various classroom activities.

A useful approach that encourages children to talk and also develops their self-esteem is to pair them with children in a younger class to provide help with simple, familiar activities such as looking at books together or showing them how to use classroom tools or equipment. This is an effective way of giving children practice in non-demanding situations, and can do much to improve their willingness to talk spontaneously. Pairing children will be even more effective if they are one of a group which is helping in the lower class, and are not singled out from their peers. Rustin and Kuhr (1989) give a comprehensive range of games and exercises to help promote the social skills of children with expressive language difficulties.

# Children who stammer

A few children have difficulty speaking fluently; they may repeat words or syllables several times, or even come to a complete block when trying to produce some sounds. This is not uncommon in nursery-age children, and usually fades spontaneously and quite quickly. However, some children experience more persistent difficulties, and once children begin to be aware of their stammering, or other people start to respond differently to them, looking embarrassed, turning away or filling in 'blocked' words, they are likely to become self-conscious and anxious. It is the presence of a more or less continuous state of anxiety when faced with the need to communicate that can give the stammering child significant problems in the classroom.

While there is no clear link between stammering and learning difficulties, educational progress can be affected by a persistent stammer. The most obvious problem arises in learning to read. Reading aloud to the teacher can be particularly stressful, and children may try to avoid such contact. But more serious problems can arise from the habits they establish to try to deal with their stammer. They may fail to listen to the teacher because they are anxiously rehearsing what they will or will not say if they are asked to speak. They may refuse to answer questions, claim they do not know answers to questions when they really do, or even give inappropriate answers in order to avoid saying words they perceive as 'difficult'. Children who stammer may eventually come to fear asking questions or joining in any conversations with their peers or teachers, thereby seriously reducing their active participation in learning.

It is not difficult to see how children who stammer become a source of stress for their teachers, but they can do much to support children in school. While it is not possible to control social interaction all the time, adults can establish an atmosphere in which positive and sympathetic attitudes to children are encouraged and negative behaviour is not accepted. If the teacher does not react to the stammer, but waits for sentences to be completed, encourages but does not force children to join in group activities, and shows an interest in what children say and do, other children are likely to behave in the same way. The strategies to help children with poor expressive language described above will also help these children. Such is the seriousness of stammering that any child over 4 who shows more than usual repetition of words or is having difficulty getting words out should be referred to a speech and language therapist for advice and possible intervention. A helpful discussion of ways in which teachers can help children is provided by Byrne (1991).

# Children with comprehension difficulties

Understanding what others say to us is a complex task that takes many years to perfect. Adults take account of this when talking to young children, regulating the length of their sentences and talking more slowly if children do not appear to be following what is being said. So automatic is this process that most adults seldom notice differences in children, and it is not widely appreciated that children vary considerably in the rate at which they learn to make sense of what others say, and that some are significantly slower than others learning to attend to, or understand, speech.

Failure to take in what has been said is commonplace among young children, however, and adults acquire many strategies for gaining and holding their attention. Most of those learning slowly are helped by these measures and will eventually catch up with their peers. But there are some who have a more fundamental problem in taking in spoken language. While there is no guaranteed way of identifying these children in a busy classroom, four patterns of behaviour suggest children who are experiencing difficulty.

The first and most obvious is when children are repeatedly slow or inconsistent in responding to talk: they 'switch off' or lose concentration when spoken to; they need to have instructions or questions repeated or simplified, or they respond inappropriately to what is said to them.

A second sign is if children seem excessively shy or anxious, quiet or withdrawn. This may be because they have particular difficulty settling down in a new environment, but it may also be because they do not fully understand what is being said to them.

A third sign is if children do not interact with others because they are always moving about, perhaps talking to themselves, without listening to what anyone else is saying. These children clearly have difficulty attending, but their behaviour may also be a way of concealing that they do not understand what others say.

Finally, there are children whose behaviour, and especially their interactions with both adults and children, are seen by everyone as odd or inappropriate. Their expressive language may be quite good, but they seem to have difficulty in understanding not just spoken language but other forms of communication like body language or facial expression.

Virtually all these behaviours provide evidence that children are not taking in spoken information as quickly or as easily as their peers. To add to the problem, many of these children will be speaking clearly – a pattern which often masks their comprehension difficulty.

The educational implications of comprehension difficulties are profound. Much of the language used in the classroom in the early years is simple and familiar, and will often be supported by concrete experience and practical activity. As children progress through the infant years, however, the language used becomes less about the 'here and now' and increasingly about the past and the future, and it is assumed that children will be able to understand an increasing amount of what is said to them without contextual cues. This change puts great demands on children's linguistic skills, and children experiencing difficulty are likely to fall ever further behind in every curriculum area. Even if their use of the basic grammatical system is established, they continue to be slow to establish complex sentence constructions and acquire new vocabulary, and show the same difficulty with the higher-order skills experienced by children with expressive problems.

Children's acquisition of written language varies, and while some have difficulty with reading, others make quite good progress initially, but commonly have difficulty understanding what they read. Similarly, children may appear to establish the mechanics of writing but have great difficulty producing grammatical sentences, and even more difficulty producing an extended sequence of ideas. They commonly make progress with the computational skills of mathematics, but find problem-solving tasks difficult.

Children with comprehension difficulties are likely to experience anxiety and frustration in school. Everything that goes on is influenced, regulated and frequently evaluated by talk, and children who cannot make sense of what others are saying are likely to find life at school bewildering and worrying. They may give inappropriate responses because they have not grasped the point of what has been said, which can distance them from others, particularly their peers. They are commonly anxious much of the time, and the more difficulty they have, the less they are likely to relate to others. Unfamiliar situations are particularly stressful for some of these children. They will often only relate to adults, who are more able to scaffold social interaction for them. Haynes and Naidoo (1991), in a long-term study of children with specific language impairment, found that lack of confidence, overdependence on adult approval and attention, and excessive anxiety over failure or new situations characterised 75 per cent of their school-leavers, and was particularly marked in children with comprehension difficulties.

Perhaps the most immediate problem for teachers is that children with comprehension difficulties can be very difficult to identify. While speech difficulties and reluctance to talk are obvious, it is much more difficult to identify children who are having difficulty following what is being said, particularly those whose speech is clear. Virtually all the behaviours children demonstrate can be explained in a number of ways, including emotional adjustment difficulties, poor thinking and learning skills, or intermittent hearing difficulties. Behavioural difficulties such as extreme withdrawal or overassertiveness can easily mask underlying language difficulties, and it is not uncommon for problems to go undetected until children are failing to make educational progress. The stress for their teachers comes from having children who fail to make progress, for reasons that are not clear, and in spite of their best efforts.

Children with comprehension difficulties are particularly likely to be lacking self-confidence, and teachers will find that it can take some time to establish a positive relationship with individual children. Regular social interaction, the daily chat suggested for children with expressive difficulties, is equally important with these children. Highlighting success, however small, can help boost their self-confidence. Other strategies can help children make sense of what is being said. Classrooms, especially infant classrooms, tend to be noisy places, often with a lot of different activities going on at once. Children who are poor at attending to, or understanding, spoken language will be at a disadvantage in surroundings where it is difficult to make out what is being said. Such children benefit from sitting relatively close to the teacher, where they will follow talk more readily and the teacher will be in a good position to judge whether the child has understood what is being said. A place near the front but slightly to the side of the room is ideal, so that the child can see the teacher's face but still be aware of what other children are doing.

The level of language used in the classroom can make a considerable difference to children's ability to keep up with their peers. If speech can be delivered relatively slowly and clearly, in short, appropriate sentences, or if instructions and questions can be repeated to children individually or in small groups, in a simple form, most will be able follow what is being said. Strategies such as saying children's names before speaking to them to get their attention, and giving visual cues to supplement what is being said all help children to attend to and interpret speech. It is also important to give children with comprehension difficulties the opportunity to spend at least part of each day in a quiet area where they can listen and talk to adults or other children without being distracted or disturbed.

# Educational implications

Regular and consistent use of the approaches described above and other stress management strategies developed within schools can be beneficial in fostering communication skills and enabling children to settle and make progress. The ultimate way in which teacher's stress will be reduced, however, is by enabling the children to make educational progress.

It is essential to ensure that the children understand what is going on in the classroom, both the immediate language and the ideas assumed to be already understood in whatever topic is being taught. Such children may need to learn through concrete experience for much longer than their peers. Practical activity helps them understand the language used by others, and encourages them to talk themselves. Regular small-group work with an adult will also be essential to enable them to listen to language at a level they can follow, and to talk confidently themselves.

The content of teaching should be based on the teaching going on in the class as a whole, though it is essential to set specific language-teaching objectives at a level appropriate to individual children. Locke and Beech (1991) outline a range of ways of promoting children's listening skills and use of language through ongoing curriculum activities.

Providing sufficient repetition is one of the keys to success in learning, and setting objectives – to teach new vocabulary, for example – is one way to ensure that specific language is addressed as often as necessary. Repeating whole-class activities in small-group sessions is a productive way of providing the often extensive repetition these children need to consolidate their learning. Procedures for checking the detail of children's learning also need to be built into teaching, as this is the only way to be sure that teaching is not moving on too quickly.

Children with language difficulties need to be helped by everyone they come into contact with, and to ensure maximum effectiveness, this additional help and support should be systematic and co-ordinated. Regular discussion about the problems of individual children, and an agreed strategy for intervention, ensure that everyone who has regular contact with individual children works towards the same objectives and provides the consistency of approach these children need.

It is equally important to involve parents. They may be able to give useful additional information, for example about a child's worries, or the amount they talk at home, or how they relate to others in the family. They may also be glad of the opportunity to discuss their concerns. Teachers may feel they need to seek specialist advice from local education authority support services or from a speech and language therapist, and this will need to be discussed with the child's parents and/or the school's special needs co-ordinator.

Parents can also contribute to the overall teaching strategy if they know which aspects of language children are currently working on, and how this can be supported by conversations, stories and other activities at home. Children always benefit from the opportunity to repeat or rehearse what they have done at school; if they hear the same story or poem, or look at or draw the same pictures, and then talk about what is going on, they will be reinforcing the language that is currently being taught. Parents will usually be pleased and reassured to be involved in this way.

While the discussion of the origins of stress in teachers of children with special needs offered in Chapter 1 illuminates the complexity of the processes involved and highlights the problem of explaining the stress experienced by individuals, it is not difficult to see why children with specific language impairment may be a particular source of stress in the classroom. Teachers are unlikely to have learnt much about them in their initial training, and can all too easily come to feel that they are failing to teach effectively. Lack of knowledge about the nature of children's difficulties or how to promote their social and educational learning, paucity of written information about the educational needs of these children, and lack of support in dealing with children's difficulties can all contribute to feelings of anxiety and lack of control. The reality is that teachers have much to offer children with specific language impairment through their everyday involvement with them in school.

# References

Aubrey, C. (1994) 'Who teaches the teachers?' *Special Children*, 78, 20–2.

Baker, L. and Cantwell, D.P. (1992) 'Language acquisition, cognitive development and emotional disorder in childhood', in Nelson, K.E. (ed.) *Children's Language*, Vol.3, Hillsdale, NJ: Lawrence Erlbaum.

Bishop, D. (1992) 'The biological basis of specific language impairment', in Fletcher, P. and Hall, D. (eds) *Specific Speech and Language Disorders in Children*, London: Whurr Publishers.

Byrne, R. (1991) *Let's Talk about Stammering*, London: Association for Stammerers.

Crystal, D. (1984) *Language Handicap in Children*, Stratford-upon-Avon: National Council for Special Education.

DES (1990) *Education Observed: Special Needs Issues*, London: HMSO.

Fletcher, P. (1992) 'Subgroups in school-age language-impaired children', in Fletcher, P. and Hall, D. (eds) *Specific Speech and Language Disorders In Children*, London: Whurr Publishers.

Grunwell, P. (ed.) (1990) *Developmental Speech Disorders*, London: Churchill Livingstone.

Haynes, C. and Naidoo, S. (1991) *Children with Specific Speech and Language Impairment*, Oxford: Blackwell Scientific Publications.

Locke, A. and Beech, M. (1991) *Teaching Talking*, Windsor: NFER-Nelson.

Morley, M. (1965) *The Development and Disorders of Speech in Childhood*, (2nd edn), London: Churchill Livingstone.

Ripley, K. (1986) 'The Moor House School remedial programme: An evaluation', *Child Language Teaching and Therapy*, 2, 281–300.

Rustin, L. and Kuhr, A. (1989) *Social Skills and the Speech Impaired*, London: Taylor and Francis.
Rutter, M., Tizard, J. and Whitmore, K.(1970) *Education, Health and Behaviour*, London: Longman.
Upton, G. (1992) 'No time for complacency', *Special Children*, 58, 23–7.
Webster, A. and McConnell, C. (1987) *Children with Speech and Language Difficulties*, London: Cassell.

# 7 Emotional and behaviour difficulties

*Graham Upton*

This chapter focuses on the potential for stress which working with pupils with emotional and behaviour difficulties has for teachers, and on the concomitant need for staff support and for the continuous monitoring of staff relationships with pupils and with one another. In Chapter 1, May drew attention to the considerable amount of empirical evidence which exists about the incidence of stress among teachers of pupils with special educational needs which arises from studies conducted with teachers working with pupils with emotional and behaviour difficulties. A substantial amount of the early, and now classic work of Dunham (1977a, 1977b, 1981, 1983, 1992) was carried out in this area, but since then the theme has been taken up by authors such as Pont and Reid (1985), Abbotts et al. (1991), Cohen (1995), Cockburn (1996) and Travers and Cooper (1996).

There are a number of reasons why working with pupils with emotional and behaviour difficulties might be particularly stressful. As has been argued throughout this book, teachers of all special educational needs pupils are likely to experience a high level of stress, in that, almost by definition, the children and young people in their care present additional challenges to those presented by others. Pupils with emotional and behaviour difficulties are no exception. For, as well as commonly presenting significant learning difficulties, they frequently challenge the ability of the teacher to create an effective learning environment for them and for others – an achievement which is fundamental to the task of teaching and the job satisfaction of any teacher. Indeed, the current popularity of the term 'challenging' in referring to the behaviour of these pupils could be seen as acknowledgement of the fact that they present greater challenges than other groups.

## Behaviour difficulties

The conceptualisation of behaviour difficulties as 'challenging' is a positive construction of reality, in that it highlights the possibility of teachers being able to deal with, and ameliorate, the problems with which they are confronted. In reality, meeting the challenges posed by difficult behaviour is not necessarily what most teachers see as their primary task, and ignores the fact that dealing with behaviour difficulties can be extremely emotionally demanding. In his various studies of teacher stress, Dunham has graphically described the stress which teachers can experience from this source. In particular, he commented on the insecurity staff report as arising from the unpredictability of behaviour and the vulnerability that can ensue from feelings of uncertainty about the effectiveness of their own coping resources. He describes, for example, the behaviour of an infant school child:

> who joined the class in mid-term and caused total disruption. He tore pictures from the wall, threw children's games across the room, scribbled over their work and painting and could not sit beside children without doing something to them. He pinched their faces, pulled their hair, kicked or punched them and put his hand up girls' skirts. If he felt the least bit rejected or ignored he would inflict injury on himself. Usually, this would be biting and scratching his hand until he drew blood. He would scream with pain but refuse to take his hand out of his mouth. (Dunham, 1992, p.48)

Not surprisingly, he goes on to talk of the teacher as having to 'keep an eye on him for every second of the day' and as having been 'under extreme stress for the whole of the time he was in her class'.

The strain which severe behaviour difficulties can impose on a teacher are highlighted equally graphically by Cockburn (1996), who describes a particularly awkward situation faced by a headteacher:

> I had this child in my room and he had to be carried yelling and screaming to my room. He was desperately trying to get out of the door, and normally if I just sit by the door and carry on with some work the child just blows it all out and calms down then you can talk with them. But this particular child, he proceeded to kick and bang and hit the door, and me. He was making real swipes for me. He started throwing things about the room and not just kind of gently tipping things up but actually with real force, actually throwing things so that things were hitting the window – a great box of Lego. The only thing I could do to control him – because my initial reaction was, well let him throw a few things about and get it out of his system and he'll be OK, but it didn't stop, and for an hour he was in my room in an extremely disturbed state and I ended up having to hold his hands, physically restraining him, which I don't like to do to a child, because if I didn't he was going to hurt himself, or hurt me or damage things in the room. I've never been in that

situation before. And when he'd finally calmed down and we'd read a book together and it was all resolved, I was really shaking. It was one of the most stressful situations I'd ever been in. He was in such a state and so strong that I couldn't even get out of my room to contact another member of staff or the secretary or anything, and it was awful. I think that was one of the most stressful experiences I've ever experienced. (pp.60–1)

Support for such anecdotal evidence that behaviour difficulties are a major source of stress for teachers is provided by the recent findings of Travers and Cooper (1996), who identified ten separate 'teacher stress' factors based on a factor analysis of the questionnaire responses of 1,782 teachers, largely drawn from the secondary sector. The first and major factor to be identified contained ten items, all of which refer to problem behaviours and the problems of dealing with those behaviours.

Further evidence comes from the Elton Report (DES and WO, 1989). In a survey involving over 3,500 teachers which was commissioned for the report, it was found that in response to a questionnaire which asked them to report on their experience in the classroom and around the school during the previous week:

The vast majority of primary and secondary teachers reported that, at some point, the flow of their lessons had been impeded or disrupted by having to deal with minor discipline problems. Pupils 'talking out of turn', 'hindering other pupils', 'making unnecessary (non-verbal) noise' and 'calculated idleness or work avoidance' were the most commonly reported forms of bad behaviour in class. 'Showing lack of concern for others', 'unruliness while waiting' and 'running in the corridors' were the most frequently mentioned forms of bad behaviour encountered during the course of teachers' duties around the school. One in four teachers reported having to deal with such behaviour on a daily basis. 'Verbal abuse towards other pupils', 'general rowdiness' and 'cheeky or impertinent remarks or responses' were also encountered frequently by both primary and secondary teachers. Primary teachers made special mention of having to handle 'physical aggression towards other pupils', both in the classroom and around the school. (pp.61–2)

The significance for teachers of this high incidence of behaviour difficulties was revealed in follow-up interviews with the teachers, wherein it was found 'that while teachers are dealing with these problems as a matter of routine, their cumulative effects are wearing and contribute to a sense of stress and growing frustration' (pp.61–2).

# Emotional difficulties

While not as common a phenomenon, emotional difficulties can be equally troublesome, even if they don't constitute the same sort of challenge to teachers as overt problematic behaviour. Coping with withdrawn and deeply disturbed pupils can be a source of real stress. The pressures which teachers can experience when faced with problems which they don't understand and for which they are not trained are well illustrated in another extract from Dunham (1992):

> He is a Year 7 boy who is an overweight and unattractive child. He continually pesters staff at every opportunity and demands attention with repetitive questions. He is inclined to day dream in class but pretends to work hard. Older children plague him and every playtime he seeks refuge by following the staff on duty. He seldom plays with his peers but when he does he causes embarrassment by touching and kissing them and by making occasional declarations of love. His [sic] is the youngest child of overbearing parents. What can we do to help him before our patience has worn thin? (pp.51–2)

Answers to some of these questions are provided by Greenhalgh (1994) in terms of enhanced knowledge and therapeutic skills, but the stress which teachers experience in cases of this kind is often greatly exacerbated by their awareness of the distressing home situations from which some of these pupils come.

A primary school headteacher is quoted by Dunham as saying:

> Some days I despair when I see the pupils' home circumstances. Some of the children just haven't got a chance. That's when I get a feeling of deep frustration and wonder if anything I have tried to do will have any long term effect. (1992, p.53)

The desire to look after them and try to compensate for pupils' previous deprivation can be extremely emotionally draining and upsetting. Equally, the extent to which economic and social factors can be a cause of stress for teachers are addressed in Chapter 10 by Martin Brown, while the distress which can be experienced by teachers in cases of physical and sexual abuse is explored by Neil Hall in Chapter 11. Both of these chapters have obvious relevance to the present one.

# Systemic considerations

It is hard to imagine anyone being unaffected by interactions such as those described above, but the stress involved in working in situations such as this is not simply about coping with difficult behaviour. It is more complex than this. For emotional and behaviour difficulties are not simply characteristics of the individual but are products of social interaction. This applies equally to their origins and to their occurrence at any particular time, and in the eco-system of the classroom, the teacher is invariably 'involved' in a fundamentally different way than is the case in relation to any other area of special educational needs. (For a discussion of the systemic understanding of emotional and behaviour difficulties, see Cooper and Upton, 1990.)

To begin with, the classification of any behaviour as 'problematic' is a highly subjective issue, and teachers differ enormously in terms of what they consider to be acceptable behaviour. Thus, behaviour which one teacher sees as rude and disrespectful may be regarded by another as humorous. Furthermore, these individual variations between teachers are often reflected in differences in levels of tolerance between schools in relation, for example, to matters such as the types of clothes which are acceptable and the amount of jewellery which pupils are allowed to wear. In this sense, the expectations of teachers, and of their schools, are crucial to the extent to which any particular behaviour pattern – or pupil, for that matter – is regarded as a problem, and to the level of stress its occurrence occasions for the teacher.

What's more, it is not uncommon for a pupil's behaviour to vary considerably with different teachers, and for pupils to behave differently at home to the way in which they behave at school. Traditionally, such differences were largely explained in terms of inconsistencies in the individual's behaviour, family or peer influence, or as the effects of environmental factors. More recently, the study of school differences has suggested that schools and teachers must be seen as possible causative factors in the occurrence of behaviour problems. This is not to 'blame' teachers for the occurrence of behaviour difficulties, but it would be dishonest to pretend that all teachers possess an equally high level of teaching competence. And, as has been noted above, some of the stress which teachers experience when confronted by emotional and behaviour difficulties comes from awareness of the limits of their ability to understand and deal with difficulty as it arises. Such feelings must inevitably be compounded in situations where the teacher is also aware that the problem exists partly because he or she has had a part to play in creating the situation in the first place, or when it is apparent that one's colleagues are not experiencing the same degree of difficulty with a particular pupil or group of pupils.

But the 'involvement' of teachers in emotional and behaviour difficulties goes even deeper than this. It is inevitable that when confronted with emotional and behaviour difficulties, issues from the teacher's own life will impinge upon, and be affected by, those difficulties. Thus the teacher who has had an unhappy childhood, or who was brought up in extremely difficult family circumstances, cannot fail to be 'moved' by the child who is showing the effects of a similar experience. Similarly, the teacher who is currently experiencing 'problems in living' as a result, for example, of bereavement or a breakdown in a personal relationship, may well have a reduced ability to tolerate, and be supportive of, a pupil's distress or disruption.

The potential for stress in working with pupils with emotional and behaviour difficulties is also exacerbated by the fact that in their relationships with different pupils, staff need to adopt a variety of roles – to meet one pupil's needs, a staff member may need to be functioning as a nurturing parent, for another as a disciplinarian, and for yet others more as a friend and confidant. While the nature of the role adopted by the member of staff (and by the pupils) is usually an unconscious product of that interaction, the role adopted by the member of staff may be more or less appropriate to the therapeutic needs of the pupil. In itself, this is a difficult balance to achieve and is inherently stressful, but it brings with it additional dangers of 'getting it wrong'. For example, an adolescent girl who comes from a turbulent family background wherein she has been the subject of violence and/or sexual mistreatment by her father may not be helped by involvement with a male member of staff who relates to her in a paternal or stereotypically masculine ('macho') manner. In turn, this will affect the girl's relationship with the teacher, and in due course, possibly result in escalating conflict and severe feelings of failure for the teacher.

Staff relationships are also important, especially in small special schools or units, where the intensity of staff interactions can easily result in conflict. Working relationships with colleagues can, as Galloway (1990) points out, 'compound the stress inherent in classroom teaching or can help create a climate which is both stimulating and supportive' (p.110).

# Staff support

All of the above considerations suggest the need for a staff support system. The need for support when working with children (and adults) who exhibit emotional and behaviour difficulties, and the concomitant need for the continuous monitoring of staff relationships with clients and with one another, has long been recognised in the traditional therapeutic disciplines. Most commonly, these issues have been debated in relation to psychoanalytic practice – where it has long been seen as a requirement that anyone working as an analyst should have undergone analysis themselves – and the child guidance approach, with its offshoot of staff support teams (usually a psychiatrist, a psychologist and a social worker) being attached to educational establishments. But the need for and importance of working in staff groups has been recognised by other professionals in psychotherapeutic work, where the concept has been widely accepted (see, for example, Speed et al., 1982; Jones, 1993).

The importance of staff support for teachers of pupils with special educational needs is referred to in other chapters of this book, and the way in which this might be provided in mainstream schools will be explored at length in Chapter 12. But it is arguable that this is a particularly significant issue when working with pupils who exhibit emotional and behaviour difficulties, and that special measures are required. Furthermore, recent developments in special educational provisions for this group would seem to make this a more pressing concern than it has perhaps been in the past. When special provision for those with emotional and behaviour difficulties was limited to a small number of highly-specialised institutions, these were often run by people with specialised skills and with trained psychotherapeutic supervision (see Bridgeland, 1971). In many of these 'pioneer' institutions, the concept of self-awareness and support was given a high priority. With the closure of some of these specialised settings, with the greater emphasis that has been placed on curriculum issues since the introduction of the National Curriculum and with the reduction of opportunities for specialised in-service training, many people are now working in situations approaching isolation, or with colleagues who possess a bare minimum of therapeutic skills – this would seem to be particularly true of staff working in special units within the ordinary school sector, but is probably also true in many special schools. In such situations, staff support systems seem to be vital.

# A staff support system

It can be argued that the provision of staff support and the monitoring of staff interaction requires specialised skills, and the utilisation of consultant psychotherapeutic personnel is an ideal means of making such provision (see, for example, Marks and Pennycook, 1986; Dowling and Osborne, 1994). But economic realities suggest that this position is unlikely to be realisable in the vast majority of schools, special as well as mainstream. None the less, in the absence of such support, much can still be done to provide effective self-help and self-generated support (see, for example, Hodgkinson, 1985; Lanyado, 1989). A prerequisite to the successful implementation and operation of any such system, though, is a commitment to openness and honesty. This is obviously not exclusively a 'professional' attribute, but as a group, teachers have a strong tradition of classroom privacy, and unlike other professional groups involved in therapeutic work (social workers, psychiatrists and psychologists), teachers often seem to find it difficult to 'open up' and to engage in this process of professional analysis.

Dunham (1992), in introducing his case for staff support as a means of helping teachers deal with stress, cites this tendency to isolationism, and quotes from the research of Galloway et al. (1982):

Teaching can be an extraordinarily lonely profession. The loneliness of the classroom is compounded by that of the staffroom. Disruptive behaviour is the most
striking example of stress which too often has to be borne in painful isolation. For
many teachers, admitting to bad classroom discipline is paramount to admitting
that they are bad teachers. (p.135)

Nevertheless, given a commitment to open and honest communication, staff
can provide one another with a great deal of support in easy and informal
ways. Such an openness will be reflected in the quality of personal relationships and staffroom discussions, as well as on more formal occasions such as
staff meetings and case conferences. In addition, staff support must be seen
as being part of the role of the headteacher and other senior staff, and as an
area with which any staff appraisal system should be concerned. However,
there are ways in which such interaction can be taken to deeper and more
intense levels than often seems to occur. In particular, there are two
approaches which the writer feels can constitute such an extension of informal support and which can be implemented with only a moderate degree of
staff training. These are 'groupwork' and 'counselling'.

## Groupwork

Groupwork can provide an excellent medium for monitoring staff interaction
with pupils and the resolution of staff conflict which Galloway (1990) points
out 'can compound the stress inherent in classroom teaching' (p.110). Group
meetings, be they staff meetings or case conferences, are an integral part of
most educational institutions, and group therapy is a widely adopted therapeutic model. Groupwork has also long been referred to as a means of providing staff support in schools (see, for example, Clifford, 1980). In Chapter
12, Daniels and Norwich argue for the use of what they term 'teacher support
teams' as a means of supporting special needs teachers in general. Similarly,
Mead and Timmins (1993) discuss the use of 'peer support groups' as a
means of 'reducing the pressures of school life' (p.111).

However, the honest sharing of problems by staff in a group situation is
not easily achieved, and aspects of the work situation can, in fact, militate
against such sharing. A young member of staff may, quite understandably,
be reluctant to discuss problems in front of senior staff, while senior staff
may, in turn, find it equally hard to admit their own difficulties. The trust
required for the honest exchange of experience in a hierarchical institution
usually takes a long time to establish, and initial group meetings may be tor-
tuous and punctuated by awkward silences and superficial chat. In the initial
stages of establishing a staff group, consideration may profitably be given
to the use of 'non-threatening' activities which can facilitate the gradual
development of trust, and exercises can be devised to focus on specific

school-related issues which give rise to stress. For example, staff can be asked simply to identify major stress points and to share with one another how they experience and cope with that stress. This can serve to give staff insight into one another's problems, and can also lead to the identification of factors in the school, or in staff relationships, which exaggerate or mitigate the stress which staff experience and which can be followed up in subsequent sessions in more detail.

A staff group of this kind can be 'leaderless', especially in situations where a number of staff members have groupwork skills. However, while such an approach may be appropriate in a self-help therapy group, in a staff support group which has a specific task orientation, a leader is more likely to result in the group working effectively and efficiently, as well as keeping to its brief of providing staff support. Clearly, the leader of such a group must have sound group leadership skills, and ideally, should have had some leadership training. There are many styles of group leadership, and the role which any leader adopts must be a comfortable one for that person. But if a staff group is to be effective in enabling staff to help one another deal with stress, it is the interaction between members of staff that is most important, and it is therefore appropriate that the group leader's prime task should be to encourage and intensify that interaction. Useful guidelines for the facilitation of groups to generate this sort of support are provided by Heron (1993).

In practical terms, a staff group will need to meet regularly, and for a sufficient period of time on each occasion, if all members of the group are to have an opportunity to explore issues that they find stressful reasonably close to the time at which they arise. Just how long will be needed will depend on the size of the group, but a group of three or four people will probably need to think in terms of allowing at least an hour each time they meet and of meeting, say, once every two or three weeks if the ongoing nature of these issues is to be taken into account. Once a month may commend itself as more practicable to many teachers, but $1\frac{1}{2}$ hours may then be needed to 'catch up' and give everyone a fair chance of raising issues that are troubling them.

Such an arrangement obviously requires a considerable commitment of staff time. This can sometimes be accommodated into school routines (e.g. in residential schools) but more commonly probably has to be seen as an out-of-hours commitment. 'Baker' days can be used to create space for this sort of activity, although these have obvious limitations in terms of facilitating regular support.

Given the extent to which stress is a common experience for teachers, the potential for 'self-help' is considerable, although this requires a willingness to communicate and the motivation to work together. But if the conditions are met, groupwork, as part of a staff support system, can provide a unique opportunity for staff to share experiences and benefit from the reservoir of expertise which exists in any school.

## Counselling

One of the major points to emerge from the study by Travers and Cooper (1996) was 'that the profession needs the introduction of a counselling service to enable staff to become involved in attempts to reduce the high levels of mental ill health that are prevalent in teachers' (p.168). Elsewhere, the present author has argued for the use of external consultants in helping teachers to understand the nature of some of the difficulties they face and the nature of their involvement with them (Upton, 1993). While both of these suggestions have much to commend them, the financial exigencies within which most schools work would seem to render them unrealistic and unlikely to be implementable other than in specialist situations or on a very small scale. However, models do exist whereby it may be possible for counselling support to be provided by teachers themselves on a peer-mediated basis.

Re-evaluation counselling, or 'co-counselling' as it has sometimes been called, is one such model which merits consideration. This is an approach which enjoyed great popularity during the 1970s (for descriptions of its origins, see Scheff, 1972; Somers, 1972; Heron, 1973). The basic idea is that two people can exchange effective support by meeting regularly with a commitment to helping one another to deal with emotional issues. More specifically, it requires that those two people meet in a spirit of equality, wherein neither person functions in a position of authority. Rather, the two people set out to help one another and take turns in helping and being helped.

In practical terms, counselling of this kind could be incorporated into a staff support system, either within a school or between schools and units, whereby members of staff could be paired and arrangements made for them to meet regularly for counselling sessions. Such sessions need not be long (half an hour or an hour every two weeks may be enough), but the time allocated should be agreed in advance and then strictly adhered to, as well as ensuring that they are held at a time and in a place where the sessions cannot be interrupted. The agenda for these meetings should be flexible to meet the needs of the staff involved, but care must be taken to ensure that in every session, each member of the pair has an equal opportunity to explore his or her own personal issues. Thus, in a half-hour session, it might be agreed that the focus for fifteen minutes may be one member of the pair and then for fifteen minutes on the other.

The nature of the interaction which takes place in such sessions has been seen by advocates of the model as being enhanced if the participants adopt an approach similar to that described as non-directive or client-centred counselling (Rogers, 1979 still remains the best elaboration of this approach). In essence, this means that the person, upon whose problems the focus is, must be encouraged to explore the issues freely, while the other member of the pair adopts a role which equates to that of an interested and supportive listener. Specific suggestions of ways in which these roles can be maximally developed can be best enumerated as a list of 'dos' and 'don'ts' for the listener, as follows:

## Dos

1 Listen. This is the first thing you must do – listen with interest, with full attention.
2 Ask questions, but not for your benefit as a listener, rather to reassure the other person of your interest and to steer or guide his or her attention.
3 Permit emotional upset. This is not something to be afraid of or covered up. Rather it is a vital means of releasing tension.

## Don'ts

1 Don't be suggestive. Refrain from telling the other person what you think they should do about a problem. Answers are no good for the other person unless they have worked them out for themselves, and yours may constitute a barrier to them working out their own. Try to spend the time listening, not talking.
2 Don't react emotionally. Strong emotional reactions on your part may only add to the person's fears, just as too much sympathy can interfere with the other person's handling of problems. The most productive attitude towards the other person is that of sincere interest.
3 If the other person is upset or angry, don't be tempted to stop the expression of that emotion. A common reaction to crying, for example, is to try to get the person to stop but within this approach, such 'emotional discharge' can help to free the person from the stress which the tears express.

In the context of a staff support system, such a counselling arrangement can offer an ideal vehicle for staff to explore in private the stress and strain which was referred to earlier in this chapter as being inherent to work with pupils with behaviour problems. Worries about the appropriateness of management skills and problems in relationships with pupils and other staff can be explored in the security which such an arrangement provides. The successful operation of a counselling scheme clearly requires some knowledge of appropriate counselling skills, but these are skills which staff working with pupils with behaviour problems are frequently called upon to exercise with their pupils and about which there is no shortage of supportive material (see, for example, Bovair and McLaughlin, 1993).

Nevertheless, in the initial stages of the implementation of a counselling programme, guidance will need to be given to inexperienced staff, and to this end, group training meetings may be valuable to allow staff to share experiences and to discuss the use of the approach. Also during the initial phases of the counselling relationships, some pairings may prove unsatisfactory, and clearly, if productive help is to occur, such pairings may necessitate some regrouping. While initial incompatibility is sometimes most productive in helping staff to accept and work with differences, the right to opt in or out of a counselling relationship must remain at all times with the individual member of staff.

# Conclusion

In this chapter, it has been argued that emotional and behaviour difficulties constitute a particularly powerful source of stress for teachers, and that there is a need for staff support systems in schools to help staff deal with the stress that is inherent in their work. While it is reasonable to assume that much support is provided for individual teachers by their colleagues and through a school's normal pastoral and appraisal systems, it has been argued that more explicit help is needed to deal with the scale of the problems experienced by some teachers. The need for more specialised support is becoming more widely recognised, and a number of references have been cited which can provide useful guidance to anyone contemplating the introduction of such a scheme. To supplement ideas which can be found elsewhere, the use of self-help counselling and groupwork have been commended as representing potentially valuable tools in the alleviation of stress among teachers. Both of these approaches make demands on staff time and commitment, but the potential benefits for staff – and pupils – would seem to more than justify their advocacy.

# References

Abbotts, P., Clift, S. and Norris, P. (1991) 'Implementing the 1988 Education Reform Act: A study of stress levels generated in teachers and headteachers of special schools', *Maladjustment and Therapeutic Education, 9*, 1, 16–27.

Bovair, K. and McLaughlin, C. (1993) *Counselling in Schools,* London: David Fulton.

Bridgeland, M. (1971) *Pioneer Work with Maladjusted Children,* London: Staples Press.

Clifford, A. (1980) 'A support group for teachers', *Therapeutic Education, 8*, 1, 31–5.

Cockburn, A.D. (1996) *Teaching under Pressure,* London: Falmer Press.

Cohen, S. (1995) 'Is there more stress in teachers of children with emotional and behavioural difficulties? A comparison of SENs teachers working in three types of EBD schools and mainstream and SLD schools', unpublished MA dissertation, London: Institute of Education, University of London.

Cooper, P. and Upton, G. (1990) 'An ecosystemic approach to emotional and behavioural difficulties in schools', *Educational Psychology*, 10, 4, 301–21.

DES and WO (1989) *Discipline in Schools* (The Elton Report), London: HMSO.

Dowling, E. and Osborne, E. (1994) *The Family and the School*, London: Routledge.

Dunham, J. (1977a) 'Stress of working with maladjusted children', *Therapeutic Education*, 5, 2, 3–11.

Dunham, J. (1977b) 'The effects of disruptive behaviour on teachers', *Educational Review*, 29, 181–7.

Dunham, J. (1981) 'Disruptive pupils and teacher stress', *Education Research*, 23, 3, 205–13.

Dunham, J. (1983) 'Coping with stress in school', *Special Education*, 10, 2, 6–9.

Dunham, J. (1992) *Stress in Teaching* (2nd edn), London: Routledge.

Galloway, D. (1990) *Pupil Welfare and Counselling*, London: Longman.

Galloway, D., Ball, T., Blomfield, D. and Seyd, R. (1982) *Schools and Disruptive Pupils*, London: Longman.

Greenhalgh, P. (1994) *Emotional Growth and Learning*, London: Routledge.

Hanko, G. (1990) *Special Needs in Ordinary Schools: Supporting Teachers*, Oxford: Blackwell.

Heron, J. (1973) 'Re-evaluation counselling: Personal growth through mutual aid', *British Journal of Guidance and Counselling*, 1, 2, 26–36.

Heron, J. (1993) *Group Facilitation*, London: Kogan Page.

Hodgkinson, P.E. (1985) 'Staff support systems in the residential treatment of adolescents', *Maladjustment and Therapeutic Education*, 3, 1, 43–9.

Jones, E. (1993) *Family Systems Therapy*, Chichester: John Wiley.

Lanyado, M. (1989) 'United we stand . . . ? Stress in residential work with disturbed children', *Maladjustment and Therapeutic Education*, 7, 3, 136–46.

Marks, F.M. and Pennycook, W. (1986) 'The value of psychiatric consultation to a tutorial class teacher', *Maladjustment and Therapeutic Education*, 4, 1, 54–8.

Mead, C. and Timmins, P. (1993) 'Peer support groups and whole school development', in Bovair, K. and McLaughlin, C. (eds) *Counselling in Schools*, London: David Fulton.

Pont, H. and Reid, G. (1985) 'Stress in special education: The need for transactional data', *Scottish Educational Review*, 30, 3–14.

Rogers, C.R. (1979) *Client Centred Therapy*, London: Constable.

Scheff, T.J. (1972) 'Re-evaluation counselling: Social implications', *Journal of Humanistic Psychology*, 12, 1, 58–71.

Somers, B.J. (1972) 'Re-evaluation therapy: Theoretical framework', *Journal of Humanistic Psychology*, 12, 1, 42–57.

Speed, B., Seligman, P., Kingston, P. and Cade, B. (1982) 'A team approach to therapy', *Journal of Family Therapy*, 4, 3, 271–84.

Travers, C.J. and Cooper, C.L. (1996) Teachers under Pressure, London: Routledge.

Upton, G. (1993) 'Putting problems in context – the family and the school', in Bovair, K. and McLaughlin, C. (eds) *Counselling in Schools*, London: David Fulton.

# 8 Multiple disabilities

*Jean Ware*

## Introduction

This chapter is concerned mainly with the stresses experienced by teachers of pupils with severe and profound learning difficulties (SLDs and PLDs). It takes up the theme of Chapter 1 by examining the potential causes of stress for teachers in this area of special education, and by comparing the stresses experienced by these teachers with those experienced by mainstream teachers and other teachers of pupils with special educational needs.

## Severe and profound learning difficulties

It is always difficult to define learning difficulties – particularly where those learning difficulties are severe – in a way which is clear and yet does not concentrate on what people with such difficulties are unable to do.

The term 'severe learning difficulties' is used to refer to a wide variety of people with intellectual impairments, some of whom may, as adults, be able to function independently in the community, and some of whom will need an intensive level of support throughout their lives. In very crude terms, a child with severe learning difficulties would function less well than someone half their age; however, evidence shows that people with severe learning difficulties are more likely than the majority of the population to function at very different levels in different areas (MacPherson and Butterworth, 1988). A person with severe learning difficulties generally has an IQ score of less than 50–55, and is likely to have some organic brain damage.

Within education in England and Wales, 'profound learning difficulties' is regarded as a subdivision of 'severe learning difficulties', and the term is used to refer to those with the most severe impairments. Generally, a person with profound learning difficulties will have an IQ of less than 20–25, but, in addition, for adults with profound learning difficulties, a rule of thumb is often applied which includes only those functioning at or below a developmental age of 2 years as having profound learning difficulties.

# Multiple impairment

To describe someone as 'multiply-impaired' means that they have two or more severe impairments (a severe impairment is one which by itself would constitute a hindrance to learning such as to lead to the necessity for special methods to ensure development – De Jong, 1985). Thus someone who is multiply-impaired does not necessarily have learning difficulties. However, a phenomenon known as the 'association of impairments' (i.e. a person who has one impairment has a higher than average chance of having additional impairments), which is especially prevalent among people with severe and profound learning difficulties, means that there is a large degree of overlap between multiple impairment and severe and profound learning difficulties. In fact, the majority of children with severe learning difficulties will have at least one additional impairment (Kelleher and Mulcahy, 1985). Within education, children who have both profound learning difficulties and other severe impairments are usually described as having profound and multiple learning difficulties (PMLDs), and this group of pupils (which constitutes between 25 and 40 per cent of the pupils in SLD schools) is generally acknowledged to present a special challenge to teachers.

Although the 1981 Education Act gave all children the right to be educated in mainstream schools, subject to certain conditions, most children with severe learning difficulties are still educated in separate special schools (or, in Wales, in units attached to mainstream schools), so in this chapter I shall concentrate on the stress experienced by teachers in such separate special provision. This is not to imply that working with pupils with severe or profound learning difficulties in integrated settings does not have its own particular stresses, merely that the majority of teachers of such pupils still work in largely non-integrated environments (but see below).

# Previous studies of stress in teachers of pupils with SLDs

There is a huge volume of literature on teacher stress, both from a research perspective (e.g. Dunham, 1980, 1981; Kyriacou, 1987; Rees, 1990; Campbell et al., 1991) and from the perspective of practical guidance on strategies for reducing and coping with stress (e.g. Cook, 1992), with some books covering both perspectives (e.g. Dunham, 1992). However, this literature is largely concerned with teachers in mainstream schools, and as is noted in Chapter 1, much less has been published on the particular stresses experienced by teachers of pupils with special educational needs, even where these teachers work in mainstream schools. Literature on teacher stress which is specifically concerned with teachers of pupils with severe or profound learning disabilities is even scarcer; indeed, I have only been able to find two articles in the academic literature worldwide (Koch, 1981; Karr and Landerholm, 1991), and both these, perhaps not surprisingly, refer to the situation in the United States.

Neither of these articles is based on research among teachers, with Koch being mainly concerned with the adaptation of the concept of 'Quality of Working Life' to schools as organisations, while Karr and Landerholm are concerned with the relationship between parent participation in early intervention programmes and stress in teachers who work in such programmes. Karr and Landerholm suggest that teachers become frustrated when parents do not participate in their children's education as expected, and suggest that this stress can be reduced by increasing teachers' understanding of the parents' problems and stresses, with benefits to all concerned. However, Karr and Landerholm's article is also interesting in that it highlights the possible differences between causes of stress in relationships with parents for teachers of pupils with severe disabilities and teachers of pupils without such disabilities, where stresses may often result from disagreement with parents about discipline or parental desires to see their child 'pushed harder'.

It seems, then, that researchers have largely ignored the stresses experienced by teachers of pupils with SLDs and PLDs. In contrast, there is a wealth of literature on the stresses experienced by those working with people with severe disabilities in other situations – see, for example, the comprehensive literature reviews by Hatton et al. (1995) and Rose (1995) – on stress in direct care staff and the research of Todis and Singer (1991) with fosterparents.

In examining the potential impact of stress on teachers of pupils with severe learning difficulties, it is therefore necessary to turn both to the literature on teacher stress in general and to that on the stress experienced by staff working with people with severe learning disabilities in non-educational situations, and in addition to examine possible causes of stress in teaching pupils with SLDs and PLDs.

# Possible causes of stress in teachers of pupils with SLDs

General literature in the field of severe and profound learning difficulties suggests that some possible causes of stress among teachers are:

- the lack of progress made by some pupils;
- coping with pupils' medical conditions, especially terminal illness;
- pupils' challenging behaviour;
- working with other adults, such as visiting professionals and classroom assistants, and liaising with mainstream colleagues to promote integrated sessions.

## Lack of progress

Evans and Ware (1987), in their interviews with teachers who worked in 'special care classes', found that at least some of these teachers had given up believing in the ability of the children in their charge to learn, and this contributed to a general sense of low morale. For example, one teacher said:

> We have to do a three-weekly prediction of what we are hoping to teach – well, it's just not relevant to these children. (Evans and Ware, 1987, p.132)

Another said:

> I used to record every day, but there's no point when you're not getting anywhere – it's disheartening. (Evans and Ware, 1987, p.132)

On the other hand, some of the teachers did believe the children could learn, and were enthusiastic about their work:

> The longer I work with these children the more I believe they can actually learn. (Evans and Ware, 1987, p.133)

These views suggest that demonstrable learning in their pupils is as important to teachers who work in SLD schools as it is to mainstream teachers, and that we might therefore expect children's difficulties in learning to be a source of stress for teachers of children with SLDs. Of course, Evans and Ware's interviews were conducted well before the advent of the National Curriculum, and when this was introduced, many SLD schools instituted new, and sometimes complex, recording systems. Evidence from work in mainstream schools suggests that such complex schemes add considerably to the stress experienced by teachers (e.g. Campbell et al., 1991). It may well be that this stress is exacerbated where time-consuming recording appears to demonstrate that no progress has been made.

## Coping with medical conditions and terminal illness

Working with children who are medically vulnerable has become an increasing part of teaching in SLD schools since the closure of much hospital provision. The presence of children who have severe epilepsy or other problems likely to lead to medical emergencies may well be stressful for the staff who work with them; anecdotal reports suggest that the anticipation of an event is more stressful than its actual occurrence.

Evans and Ware (1987) found that about 10 per cent of the children in the special care units they surveyed were believed to have conditions which were degenerative and might lead to the child's death during the school years. Although the recent removal of tuberose sclerosis from among the group of degenerative diseases would reduce this figure somewhat, nevertheless, working with children who may not live to reach adulthood is likely to be part of the experience of most teachers in SLD schools at some time. The stress and grief caused to mainstream teachers (and pupils) when a pupil dies suddenly is recognised, and counselling and support services are rightly provided in this situation. By contrast, in most authorities, little is done to help staff or pupils in SLD schools to deal with the death of a pupil, although there appears to be no reason to believe that the stress and grief experienced will be any less. On the more positive side, there is some work which attempts to address the issue of helping people with learning difficulties cope with grief and loss (e.g. Hollins and Sireling, 1989a, 1989b), and more recent work, especially that by Cathcart (e.g. 1991, 1994), is attempting to address the issue of supporting staff as well as clients, and the British Institute of Learning Disabilities is promoting greater awareness of these issues.

## Challenging behaviour

In a recent survey of SLD schools (Ware, 1995), 13 per cent of pupils were said by headteachers to exhibit challenging behaviour. The presence of pupils displaying such behaviours might well cause stress to the staff working with them.

## Working with other adults

In the past, it has been suggested that teachers may feel inhibited by the presence of other adults in the classroom (NUT, 1962, 1978). However, Thomas (1987) and Clayton (1993) both suggest that teachers are becoming increasingly accustomed to the presence of other adults, since numbers of classroom assistants have increased and therapists more frequently work in the classroom rather than withdrawing children from it. Statistics on numbers of assistants, other professionals involved and integration schemes seem to suggest that in general terms, teachers of pupils with SLDs and PLDs are particularly likely to have to work with a large number of other adults in a range of different roles, but there is little published work specifically about this issue. However, Yard (1993), in a study of teachers and assistants in eight SLD schools, found that three-quarters of the teachers were currently experiencing difficulties working with other adults, and 1 in 8 was having difficulty in working with assistants. Yard also found that only 21 per cent of teachers had received guidance on working with assistants during their initial training, whereas half those who had not received such training would have liked to. Yard did not ask teachers whether the difficulties they experienced in working with other adults created stress, and there is insufficient evidence to decide whether teachers in SLD schools are likely to find that working with other adults is a particular cause of stress. However, work in mainstream schools suggests that relationships within schools can be a major stress factor (Rees, 1990).

## Stress in teachers in mainstream and special schools

A number of points of particular interest emerge when we examine the literature on mainstream teacher stress relating to particular causes of stress, changes in levels of stress experienced by teachers over recent years, organisational issues, and the particular problems for staff in small schools.

Studies in the literature of causes of stress for teachers in mainstream schools have consistently found that pupils' behaviour and pupils' level of functioning are significant causes of stress. For example, Pratt (1978) identified 'recalcitrant children' as causing most stress in the primary school teachers he surveyed, while 'children had learning difficulties' was the sixth most frequently used item on his stress inventory. Pratt also cites earlier studies (Rudd and Wiseman, 1962; Cruikshank et al., 1973) which came to similar conclusions. More recently, Dodgson (1987) has suggested that pupils' learning difficulties challenge teachers' own view of what makes a good teacher.

By 1990, however, although behavioural problems were still among the ten most important causes of stress for teachers, they had been overtaken in importance by a number of issues to do with educational reforms (including the National Curriculum and pupil assessment) (Travers and Cooper, 1990). Dunham (1992) suggests that his research demonstrates that the stresses on mainstream teachers have been significantly increased by the implementation of the 1988 Education Reform Act. This is supported by a study of primary teachers by Campbell et al. (1991), who found that the average hours worked per week by primary teachers had increased from 49.6 in 1990 to 54.6 in 1991, and that this was accompanied by low morale and symptoms of stress.

Furthermore, and very importantly, there is a wealth of evidence to suggest that organisational factors within the school can be significant sources of stress for teachers. For example, Dunham suggests that staff with pastoral care responsibilities experience stress when there is no clear strategy for dealing with discipline problems, and that conversely, organisational support in tackling such problems can enhance teachers' self-confidence and coping abilities.

Campbell et al. (1991) also found that staff stress (in relation to the introduction of the National Curriculum) was considerably increased in schools which were poorly organised and in authorities where teachers perceived the related training to be poor. By contrast, those in well-managed schools and authorities felt that the changes in education were causing few problems:

> These were in a minority, but they showed how, under more effective management and with high quality training, the stress could be reduced and the skills and confidence of the teachers could be boosted. (Campbell et al., 1991, p.47)

Finally, Dunham suggests that senior staff in small schools may experience particular stress from trying to carry a full teaching load in addition to heavy administrative duties. Some staff in this position also report that they feel isolated, and that having to make decisions without being able to consult with another adult is stressful (Dunham, 1992). As most SLD schools are small, it is possible that many senior staff experience similar problems, and this may be especially true when provision is in small units attached to mainstream schools.

# Stresses on care staff working with people with SLDs in community and residential situations

As Rose (1995) states, within the fields of social and the health services, there has been an increasing interest in recent years in factors which may affect the lives of people with learning disabilities including staff stress. As in mainstream teaching, the impact of stress on job performance and teacher turnover rates are two reasons for this interest.

Rose's review of the literature suggests that for staff working in services that provide for more than 20 people with learning difficulties in one location, work is moderately stressful. This contrasts with the findings from mainstream teaching (see above) which suggest that teaching (at least in mainstream schools) is among the most stressful of professions, and has become increasingly so over the past six or seven years (Dunham, 1992).

Among factors found to influence stress in residential staff, interestingly, the characteristics of the residents themselves are only infrequently stated to be a cause of stress. Both behaviour problems and lack of progress among residents are only sometimes found to be sources of stress. Compared with the situation in mainstream schools, where both these factors consistently emerge as among the most important causes of stress (e.g. Dunham, 1992), the behaviour and progress of residents seem to be less important for staff working with people with learning disabilities. As for mainstream teachers, however, organisational factors are a significant cause of stress for care staff.

These differences between the causes of stress for mainstream teachers and staff working with people with learning disabilities in non-school contexts make it difficult to predict what will be the main sources of stress for teachers of pupils with severe learning disabilities, and thus difficult to know how best they might be supported in coping with these stresses. In addition, it is not clear whether the recent education reforms, and in particular the advent of the National Curriculum, have had a similar impact on teachers in SLD schools to their mainstream peers. The literature on the National Curriculum and SLD schools suggests that implementation may have been more stressful for SLD teachers because, unlike their mainstream colleagues, many of them doubt its relevance and utility (e.g. Emblem and Conti-Ramsden, 1990) Indeed, some teachers appear to regard the recent reforms as questioning the underlying philosophy of special education. On the other hand, there can be no doubt that the increase in workload due to National Curriculum assessment has not been as great for teachers in SLD schools as it has been for some of their mainstream colleagues. However, the perceived inappropriateness of most of the assessment procedures may have further increased stress for these teachers.

# A small-scale study of stress in teachers of pupils with SLDs

Because of the paucity of literature on stress in teachers of pupils with special needs, a questionnaire was constructed by extracting relevant items from Section 10 of *A Survey on Working in Services for People with Learning Disabilities* (Hester Adrian Research Centre, no date) and adding five additional items selected from the teacher stress literature (see Figure 8.1). This questionnaire was then piloted with ten teachers of pupils with special needs in main-

- Behavioural problems among pupils*
- Relationships with pupils' parents*
- Visiting staff (e.g. physiotherapist, social worker, psychologist)*
- Attendance at many time-consuming meetings*
- The preparation of individual learning material*
- The physical work conditions
- The workload
- Lack of sufficient staff and resources
- Doing domestic tasks
- Uncertainty about what the job involves
- Doing paperwork/administration
- Lack of support from outside work
- Lack of support from management
- Too much routine
- The hours of the job
- Lack of support from colleagues
- Lack of job security
- Lack of appropriate financial reward
- The school's rules and regulations
- The emotional impact of the job
- Lack of training opportunities
- Lack of promotion prospects
- Lack of support from immediate superior
- Conflicts between home and work

*Note:* *Items selected from teacher stress literature.

**Figure 8.1   Questionnaire items**

stream comprehensive schools in South Wales (Connor, 1995). This small-scale survey found that for this group of teachers, as for other mainstream teachers, pupil behaviour was considered to be a major cause of stress, 4 out of the 10 teachers saying that pupil behaviour caused them a great deal of stress, and another 2 that it caused at least a moderate amount of stress. However, pupil behaviour was exceeded as a stressor by doing paperwork or administration, which also caused a great deal of stress for 4 teachers, with another 3 saying that it caused them a lot of stress. Comparison of the findings of this survey with Travers and Cooper's (1990) survey of teachers in comprehensive schools and with Dunham's reports of stress-causing factors in a number of schools where he had conducted workshops for the staff (Dunham, 1992) suggests that this questionnaire is a valid measure of teacher stress.

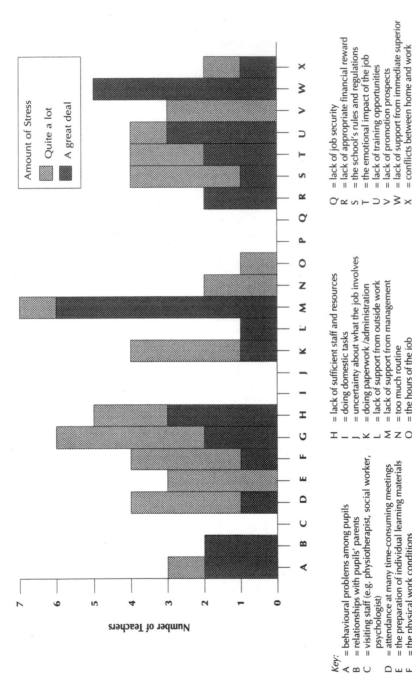

Key:

A = behavioural problems among pupils
B = relationships with pupils' parents
C = visiting staff (e.g. physiotherapist, social worker, psychologist)
D = attendance at many time-consuming meetings
E = the preparation of individual learning materials
F = the physical work conditions
G = the workload

H = lack of sufficient staff and resources
I = doing domestic tasks
J = uncertainty about what the job involves
K = doing paperwork/administration
L = lack of support from outside work
M = lack of support from management
N = too much routine
O = the hours of the job
P = lack of support from colleagues

Q = lack of job security
R = lack of appropriate financial reward
S = the school's rules and regulations
T = the emotional impact of the job
U = lack of training opportunities
V = lack of promotion prospects
W = lack of support from immediate superior
X = conflicts between home and work

**Figure 8.2    Causes of stress in an SLD school**

This questionnaire was then given to teachers in a school for pupils with severe learning disabilities, where other evidence (e.g. staff absence rates) suggested that overall levels of stress were high. There were 11 teachers in the school, and 7 of them returned completed questionnaires.

This questionnaire did not include questions about the possible stresses caused by pupils' medical conditions or potential early death, which had been identified as potential causes of stress for teachers of pupils with SLDs and PLDs. However, it was not felt appropriate to add questions on such sensitive issues in a postal questionnaire, since it would not be possible to support staff in dealing with the feelings raised by such questions.

Interestingly, although 16 per cent of the pupils in this school had challenging behaviour and 25 per cent of them profound and multiple learning disabilities, neither pupils' behaviour nor the preparation of individual learning materials were seen by most staff as particular causes of stress (see Figure 8.2). No member of staff reported that preparation of individual learning materials caused a great deal of stress, while responses to the question about pupils' behavioural problems appeared from the additional comments made by the teachers to depend partly on the particular pupils in the class, and partly on a perceived lack of support by the organisation in dealing with such problems. These teachers, then, are more similar to other staff working with people with learning disabilities than to mainstream teachers (including special needs teachers) in the extent to which they see pupil behaviour and difficulties in learning as stressful.

By contrast, organisational issues – lack of support from management and lack of support from immediate superior – were both seen as causing a great deal of stress by four or more teachers. In addition, lack of sufficient staff and resources and the workload were seen as causing a great deal or a lot of stress by at least 5 of the 7 teachers. The school's rules and regulations caused a great deal or a lot of stress to 4 of the 7 teachers. Thus, the results of this small study tend to support the view that it is organisational factors which are of greatest importance in exacerbating or alleviating staff stress, in SLD as in mainstream schools.

In addition to these directly organisational issues, 4 of the 7 teachers saw the physical work conditions, the emotional impact of the job, lack of training opportunities, paperwork and administration and attendance at time-consuming meetings as causing at least a lot of stress.

Both the reduction in training opportunities open to teachers in SLD schools and the increase in the amount of paperwork and meetings required are largely results of the recent education reforms. Like mainstream schools (Campbell et al., 1991), SLD schools have tended to develop complex recording systems to cope with the demands of the National Curriculum (see above), and recent special needs legislation has also increased the paperwork required.

The reduction in the availability of training opportunities is something which has particularly affected teachers in SLD schools, who in the past stood a reasonable chance of being seconded to full-time specialist training if they so wished, and now are likely to have to study part-time and in their own time in order to receive such training. It is not surprising, therefore, that some of these teachers saw lack of training opportunities as stressful. It is worth noting that these results probably represent an underestimate of the stress caused by lack of training opportunities, since the three teachers who did not feel that this caused them stress already had a specialist qualification (or in one case, was working towards one). It would be interesting and worthwhile to investigate whether there is any relationship between specialist training and teachers' ability to cope with the stresses of working with pupils with SLDs, but the present study was too small to compare those with and without specialist qualifications. However, evidence from other studies where teachers have reported on the value of in-service training suggests that training may be important in enabling teachers to appreciate their pupils' learning fully, and that this in turn makes the job of teaching pupils with SLDs and PLDs more satisfying (e.g. Ware, 1994, p.147). Similarly, Hatton and Emerson (1993) suggest that training may have a general effect in influencing job satisfaction for staff in a service for people with multiple disabilities.

Relationships with colleagues and with visiting staff were said to cause no more than a moderate amount of stress by any of the teachers, and relationships with parents were a major cause of stress for only two of them. The responses of these teachers to the potential for stress in relationships with colleagues and parents were, in fact, very similar to special needs teachers in mainstream schools. The evidence from this study does not support the view that working with a variety of other adults causes relationship difficulties and consequently stress for teachers in SLD schools.

Teachers who made additional comments in the main stressed organisational and support issues, although the pressure caused by the recent changes in education were also mentioned. No additional comments were made about pupils' difficulties in learning, and the SLD teachers were also similar to their mainstream special needs colleagues in reporting that the preparation of individual learning materials was not particularly stressful. The reactions of these teachers to their pupils' difficulties in learning appear to be different from those interviewed by Evans and Ware (1987); however, this difference may simply be due to the fact that the pupils taught by teachers in the current study mainly had SLDs rather than PMLDs. It may also be that the extreme amount of stress caused to these teachers by organisational factors made other issues pale into insignificance; however, the similarities with special needs teachers in mainstream schools suggest that this is not the case.

Although no firm conclusions can be drawn from such a small study, the similarities between SLD teachers and residential staff in not finding pupil characteristics particularly stressful, and between SLD and mainstream teachers in finding both general organisational issues and some of the changes occasioned by the recent education reforms major causes of stress, need further investigation. However, these similarities suggest that strategies which have proved successful in reducing staff stress in mainstream schools or non-educational settings for people with learning disabilities or in helping the staff in these settings to cope with stress may be useful for staff in SLD schools.

# Strategies for reducing and coping with stress

Practical manuals on teacher stress (e.g. Cook, 1992) suggest a variety of stress-reducing strategies which can be employed on a personal basis. Kyriacou (1980) summarises these strategies as:

- get things in perspective;
- analyse yourself and your situation;
- recognise your limitations;
- pamper yourself;
- relax.

Further details of how to apply these strategies can be found in much of the practical literature; this section therefore concentrates on organisational issues.

## Training

The potential of good and relevant training for reducing stress has already been mentioned, both in relation to the introduction of the National Curriculum and in relation to staff working in non-educational settings. Schools and LEAs might be able to help their SLD teachers to cope more positively by increasing access to training. Dunham (1992) also suggests that appraisal and training are important factors in preventing and reducing stress. It is a matter for concern, therefore, that evidence suggests that the amount of relevant training available to teachers in SLD schools has reduced over the past five years (Ware, 1995).

### Management and organisation

Dunham (1992) and others suggest that good management is essential for preventing teacher stress. Dunham suggests that knowing how the system works and being consulted about changes are important for preventing stress. Hatton and Emerson (1993) similarly suggest that staff who participate in organisational decisions are less likely to experience stress than those who feel powerless and alienated. At a more mundane level, meetings need to have clear purposes and procedures if they are not to cause stress.

### Matching aims and attitudes

Both Dunham (1992) and Hatton and Emerson (1993) suggest that individuals are less likely to experience stress if they are in sympathy with the aims and attitudes of the organisation in which they work. In addition, the much-cited work by Allen et al. (1990) and Thomson (1987) suggests that differences between staff and organisational perceptions of clients' abilities can be a major source of stress. Selection and induction of teachers for work in SLD schools may help in preventing stress arising in this way.

# Conclusion

More research is needed into the stress experienced by teachers working with pupils with SLDs, its causes, positive coping strategies teachers can employ, and organisational strategies which can be utilised by LEAs and schools to reduce stress for these staff. Further research is needed to examine the impact of pupils' medical conditions on staff stress. In the mean time however, the evidence suggests that better access to relevant training, at both induction and inservice levels and clear organisational procedures to support staff in their roles, will enable them to cope more effectively with those aspects of their role which might otherwise prove particularly stressful.

# Acknowledgements

The author would like to thank Alison Connor, who collected some of the literature for this study and carried out the survey of special needs teachers in mainstream comprehensives, Keith Park, who helped in the data collection from SLD teachers, and the staff who completed the questionnaires.

# References

Allen, P., Pahl, J. and Quine, L. (1990) *Care Staff in Transition: The Impact on Staff of Changing Services for People with Mental Handicaps*, London: HMSO.

Campbell, R.J., Evans, L., St.J. Neill, S.R. and Packwood, A. (1991) *Workloads, Achievement and Stress: Two follow-up studies of Teacher Time in Key Stage 1*, Warwick: Policy Analysis Unit, Department of Education, University of Warwick.

Cathcart, F. (1991) 'Bereavement and mental handicap', *Bereavement Care*, 10, 9.

Cathcart, F. (1994) *Understanding Death and Dying*, Worcester: British Institute of Learning Disabilities.

Clayton, T. (1993) 'From domestic helper to "assistant teacher" – the changing role of the British classroom assistant', *European Journal of Special Needs Education*, 8, 1, 32–44.

Connor, A. (1995) 'The causes of stress amongst special educational needs teachers', assignment submitted in part fulfilment of the MEd degree, Cardiff: School of Education, University of Wales at Cardiff.

Cook, R. (1992) *The Prevention and Management of Stress: A Manual for Teachers*, Harlow: Longman.

Cruikshank, D.R., Kennedy, J.J. and Meyrs, B. (1973) 'Perceived problems of secondary school teachers', *Journal of Educational Research*, 68, 154–9.

De Jong, C.G.A. (1985) 'Children in a dementia process: Emotional aspects', paper presented at the Delhi Conference of the IASSMD (International Association for the Scientific Study of Mental Deficiency), March.

Dodgson, H. (1987) 'Ritual in a reception class: An ethnographic study', unpublished MEd dissertation, Liverpool: University of Liverpool.

Dunham, J. (1980) 'An exploratory comparative study of staff stress in English and German comprehensive schools', *Educational Review*, 32, 11–20.

Dunham, J. (1981) 'Disruptive pupils and teacher stress', *Educational Research*, 23, 3, 205–13.

Dunham, J. (1992) *Stress in Teaching* (2nd edn), London: Routledge.

Emblem, B. and Conti-Ramsden, G. (1990) 'Towards Level 1: Reality or illusion', *British Journal of Special Education*, 17, 88–90.

Evans, P. and Ware, J. (1987) *'Special Care' Provision: The Education of Children With Profound and Multiple Learning Difficulties*, Windsor: NFER-Nelson.

Hatton, C. and Emerson, E. (1993) 'Organisational predictors of staff stress, satisfaction, and intended turnover in a service for people with multiple disabilities', *Mental Retardation*, 31, 6, 388–95.

Hatton, C., Rashes, R., Caine, A. and Emerson, E. (1995) 'Stressors, coping strategies and stress-related outcomes among direct care staff in staffed houses for people with learning disabilities', *Mental Handicap Research*, 8, 4, 252–71.

Hester Adrian Research Centre (no date) *A Survey on Working in Services for People with Learning Disabilities*, Manchester: Hester Adrian Research Centre, University of Manchester.

Hollins, S. and Sireling, L. (1989a) *When Dad Died*, London: St Georges Hospital Medical School.

Hollins, S. and Sireling, L. (1989b) *When Mum Died*, London: St Georges Hospital Medical School.

Karr, J.A. and Landerholm, E. (1991) 'Reducing staff stress/burnout by changing staff expectations in dealing with parents', ED351128.

Kelleher, A. and Mulcahy, M. (1985) 'Patterns of disability in the mentally handicapped', in Berg, J.M. and DeJong, J. (eds) *Science and Service in Mental Retardation*, London: Methuen.

Koch, E.L. (1981) 'Quality of Working Life (QWL) applied to educational organisations', paper presented at the Annual Meeting of the National Conference of Professors of Educational Administration, Seattle, WA, August.

Kyriacou, C. (1980) 'Coping action and organisation stress among school teachers', *Research in Education*, 24, 57–61.

Kyriacou, C. (1987) 'Teacher stress and burnout: An international review', *Educational Research*, 29, 2, 146–52.

MacPherson, F. and Butterworth, G. (1988) 'Sensorimotor intelligence in severely mentally handicapped children', *Journal of Mental Deficiency Research*, 32, 465–78.

NUT (1962) *The State of Our Schools: A Report of the Findings of the National Survey of Schools, Part 1*, London: NUT.

NUT (1978) *Ancillary Provision in Special Schools*, London: NUT.

Pratt, J. (1978) 'Perceived stress among teachers: The effect of age and background of children taught', *Educational Review*, 30, 1, 3–14.

Rees, F. (1990) *Teacher Stress: An Exploratory Study*, Windsor: NFER.

Rose, J. (1995) 'Stress and residential staff: Towards an integration of existing research', *Mental Handicap Research*, 8, 4, 220–36.

Rudd, W.G.A. and Wiseman, S. (1962) 'Sources of dissatisfaction among a group of teachers', *British Journal of Educational Psychology*, 32, 275–91.

Thomas, G. (1987) 'Other adults in the classroom: Opportunities or problems?', *Links*, 12, 3, 19–21.

Thomson, S. (1987) 'Stress in staff working with mentally handicapped people', in Payne, R. and Firth-Cozens, J. (eds) *Stress in Health Professionals*, Chichester: John Wiley.

Todis, B. and Singer, G. (1991) 'Stress and stress management in families with adopted children who have severe disabilities', *Journal of the Association for Persons with Severe Handicaps*, 16, 1, 3–13.

Travers, C. and Cooper, C. (1990) *Survey on Occupational Stress Among Teachers in the United Kingdom*, Manchester: Institute of Science and Technology, University of Manchester.

Ware, J. (1994) 'Using interaction in the education of pupils with PMLDs (i) Creating contingency-sensitive environments', in Ware, J. (ed) *Educating Children with Profound and Multiple Learning Difficulties*, London: David Fulton.

Ware, J. (1995) 'Promoting the professional development of teachers in special education through inservice training', paper presented at the International Special Education Congress, Birmingham, April (available from the author at School of Education, University of Wales, Cardiff).

Yard, P. (1993) 'Should teachers be trained to work with classroom assistants?', study submitted in part fulfilment of the requirements of the degree of BSc Hons in Psychology, Enfield: Middlesex University.

# Part II

## General considerations

# 9 Ethnic minorities

*Cecile Wright*

It is now well established that the social background of pupils is likely to shape their experience both at the level of the school and the classroom, particularly in their dealings with teachers. An examination of contemporary educational discourse over the last three decades reveals that much concern has been focused on the effects of pupils' social class and gender on teachers' perceptions of pupils' conduct and ability. Studies in these areas argue that it is in the minutiae of interaction that assumptions about pupils from different social groups might have their effect. In this regard, they may substantially, if subtly, affect the treatment accorded to pupils.

Cicourel and Kitsuse (1971), for example, found that teachers generally view white pupils of working-class background as providing them with problems in the classroom. As a consequence, working-class pupils were more likely to be classified by teachers as exhibiting conduct problems. There is also evidence to suggest that teachers' treatment of pupils differs according to their gender. Both Stanworth (1983) and Spender (1983) found that girls received less attention from their teachers compared with boys.

Studies which attest to the view of teacher bias in their responses to pupils from different social groups argue that this bias stems from teachers' typifications, which may give rise to a particular type of treatment, attitudes, perceptions of pupils' behaviour, and ultimately, the application of disciplinary practices which may be academically disadvantageous.

There seems to be a great deal of evidence concerned with responses of teachers of white working-class pupils and girls. By contrast, little detailed work has been focused upon the views and reactions of teachers either at the level of the school or classroom within the multi-ethnic setting. Yet in recent years, a particular concern among practitioners has been that teachers' expectations regarding pupils from ethnic groups will have a negative impact on their behaviour and performance, notably a sort of self-fulfilling prophecy.

Indeed, during the 1980s, in an attempt to address this issue, a growing number of local education authorities adopted multicultural policy statements (Connolly, 1992), and multicultural education was given a more significant place in teacher training.

This chapter brings together my own research over recent years in an attempt to explore teachers' reactions to ethnically mixed classroom settings. What follows is an attempt to throw some light on this issue by drawing on the findings of two studies with an overall aim of investigating the school experience of ethnic minority pupils. The first study investigated black pupils' school experience in their last two years of compulsory education, whereas the second study was concerned with very young black children at the start of their school career. Although the studies were not originally undertaken as part of a single investigation, they do represent a unity of concern and of thought relating to ethnic minority pupils' experience of school and the specific problems which teachers feel they face within the multi-ethnic classroom. In preparing this chapter, I have drawn on Wright (1986, 1987, 1992, 1993). Throughout the chapter, 'black' is used to refer to children of African-Caribbean and South Asian origin. In the case studies, all the personal names used are pseudonyms; the two comprehensive schools referred to have been given the pseudonyms Landley and Upton, and the primary schools referred to have been given the pseudonyms Adelle, Bridgeway and Castle.

# Teachers' attitudes, expectations and classroom interaction

Clearly, the education which children receive depends most immediately on the teacher in the classroom. Besides, it is well established that teachers are powerful agents in their social relationships with children. Their attitudes and treatment of them have been shown to affect children's behaviour, and ultimately, their access to effective learning.

The findings presented below describe classroom interactions between teachers and ethnic minority pupils within both primary and secondary settings. Teachers' views and behaviour are examined firstly within the secondary school classroom, followed by a similar look at evidence from a primary school context.

## Secondary school classroom setting

For secondary schools, the issues of control and discipline were observed to be paramount in the minds of teachers, particularly in their interactions with pupils of African-Caribbean origin. The classroom encounter reported below illustrates a typical interaction between the teacher and the individual African-Caribbean pupil. These encounters were observed to be frequently characterised by confrontation and conflict. Classroom interaction between teachers and African-Caribbean pupils often takes the form of the teachers enforcing their authority and/or expressing criticism. This point is illustrated by the observation of Ms Simms's lesson.

## English language (Ms Simms)

This class of middle-ability band students was being taught English language as a form group. The group comprised three Asian girls, six Asian boys, one African-Caribbean boy, six African-Caribbean girls, three white girls and eight white boys. There was a noisy start to most lessons, and it often took the teacher several attempts to secure silence.

The teacher reported:

> I really dislike this group, they are the worst group I have in terms of behaviour and motivation. The problem is, a certain group of students, they make things very difficult. I'm referring to the group of four West Indian girls who sit together. I suppose it's something to do with group dynamics. On their own they are reasonable. This group of girls are always in trouble with other teachers and their parents have constantly to be brought in.

In addition to perceiving the African-Caribbean girls as a threat to her classroom management skills, the teacher also held the African-Caribbean girls directly responsible for what she considered to be her inability to establish conducive learning conditions. As she states: 'If this group of West Indian girls were not in the class, I feel I'd be able to do a much more effective teaching job with the others.'

Such a deduction on the part of the teacher, it may be assumed, cannot be conducive to enhancing a good teacher–pupil relationship. Indeed, observations showed the classroom relations between most of the African-Caribbean girls in this class and the teacher to be based on frequent, open confrontations, which generally took the form illustrated in the classroom incident described below.

*The teacher is already in the classroom when the pupils arrive for the lesson. The pupils arrive five minutes later than normal because they have been to assembly.*

*Teacher:*   Sit down quietly 4L.
    *The teacher stands at her desk waiting for the students to settle down.*
*Teacher:*   Will you all settle down quickly, I've waited long enough. On the

board is a comprehension question taken from last year's CSE English language paper. I would like you to work through this question, work in your English folder. I will collect your work for marking at the end of the lesson. Now please get on quietly.

*The pupils work in silence. The turning of pages and a pupil tapping a pen on a desk are the only sounds. The teacher is sitting at her desk at the front of the room marking a pile of books. The silence continues for ten minutes; then a chair scrapes as an Asian girl leans forward to talk to the white girl sitting in front; four other students begin to talk. There is low level noise in the classroom.*

Teacher:    (*looks up from her marking and barks at the whole class*) Right, quiet please and get on with your work.

*The silence resumes, and then is broken by an Asian girl talking aloud to an African-Caribbean boy.*

Kulwinder (Asian girl):   Hey, Vincent, when will we be having our maths exam?

*Other students begin talking among themselves. The teacher looks up from her marking as a result of the increasing classroom noise. She looks to the back of the classroom where four African-Caribbean girls sit talking among themselves.*

Teacher:                             (*in a raised voice*) Will you four girls stop talking and get on with your work.
Barbara (African-Caribbean):   We *are* working, we're just talking about the question.
Jean (African-Caribbean):       It's not only us talking. What about her (*pointing to Kulwinder*) shouting? Why do you always pick on us?

*While the teacher is talking to the African-Caribbean girls, three white boys sit playing with a pocket computer game, which the girls have noticed.*

Teacher:    Whenever I look up you're always talking.
Barbara:    That's 'cause you only see us, everybody else is talking. Look at them (*pointing to the boys playing with the computer game*) they're not even working. (*turning to the other African-Caribbean girls and talking in a loud whisper*) Damn facety.

*The African-Caribbeans burst into laughter at Barbara's comment to them.*

*Teacher:*     *(shrilly)* Barbara and Jean, will you leave the room.

*The girls leave the room, closing the door loudly behind them.*

*Teacher:*     *(to the class)* Will the rest of you settle down now, and get on with your work. I'll be gone for just a few minutes.

*The teacher leaves the room.*

In an interview with the teacher after the lesson, she had this to say about the two African-Caribbean girls and the incident which had led her to send them out of the lesson.

*Teacher:*     Well I'd say perhaps I have more problems with them than most of the class, perhaps they are the ones whom I'm usually driven to send to Mrs Crane [deputy headteacher for discipline]. I'll put up with so much but they're inclined to become very rude some-times, which others wouldn't do. They know their limits but those two frequently go over them. It's difficult because I've tried hav-ing them sitting separately which doesn't seem to improve things because then they just become resentful and will try then to kind of communicate across the room, which is almost worse than this business here. As I've said before they're quite good workers, when they get down to it they enjoy the actual work and usually get good marks. Their work is generally handed in on time and nicely presented. As I've said, I've sent them out quite frequently and I know lots of other teachers have the same problems. I'm not sure what the solution is. I believe things are being done with them.

*C.W.:*     What happened when you sent Barbara and Jean out of the lesson and you followed them out?

*Teacher:*     I sent them down to Mrs Crane. I told them to take a note and just wait outside her room. They got into so much trouble last term, she [the deputy headteacher] threatened to bring their parents up. I don't know if it actually got to that. I never know quite what to expect, what sort of mood they will be in, they are either in a bad mood or a good mood. Yes, I can't really, and I find it difficult because I resent having to jolly them along, which I do slightly. Because if I just home in on them straight away at the beginning of the lesson and normally they do start their chattering and things right away. Well I try to put up with so much. They react, they just resent it, if I do tell them off. But then I mean they do accept it. In the past when I've sent them off to Mrs Crane, and after, perhaps, a blazing row, or having brought her up here [to the classroom], and we have a big confrontation and I expect them to be quite cool for weeks afterwards, or really rude. And they haven't been at all. Really I have no reason to believe that they would not come in as charming as anything next lesson, or they'll be troublesome, it just depends on them more than me.

This classroom observation reveals a tendency for the teacher to pick on a group of African-Caribbean girls and to promote confrontation, yet at the same time blaming the girls for an inability to establish conducive learning conditions. She invariably expected them to be difficult so that she would be in confrontation with them, and played down opportunities for conciliation. She recognised their academic abilities, but these received only secondary consideration. Observations of other classes in the school suggested that this attitude and expectation were fairly common among the staff, with the result that the academic assessment of both African-Caribbean boys and girls was influenced more by behavioural considerations than by cognitive criteria.

In their conversations, pupils themselves talk freely of the criticisms and directions that seem to make up the content of their classroom experience.

## Primary school classroom setting

It seemed clear from observations of teachers working within the ethnically-mixed primary classroom that their reactions appeared to have been shaped by their perception of children's linguistic proficiency on one hand, and their social behaviour on the other. The first issue was of particular concern for teachers in their interaction with children of Asian origin, whereas the latter issue tended to be associated with children of African-Caribbean origin.

### The Asian child in the classroom

In the nursery units, children came together as a group each day for 'story time' and (English) language work. Through effective discussion and questioning, by talking about stories, songs, objects, and so on, the teacher encouraged the children to extend their spoken English.

In these formal sessions, the Asian children were generally observed to be excluded from the discussions because of the assumption that they could not understand or speak English. On the occasions when the Asian children were encouraged to participate in a group discussion, teachers often communicated with them using basic telegraphic language. When this strategy failed to get any response, the teachers would quickly lose patience with the children and would then ignore them. This was also the observation of the black nursery nurses working in the nursery units, as the following comment from Bridgeway School reveals:

> They [white teachers] have got this way of talking to them [Asian children] in a really simple way ... cutting half the sentences, 'Me no do that' sort of thing, and that is not standard English. And they've [teachers] got this way of saying words, 'That naughty' and they miss words out and it really does seem stupid ... I feel that it's not my place to say 'Well that's a silly way to speak to children.' I worry about what it tells the white children who think that Asian children are odd anyway.

Teachers often expressed open irritation or frustration when they felt that the Asian children's poor English language skills interfered with their teaching. The scenario below illustrates experiences common to the schools observed.

*In a classroom in Adelle School, 5–6 year-olds are working on a number of activities. The class teacher calls children out individually to listen to them read. She asks an Asian girl, recently arrived from Pakistan and in the school for less than a term, to come to her desk.*

*Teacher:*    *(to Asian girl)* Right, lets see what you can do. *(teacher opens book, pointing to a picture)* This is a flower, say flower.

*Rehana nods nervously, appears a little confused.*

*Teacher:*    This is a flower. After me, FLOWER.

*Pupil doesn't respond.*

*Teacher:*    *(calls for assistance from one of the Asian pupils)* Zareeda, would you come here a minute. *(Zareeda walks over to the teacher's desk)* What is the Urdu word for 'flower'? *(Zareeda fidgets nervously)* Tell her in Urdu that this is a flower.

*Zareeda looks very embarrassed, refuses to speak. A few children gather around the teacher's desk. Zareeda hides her face from the children who have gathered around the teacher's desk.*

*Teacher:*    Come on Zareeda, what is the Urdu word?

*Zareeda refuses to co-operate with the teacher, stands at the teacher's desk with head lowered, looking quite distraught.*

*Teacher:*    Zareeda, if you're embarrassed, whisper the word to me.

*Zareeda does not respond.*

Teacher:    *(visibly irritated)* Well, Zareeda, you're supposed to be helping, that's not the attitude in this school, we help our friends. You're supposed to be helping me teach Rehana English ... *(to the Asian girls)* Go and sit down, both of you ... I'll go next door and see if one of those other Asian children can help me. *(teacher leaves the room)*

*The incident has attracted the attention of the whole class. While the teacher is inter-acting with the Asian girls, the white children are overheard making despairing remarks about 'Pakis'.*

In the classroom, many of the Asian children displayed a quiet and controlled demeanour. In comparison with other children, they appeared subdued. There was a sense in which the Asian girls seemed invisible to the teachers. They were rarely invited to answer questions and take a lead in activities in the classroom. Interestingly, for children of this age group, greater classroom co-operation was observed between Asian boys and girls than was the case for other pupil groups. In the classroom, these children operated as a closed group.

Initially, such a reaction to their classroom experience was in itself perceived to be a problem by some teachers, as reflected in this comment from a teacher at Bridgeway School:

The Asian children tend to be self-isolating. I have to deliberately separate that group. They tend to ignore all other children ... are not too happy sitting next to anybody else and see themselves as their own little group. Now they tend to converse in their own language. I'm afraid I have to say 'Now come on, stop.'

When asked to explain why Asian children conversing in their mother tongue in the classroom was a concern, she pointed out:

Because I don't know what is being said. It could be something against one of the other children in the class. I mean, I've no idea what is going on. Often one [Asian child] will come up to me and say 'Miss he's swearing,' that kind of thing. They always tell on each other of course. But no, I don't encourage that, at least not in the normal classroom situation. They [Asian children] do go as a special group to Mrs Reeves [English as a second language support teacher] and she does special stories in Urdu with them.

Among the negative responses to Asian children expressed by teachers was also open disapproval of their customs and traditions, often considered to pose problems for classroom management. Such disapproval added to the negative experiences of school of some of these children, precisely because of the contradictory expectations of home and school.

Preparing for physical education lessons, for example, posed some difficulties for the Asian girls because pupils were required, particularly at the nursery school, to undress in the classroom. The girls employed a number of creative measures to acquire some privacy, such as hiding behind chairs or under desks. The teachers often showed total disregard for the feelings of these children, openly disapproving of what they considered was oversensitive, modest behaviour on the part of the Asian girls. At the end of the PE lesson, the Asian girls were the recipients of teachers' sarcasm – 'Well, don't you wish you were all as quick getting undressed?'

The anguish experienced by the Asian girls was expressed by these 7- and 8-year-olds at Adelle School.

| | |
|---|---|
| *Parvin:* | We don't like PE. I get a headache when we do PE. |
| *Rashida:* | I don't like it because we are not allowed to do it. |
| *C.W.:* | Why? |
| *Parvin:* | Because it's like my mum and dad said, her Mum and Dad, if you do PE you get Gonah. |

['Gonah' is a term used by Muslims to mean 'sin' (in the eyes of Allah)].

| | |
|---|---|
| *Rashida:* | We go to mosque and if you do PE and you just go to mosque like that, you get smacked from that lady. That's why we don't like to do PE. We don't want trouble from God for doing PE. |
| *Parvin:* | Because we don't allow other people to see our pants, so we hide behind the table when we get changed for PE. |
| *C.W.:* | What does the teacher say when you hide behind the table? |
| *Parvin:* | Sometimes she shouts. |
| *C.W.:* | Have you told the teacher about your feelings? |
| *Parvin & Rashida:* | No, no. |
| *C.W.:* | Why? |
| *Rashida:* | Because we're scared. |
| *Parvin:* | Because we don't like to, she would shout. |

The girls are expressing a fundamental conflict between the perceived expectations of their background and the requirements of the school. However, they were reluctant to share their feelings with the class teacher because of the fear of being reprimanded. Thus, the teacher was perceived as being unsupportive.

## The African-Caribbean child in the classroom

As with the Asian child, the African-Caribbean child carries a range of expectations of their behaviour and educational potential, right from the nursery class. While the Asian child may experience a pattern made up of assumed poor language skills and negativity towards their cultural background in relation to expectations for educational attainment, the African-Caribbean child's experience is often largely comprised of expectations of bad behaviour, along with disapproval, punishment and teacher insensitivity to the experience of racism. Some African-Caribbean children of Rastafarian origin also experience cultural disapproval.

An example of such assumptions revealed at a very early stage took place in a nursery group of 4-year-olds in Castle School.

| | |
|---|---|
| *Teacher:* | Let's do one song before home time. |
| *Peter (white boy):* | Humpty Dumpty. |
| *Teacher:* | No, I'm choosing today. Let's do something we have not done for a while. I know we'll do the Autumn song. What about the Autumn song we sing. Don't shout out put your hand up nicely. |
| *Mandy:* | (*shouting out*) Two little leaves on a tree. |
| *Teacher:* | She's nearly right. |
| *Marcus (African-Caribbean):* | (*with his hand up*) I know. |
| *Teacher:* | (*talking to the group*) Is she right when she says 'two little leaves on a tree'? |
| *Whole group:* | No. |
| *Teacher:* | What is it Peter? |
| *Peter:* | Four. |
| *Teacher:* | Nearly right. |
| *Marcus:* | (*waving his hand for attention*) Five. |
| *Teacher:* | Don't shout out Marcus, do you know Susan? |
| *Susan (white girl):* | Five. |
| *Teacher:* | (*holding up one hand*) Good, five, because we have got how many fingers on this hand? |
| *Whole group:* | Five. |
| *Teacher:* | OK, let's only have one hand because we've only got five leaves. How many would we have if we had too many? Don't shout, hands up. |
| *Mandy:* | (*shouting out*) One, two, three, four, five, six, seven, eight, nine, ten. |
| *Teacher:* | Good, OK how many fingers have we got? |

| | |
|---|---|
| *Marcus:* | Five. |
| *Teacher:* | Don't shout out Marcus, put your hand up. Deane, how many? |
| *Deane:* | Five. |
| *Teacher:* | That's right, we're going to use five today, what makes them dance about, these leaves? |
| *Peter:* | *(shouting out)* The wind. |
| *Teacher:* | That's right. Ready here we go. |

*Teacher and children sing: 'Five little leaves so bright and gay, dancing about on a tree one day. The wind came blowing through the town, whoooo, whoooo, one leaf came tumbling down.'*

| | |
|---|---|
| *Teacher:* | How many have we got left? |
| *Deane:* | *(shouting out)* One. |
| *Marcus:* | *(raising his hand enthusiastically)* Four. |
| *Teacher:* | *(to Marcus)* Shush. Let's count, one, two, three, four. |
| *Teacher:* | How many, Deane? |
| *Deane:* | Four. |
| *Teacher:* | Good, right, let's do the next bit. |

*Teacher and children sing the next two verses.*

| | |
|---|---|
| *Teacher:* | How many have we got left, Peter? |
| *Peter:* | Don't know. |
| *Mandy:* | Two. |
| *Teacher:* | I know that you know, Mandy. |
| *Marcus:* | Two. |
| *Teacher:* | *(stern voice)* I'm not asking you, I'm asking Peter, don't shout out. We'll help Peter, shall we. Look at my fingers, how many? One, two. How many, Peter? |
| *Peter:* | Two. |
| *Teacher:* | Very good. Let's do the next bit. |

*Teacher and children sing the next verse; at the end of the verse:*

| | |
|---|---|
| *Teacher:* | How many have we got left, Susan? |
| *Susan:* | One. |
| *Teacher:* | Good, lets all count, one. Let's do the last bit. |

*Teacher and children sing the last verse. At the end of the verse:*

| | |
|---|---|
| *Teacher:* | How many have we got left? |

| | |
|---|---|
| *Whole group:* | None. |
| *Teacher:* | That's right there are no leaves left. Marcus, will you stop fidgeting and sit nicely. |

Marcus was frequently the recipient of teacher control and criticism. He was often singled out for criticism, even though several pupils of different ethnic origins were engaged in the same behaviour.

In a conversation about the above observation, the African-Caribbean nursery nurse attached to the unit commented:

> Marcus really likes answering questions about things. I can imagine he's quite good at that because he's always got plenty to say ... but they [white teachers] see the black children as a problem here.

Black nursery nurses in another nursery unit of Bridgeway School also expressed concern about the attitudes of white colleagues towards African-Caribbean boys in particular. One of them pointed out:

> The Head of the Nursery is forever saying how difficult it is to control the black children in the nursery, because they only responded to being hit ... there is an attitude that they all get beaten up at home and they're all used to getting a good slap or good punch. There are one or two [black children] that they are quite positive about ... they happen to be girls. I think it is a very sexist nursery. That black girls, they are positive about, are thought to be clean, well spoken, lovely personalities. As for the boys, I think boys like Joshua [Rastafarian] and Calvin who have recently moved into the reception class, they were labelled disruptive. When Fay [African-Caribbean nursery nurse] was there she really got these two children to settle, because they had somebody to relate to, that understood them, realised that they weren't troublemakers. They just needed somebody to settle them, especially Calvin, he related to her really well. Then just when he was settling down they upped and took him [transferred to the reception class] ... He went right back to stage one, he sat outside the classroom for the first few months of school apparently ... all he used to do was sit outside the classroom. I used to go over to speak to him, I'd ask him what had happened. He used to say 'The teacher said, I've been naughty, so she's put me outside.'

In contrast to the lack of attention which the Asian children often faced, African-Caribbean boys received a disproportionate amount of teachers' negative attention. For example, there was a tendency for African-Caribbean and white boys to engage in task avoidance behaviour, to fool around when they should be working, and to be generally disobedient. Teachers were observed to be more inclined to turn a blind eye to flagrant breaches of normal classroom standards when committed by white boys, or to be lenient in their disapproval. By contrast, similar conduct on the part of African-Caribbean boys was rarely overlooked by the teachers. Furthermore,

African-Caribbean boys were sometimes exclusively criticised when peers of other ethnic origins shared in the offence. Disapproval was usually instant. The punitive sanctions employed by the teachers included verbal admonishment, exclusion from the class, sending children to the headteacher, or withdrawal of privileges. African-Caribbean boys were regularly the recipients of these punitive measures, which were often made more a personal attack on the individual concerned, as in the following example from Bridgeway School.

*A class of 7–8-year-olds settle down to work after morning break. The children are seated four to a table. The classroom noise varies from low to medium level. The teacher, seated at her desk marking the children's work, keeps a vigil on a table where the following four children sit: one African-Caribbean boy (Carl), two white boys and one white girl. Every time the classroom noise level increases, the teacher looks at the African-Caribbean boy, who works effortlessly at the task set him, stopping occasionally to converse with the white boys seated at his table.*

*Teacher:*   Carl, get on with your work.

*Carl gives her a despairing sideways glance. Attends to his work. The classroom noise decreases temporarily. The classroom noise rises again. The teacher looks up from her marking and sees that Carl and the white boys seated at the table are engaged in task-avoidance behaviour.*

*Teacher:*   (shouting) Carl, stop disrupting the class, go and work outside. I'm not having you disrupting the class.

*Carl picks up his book and leaves the room, giving the teacher a despairing sideways glance.*

*Teacher:*   (addressing the class) Look at the face (referring to Carl). Go on outside. The trouble with you is that you have a chip on your shoulder.

*Carl spent the remaining school day outside the classroom, working in the corridor.*

In a conversation with the class teacher, she admitted that she had excluded Carl from the classroom on other occasions, against the policy of the school. The teacher appeared not to be concerned that Carl's exclusion from the classroom meant that he could not participate in the lesson.

# Conclusion

This chapter has focused on the findings of two studies of multi-ethnic classroom settings in an attempt to examine the content of white teachers' classroom experience across both primary and secondary contexts. Where possible, it has also attempted to emphasise the commonalties of experience across the respective settings. From the findings, it seems that for both primary and secondary teachers, the multi-ethnic classroom was frequently an extremely stressful and frustrating place to work. The source of their stress stemmed particularly from the quality of their interaction with both Asian and African-Caribbean children. Teachers genuinely perceived these pupils as potential threats to classroom management. Concerning Asian children, it seems that teachers were often beleaguered by having to respond to these children's perceived English language and cultural needs. For instance, teachers were observed to display awkwardness in interacting with Asian pupils in the classroom, Asian children were sometimes deliberately excluded from certain classroom activities (such as classroom discussions) or dealt with in a way insensitive to the children's background culture.

On the other hand, African-Caribbean children were considered a threat to classroom peace because teachers appeared to expect bad behaviour and lower educational attainment from the African-Caribbean children. These children were singled out for criticism, reprimand and vilification although white and Asian children were indulging in similar behaviour. This was shown to account for the tendency for teachers to overdiscipline African-Caribbean pupils compared with other groups within the classrooms.

On a broader note, it could be argued that the broad typifications of pupils operated by the teachers (i.e. Asian pupils being judged by technical criteria – language proficiency – and African-Caribbean pupils by social/behavioural criteria) does not point to a pathological condition in teachers. Rather, it seems to reflect a coping strategy that has become institutionalised in teacher practice and culture and school processes. Underlying this process is what sociologists term the teacher image of the 'ideal pupil' (see Becker, 1952).

In this respect, my findings indicate that teachers' comments tend to define the 'ideal pupil' more in behavioural than intellectual or academic terms, which would suggest that if pupils do not accord with, or conform to, that apparent assumption about the 'ideal pupil', or are not seen as doing so, they are more likely to be negatively labelled and stereotyped. Furthermore, my studies suggest a link between conforming behaviour and teacher approval, whereby non-conforming behaviour (where pupils are either viewed as posing a behavioural problem or not being of the 'appropriate cultural background') somewhat lowers the pupils' worth in the teachers' eyes, despite their academic worth. Moreover, since the teacher's notion of the 'ideal pupil' is inevitably culture-bound, it may be, as the classroom incidents suggest, that some groups are more likely than others to be disadvantaged by its operations.

Broadening the focus in this way enables us to appreciate the complex nature of the relationship between pupils and between teachers and pupils within the culturally diverse classroom setting. As we have seen, actual classroom practices often give rise to a great deal of concern. My findings clearly show teachers to be ill-equipped to cope with the challenges of teaching in a multicultural classroom setting. But then, what specific preparation, training or support had they received? Indeed, it has become increasingly clear that initial teacher education cannot provide all the knowledge and skills that teachers will need during their careers. In the context of the culturally diverse education setting, therefore, this is particularly applicable, as the ability of teachers to deal with changing populations and changing circumstances will be strongly influenced by a range of variables over which they may have varying degrees of influence or control. Strategies that are successful in one context do not always translate to other contexts. Thus, it is essential, as a first step in responding to teachers' evident professional needs, to offer well-resourced programmes for professional development. Within the context of multicultural classroom settings, such a teacher education programme should provide the opportunity for teachers to look closely at what happens in the classroom, and also at what it is that they are trying to achieve.

A programme of this nature might, for instance, address itself to two main areas of development – the informational and the affective – as possible ways of effecting change. In the case of the former, emphasis could be placed on teachers acquiring accurate information about management styles employed within their classroom. This could be considered in relation to a number of questions which are likely to give some indication of the nature of the relationships between teachers and pupils in the classroom. What constitutes normal classroom behaviour? Which group of children are normally well-behaved? How does the teacher react to disruptive behaviour? Which language and dialect are spoken by the children? What are the optimal conditions for supporting bilingual children in the classroom? In the case of the latter, a developmental programme might include heightening teachers' awareness of attitudinal blocks which mitigate against racial equality in the classroom. Such a programme should involve supporting and assisting teachers to identify practices and expectations at the level of both the school and the classroom which are racist in effect, if not in intent.

In sum, this chapter has focused on the challenges faced by both primary and secondary school teachers working in culturally diverse classroom settings. This challenge, at best, led to some teachers responding in an *ad hoc* manner to the demands of the context, and, at worst, teachers exhibiting frequent anxieties, frustrations, disappointment, dismay and applying inappropriate practices in their dealings with ethnic minority children. Moreover, the realisation that similar issues recurred with startling regularity in both primary and secondary contexts underlined the scale of the challenge facing schools. Thus, if the quality and the professional lives of teachers and the experience of ethnic minority children are to be radically transformed, it is argued, that as a necessary first step, support, training, improved resources and measures for helping teachers to develop alternative and more constructive responses to the challenge presented by the culturally diverse classroom setting are in need of immediate attention.

# References

Becker, H.S. (1952) 'Social class variations in the teacher–pupil relationship', *Journal of Educational Sociology*, 24, 451–65.
Cicourel, A.V. and Kitsuse, J.I. (1971) 'The social organisation of the high school and deviant adolescent careers,' in Cosin , B.R. Dale, I.R., Esland, G.M. and Swift, D.F. (eds) *School and Society*, London: Routledge and Kegan Paul.
Connolly, P. (1992) 'Playing it by the rules: The politics of research', in *'Race' and Education: British Educational Research Journal*, 18: 133–48.
Spender, D. (1983) *Invisible Women: Schooling Scandal*, London: Women's Press.
Stanworth, M. (1983) *Gender and Schooling*, London: Hutchinson.
Wright, C. (1986) 'School processes – an Ethnographic study', in Eggleston, J., Dunn, D., Anjali, M. and Wright, C., *Education for Some*, Stoke-on-Trent: Trentham Books.
Wright, C. (1987) 'Black students – white teachers', in Troyna, B. (ed.) *Racial Inequality in Education*, London: Tavistock.
Wright, C. (1992) *Race Relations in the Primary School*, London: David Fulton.
Wright, C. (1993) 'Early Education: Multiracial primary school classrooms', in Gomm, R. and Woods, P. (eds) *Educational Research in Action*, Milton Keynes: Open University Press.

# 10 Social disadvantage

*Martin Brown*

Although there is a wealth of research on environmental influences that affect children's learning, research since the 1970s has tended to focus on issues of ethnicity and gender (Shipman, 1982). As a result, the term 'social disadvantage' may require clarification. Cox (1993) suggests:

> Membership of the lower working class (that is having semi-or-unskilled jobs or being long-term unemployed) is often included in operational definitions of dis-advantage as it is associated with low incomes, poor housing and other adverse features. (p.121)

Although ethnic background and gender may compound the disadvantages faced by working-class children, the purpose of this chapter is to examine the effects that social class and related economic factors may have on children's learning, the resultant stress generated in their teachers, and to suggest some possible solutions.

## Trends in social disadvantage

There is abundant evidence that the incidence of social disadvantage is on the increase in the UK: 31 per cent of children now live in households where the income is less than half the national average, compared with 10 per cent in 1978/9 (Glyn and Miliband, 1994), while the overall number of people with an income that is below half the national average rose from 3.3 million in 1977 to 11.4 million in 1991 (Goodman and Webb, 1994).

While most families suffering social disadvantage in the UK are not living, in historical or global terms, at absolute poverty levels, welfare depends on relative material consumption as well as absolute levels of consumption

(Townsend, 1979). Almost every home contains a fridge and a television, and two-thirds of the poorest 20 per cent of households in Britain own a freezer, a telephone, central heating and a washing machine (DSS, 1992). However, as health researcher Richard Wilkinson points out:

> The tendency to overplay the significance of the material in relation to the social position represents a failure to recognise the nature of unhappiness caused by relative deprivation. Material disadvantages in themselves count for rather little compared to the low self-esteem, insecurity, depression and anxiety which relative deprivation so often engenders. Psycho-social factors can dominate one's consciousness and drain life of its value. What really damages the all important subjective quality of life is having to live in circumstances which, by comparison with others, appear as a statement of one's personal failure and inferiority. (Wilkinson, 1994, p.42)

This sense of inferiority and social exclusion leads to responses which may include mental and physical illness and antisocial forms of behaviour, which can, in turn, suggest Glyn and Miliband (1994), impose heavy costs on the rest of society. One of the costs is the increased level of stress suffered by teachers and others in daily professional contact with social disadvantage.

While the domestic policy shifts on taxation, deregulation and privatisation that have resulted in higher levels of unemployment, more part-time working and other manifestations of social disadvantage have parallels all over the developed world, certain characteristics are more pronounced in the UK. The growth of one-parent families is a Europe-wide phenomenon, but the 1992 General Household Survey (cited in LRD, 1994a) reveals that just over one-fifth of all families in the UK with dependent children are headed by a lone parent (who, in 9 out of 10 cases, is a woman). While this is a relatively high proportion compared with the rest of Europe, the real difference between Britain and Europe in this respect is lone mothers' employment prospects. Just 46 per cent of British single mothers are working or looking for work, compared with 67 per cent of mothers with partners. In Britain, mothers with partners are more likely to be in work than lone mothers. One study concluded that the reason for this was that in the UK, 'there are stronger barriers facing lone mothers entering the labour-force, in particular minimal assistance with childcare and high-effective marginal tax rates' (OECD, 1993).

The links between health and socio-economic circumstances are now well established, as are the links between stress and illness (Townsend and Davidson, 1992). Children of lone parents caught in the 'poverty trap', children of families coping with absolute as well as relative poverty, children of the long-term unemployed, and children living with parents whose situation has encouraged low self-esteem, depression and anxiety are an increasing part of the contemporary school community, and their own prospects for health, happiness and fulfilment are severely limited.

The trebling of the number of teachers leaving the profession through stress-related illness has also been noted by a number of commentators, and stress consultants such as Dunham have done valuable work in developing an awareness of strategies for managing stress that have focused on the work situation, on coping with organisational change, role conflict and ambiguity and that have projected methods of developing personal and organisational resources (Dunham, 1992). However, new evidence is now emerging that suggests that the psychological stresses of social disadvantage affect a far wider cross-section of society than was hitherto acknowledged. It will come as no surprise to teachers in daily contact with parents and children experiencing the stress of social disadvantage to learn that they themselves will share that stress, and that:

> Health in the affluent societies is now influenced less by people's absolute standard of living than their standard relative to others in society ... what affects health most is the distribution of resources within each society. (Wilkinson, 1994, p.25)

Research at the Trafford Centre for Medical Research, Sussex University, commissioned by Barnardos indicates that:

> Standards of health in developed countries are powerfully affected by how equal or unequal people's incomes are. Countries with the longest life expectancy are those with the smallest spread of incomes. (LRD, 1994b, p.125)

The report states that the deficit in life expectancy in the more unequal societies directly affects at least half the population and appears to work by reducing general immunity to disease, and that it is not the direct physiological impact of poverty that does this, but:

> what people feel their circumstances to be and what the difference in their circumstances makes them feel ... it is the social and psychological meanings attached to material differences which impact on health.
> Psychological stresses are not confined to the poor in increasingly unequal societies. The more unemployment, the more homelessness, the more houses repossessed, the more poverty, the greater will be the sense of anxiety and insecurity amongst the population at large. Meanwhile, if job opportunities, pension rights and health services appear to be crumbling, people feel there is further to fall and the risks of daily life are more worrying. (LRD, 1994b, p.125)

# Past initiatives aimed at tackling social disadvantage, and recent developments

The link between teachers' stress and pupils' social disadvantage is powerful and complex, but the link has long been recognised. In the primary sector, for example, the Plowden Report (Central Advisory Council for Education, 1967) laid emphasis on the influence of the home environment on the child's educational progress, and gave a clear message to government and local education authorities (LEAs):

> Policy makers and administrators must act in a world where other things are never equal … in a world in which the children grow up where everything influences everything else, where nothing succeeds like success and nothing fails like failure. (p.50)

The report noted that in schools serving socially disadvantaged communities, there was frequently a rapid turnover of staff, with problems of unfilled vacancies, that the permanent members of staff were 'sometimes too tired to even enjoy their own holidays', and that if issues of social justice for children living in disadvantaged neighbourhoods were to be tackled, then the demands on 'teachers who work in deprived areas with deprived children' would have to be recognised. It was accepted that too many staff experienced exhaustion and negative carry-over to life outside the school.

The Plowden proposals included the establishment of Educational Priority Areas (EPAs), where schools would receive improved resourcing, including additional allowances in teachers' salaries, since:

> teachers in such schools deserve extra recognition and reward and, to give it to them, would be one way of achieving something even more important, greater fairness between one child and another. (Central Advisory Council for Education, 1967, p.60)

Other recommendations for schools in Educational Priority Areas aimed at improving educational provision for pupils also affected teacher morale: improving staffing ratios so that no class exceeded thirty pupils, enhancing provision of teacher's aides, encouraging building improvements and fostering the expansion of nursery education and research programmes to determine the most effective measures for dealing with social inequality.

A range of criteria were proposed for the identification of the most disadvantaged areas. These included the proportion of unskilled or semi-skilled workers, the proportion of large families and single-parent families, overcrowding and relative poverty measured by the take-up of free school meals.

The government of the day funded initiatives in response to the report. The Urban Programme granted funds to local authorities to be allocated to education and other public services in designated areas, while the Educational Priority Areas research initiatives were aimed at raising educational standards and teacher morale, improving home–school links and parents' involvement in their children's education and in giving local communities a sense of responsibility.

The Plowden recommendations and their implementation were open to criticism. The blanket nature of the EPA designation resulted in inflexibility: a high proportion of socially disadvantaged pupils were unable to benefit from additional resources because they lived in the wrong location, outside an Educational Priority Area. Over time, the EPA designation became anomalous. In the light of subsequent research, the most significant recommendations of all, relating to increasing early years and nursery provision, still awaits implementation (Mortimore and Blackstone, 1982).

Despite these criticisms, there can be little doubt that the official recognition that Plowden gave to the needs of schools serving areas of social disadvantage, and the stress often faced by staff in such schools, helped improve status and self-esteem. As a teacher working at an Inner London school in an Educational Priority Area at the time, I had personal experience of the effect that the ILEA initiatives in response to Plowden had on raising staff morale. Despite many serious problems, which would be identified today as relating to professional stress and children's special educational needs, teachers not only understood that they were engaged in meaningful and socially important activities but had their need for self-esteem satisfied by the belief that their worth was recognised by all. These are both stress-reducing criteria (Dunham, 1981).

In education, as in other areas of public service, rising expectations were dashed by the economic downturn heralded by the oil crisis of the early 1970s. Member countries of the Organisation for Economic Co-operation and Development examined their options for reducing public expenditure. In Britain, the new priorities were signalled by Prime Minister Callaghan's 1976 Ruskin College speech (cited in Kelly, 1989). In the intervening years, 'value for money' – achieved through the combination of a centrally-determined curriculum and 'market forces' operated by parents exercising their rights and responsibilities – has become the new orthodoxy.

Thus it is today that parents with the time, knowledge and confidence are able to choose the 'best' state schools for their children, while those who are struggling to survive increasing social and economic problems with decreased social support have more immediate and pressing concerns than being educational 'consumers' (Brown, 1990), and 'the individual's life chances are left to the random outcome of the operation of an imperfect market' (Brighouse, 1990).

Formula-funded school budgets, primarily based on school rolls, leave little opportunity for either schools or LEAs to respond to issues like social disadvantage. League tables of national test and examination results and attendance figures based on raw scores give parents partial information that discriminates against schools serving socially disadvantaged communities.

The OFSTED inspection handbook makes only one provision for registered inspection teams to comment on an inspected school's social composition (OFSTED, 1994).

As Leonard (1988) points out, under the operation of Local Management of Schools, the most attractive pupils in cost-benefit terms are the average achievers, who can be taught in large, homogeneous teaching groups, while the most able will benefit the school through examination successes. Pupils with learning difficulties, a large proportion of whom suffer social disadvantage, are a poor investment: 'special needs pupils do not fit easily into a system which is strongly influenced (if not totally dominated) by market forces' (Leonard, 1988, p.218). The balance is firmly tilted against disadvantaged pupils. Unless a child who has special educational needs also carries the financial benefit of a statement, he or she is likely to be viewed as a burden on a school's resources.

## Social disadvantage, attainment and special educational needs

The strong correlation between social class and educational attainment has been demonstrated repeatedly over many decades (Davie et al., 1972; Essen and Wedge, 1982; Osborn and Milbank, 1987; Cox and Jones, 1983). Social disadvantage appears to affect every stage of development. In one survey, 46 per cent of the most disadvantaged children received no form of pre-school education, compared with only 10 per cent of the most advantaged (Osborn and Milbank, 1987). Among those entering the labour force between the mid-1950s and the late 1980s, the children of unskilled manual workers were one-tenth as likely to gain a university qualification as those of professional parents, and eight times as likely to have no qualifications at all (Central Statistical Office, 1993). A child born into a family of professional, administrative or managerial parents is seven times more likely to have a professional job than a child of working-class parents (Marshall and Swift, 1993).

Social class is a more powerful factor than race or ethnicity in determining educational achievement, according to one recent study which found that while male children of white, professional parents achieved on average 10 per cent better examination scores than their African-Caribbean counterparts, they scored almost twice as well as those of white manual workers (Drew and Gray, 1990).

Experiences of seemingly predetermined life expectations can promote anger and despair among pupils so affected, which may be expressed in school in behavioural terms. Dunham reports an interview with a secondary school pupil reported to have behaviour problems:

I look out of our front door at the street and wonder if I'll ever manage to get away from it all. Homework is alright for a lot of kids, especially when you've got small families and the parents understand. But tell me, how do you think I get it done in a place like ours? The kids tear the books and get jam on everything. Telly never stops. 'Use your bedroom' says the teacher. Is he kidding, it's even worse there and I share it with two others. (Dunham, 1992, p.53)

Teachers with knowledge and understanding of some of the difficulties faced by socially disadvantaged pupils may experience a sense of frustration at having to deal with the consequences of situations over which they have no control.

It is, of course, possible to overstate the effects of social disadvantage on pupils' lives. Teacher expectations can be depressed by finding too many mitigating circumstances for pupils not achieving more, and the studies of Mortimore et al. (1988) and Smith and Tomlinson (1989) have highlighted the difference that schools can make to their pupils' attainments and aspirations. Purposeful leadership from the headteacher, staff involvement in curriculum planning, consistency of teacher approach, structure in the school day, intellectually challenging teaching, maximum communication with pupils and parents and a positive work ethos were some of the recommendations of the Mortimore team for school effectiveness. Much of the variation between schools in their effects on pupils' progress and development was accounted for by differences in their policies and practices and by certain of their 'given' characteristics. Yet the fact remains that socioeconomic factors are important determinants in assessing school performance. At LEA level, 'league tables' have consistently shown affluent Southern authorities, such as Harrow, West Sussex and Surrey, as league leaders, while the bottom ten have been urban and largely inner-city.

There is an associated link between social disadvantage and special educational needs (SEN), expressed in one study as 'a tendency for children from the lower social classes, ethnic minorities, and non-English speaking backgrounds to be disproportionately represented among the population designated as retarded or learning disabled' (Pumfrey and Ward, 1991, p.61). Furthermore, these special needs tend to be associated with behavioural problems (Rutter and Madge, 1976; Essen and Wedge, 1982; Bash et al., 1985). Garner (1994), reporting on his study of two groups of 'disruptive' pupils in two schools in England and the USA noted that the research amplified the idea of a link between environmental factors and pupils being categorised as 'disruptive'. Most of the sample were experiencing high levels of stress due to social disadvantage, and all were drawn from communities that had suffered social and economic deprivation as a result of economic recession.

This might suggest an increase in behavioural disturbance in recent years, and there is some evidence to support this. The number of pupils referred out of mainstream schools on behavioural grounds has been described as a 'hidden explosion', with many more waiting within the mainstream (Stirling, 1991). But mainstream schools may be less tolerant of learning difficulties that may affect their market image or league table placing. Here, too, is a stress point for special needs teachers working in mainstream schools. Over the past three decades, there have been a number of studies that have suggested subjectivity, bias and 'labelling' of pupils (Coard, 1971; Tomlinson, 1982). The question arises whether the needs of pupils or the needs of the institution are the 'special needs' being protected by some referrals.

The number of socially disadvantaged children displaying emotional and/or behavioural difficulties puts additional demands on SEN teachers and their colleagues, as they become targets for 'displaced feelings of hostility, jealousy, disappointment, affection and dependence' (Dunham, 1981). Insecurity may be further increased by a lack of psychological knowledge, which leaves teachers feeling uncertain as to how to respond appropriately. This can be particularly acute when a pupil's hostile reaction produces a sense of personal inadequacy or is taken personally. Appropriate INSET and opportunities to discuss incidents with colleagues have not been priorities in most schools in recent years.

Unfortunately, SEN teachers' coping strategies, especially in schools with a high proportion of socially disadvantaged pupils, have been undermined by the generally diminishing availability of financial resources available to schools. My own observation is that SEN departments tend to be the least well resourced within schools, making do with the oldest furniture and equipment, and likely to be using, for example, other departments' cast-off computers. In schools serving the most socially disadvantaged, SEN departments are becoming the 'Cinderellas' of what are already 'Cinderella' schools.

The increased demands created by the legislative changes of recent years also have a sharper edge when dealing with social disadvantage. For some parents, whose life experiences have made them wary of authority, the bureaucratic procedures for SEN referrals resemble those of the social security office. Multidisciplinary review meetings that include parents can intimidate them unless there is sensitivity and empathy from other participants. Delays in issuing Statements by LEAs can appear to be a denial of rights to parents, and frequently, it is the SEN teacher who is the first to be approached by an anxious parent. Well-founded parental concerns and suspicions can lead to role ambiguity for SEN staff in dealing with socially disadvantaged families.

Another cause of stress arises from what have been described as 'feelings of alienation from values they see in the new business culture of their school' (Dunham, 1992). While marketing committees and mission statements may be accepted with cynical resignation, other aspects may cause real outrage.

An example reported to me recently concerned a secondary school pupil with special educational needs who was temporarily excluded for breaching the school's newly-introduced dress code for pupils by wearing the wrong footwear. The pupil's illiterate parents were forewarned by letter, while the SEN staff (who knew of the special family circumstances) were informed after the event. SEN teachers with intimate knowledge of pupils' histories and home backgrounds and carefully-nurtured relationships with families can feel that their expertise is no longer valued after such occurrences.

SEN staff may also feel isolated and alienated from colleagues who have unrealistic expectations about the level of support they are able to give. The pressures on class teachers from increased class sizes, the introduction of the Code of Practice (DfE, 1994) and demands for the production of more differentiated teaching materials have led to some SEN teachers being expected to undertake impossible workloads. Many are employed on part-time contracts, which can result in them missing important communications if staff notices circulate on days when they are not employed and their absence is overlooked. I know of SEN teachers who have felt guilty at being unable to attend meetings called at times when they were not employed at their schools; I know of others in secondary schools experiencing feelings of inadequacy at their inability to produce differentiated materials for specialist subjects. There is a danger of some regarding SEN staff as 'second-class teachers for second-class pupils'. Professional weaknesses, be they individual or collective, may be harder to acknowledge in the current climate of opinion, overshadowed as it is by appraisal and the possible introduction of performance-related pay. Such defensive attitudes are understandable, but serious criticisms demand serious replies. Despite 'sinister aspects' (Grice and Hanke, 1990), to date, appraisal remains no more than a tool for professional development (McMahon, 1989), which many have found a useful and worthwhile exercise (Dunham, 1992).

At an individual level, it is necessary to accept that teaching socially disadvantaged children with special educational needs is, by its very nature, likely to be demanding and stressful. A high order of personal commitment and organisational and other skills are required. However, individuals, must recognise that they cannot compensate for social injustice. The 'guilty feeling nearly all of the time that nothing has been done properly' (Dunham, 1992) is a common experience for teachers coping with socially disadvantaged pupils. Guilt can be diminished by setting realistic targets, identifying one's limitations and knowing how to be assertive:

> assertiveness is valuable ... when a member of staff is asked to undertake a new area of work despite being over-burdened or when a teacher is asked to finish a project within an unrealistic deadline. Saying 'No' to these demands is often regarded as unprofessional and the person who manages to do it often feels guilty,

but if you want to halt the severe loss of your time please practice this lovely word. (Dunham, 1992, p.182)

Effective time management is another way of alleviating stress. It is all too easy for those working with social disadvantage to be diverted into responding to immediate crises. If the diversion is clearly not part of one's job description, then it should be left to another whose job it is. Some people find that keeping a time log for a short period helps them to identify where their time is being used up. The following advice, directed at headteachers, contains some useful ideas that could be adapted:

1    Keep long-term goals in mind even while doing the smallest task.
2    Plan first thing in the morning and set priorities for the day.
3    Keep a list of specific items to be done each day, arrange them in priority order and then do your best to get the important ones done as soon as possible.
4    When under pressure ask yourself, 'Would anything disastrous happen if I didn't do this now?' If the answer is no, then don't do it.
5    Do your thinking on paper.
6    Set deadlines for yourself.
7    Delegate.
8    Generate as little paperwork as possible.
9    Recognise that some of your time will be spent on activities outside your control and don't worry about it.
10    Ask yourself hourly, 'Am I making the best use of my time right now?' (Day et al., 1990, p.93)

It is also necessary to keep one's work in perspective. Work is only one aspect of our lives (albeit an important one). We also have responsibilities to our families, friends and communities. Making time for one's life outside is essential for personal development. Personal development is not the same as professional development!

Stress alleviation cannot just be tackled at an individual level. As has been pointed out by the Education Advisory Service Committee of the Health and Safety Commission:

> Stress problems should be approached from both the organisational and individual levels with each making an important contribution. Neither strategy on its own is likely to be totally effective. (Health and Safety Executive, 1990, p.11)

Their recommendations have been presented in the form of a checklist:

● Develop a supportive culture.

- Are you countering the view that stress is a reflection of personal vulnerability?
- Are senior managers accessible to staff to discuss problems?
- Are staff encouraged to support colleagues and to talk about feelings and effects of stress?
- Is the management style co-operative rather than competitive?
- How is team spirit, a sense of belonging and sharing of aims and objectives, encouraged?
- Are induction and introduction programmes for new staff effective?
- Do you recognise individuals' fears about returning to work after sickness?
- Do staff make use of occupational health advice?
- Do you encourage group problem-solving?
- Do you emphasise prevention and preparing rather than coping with stress?
- Have staff discussed whole-school policies and action plans designed to reduce stress arising from:

  - discipline and disruptive pupils;
  - training, induction and career development;
  - workload;
  - lack of resources;
  - the state of the school;
  - staff facilities;
  - school organisation;
  - communications;
  - political and community expectations? (Harrison, 1990, p.23)

Stress, then, has to be tackled at an institutional as well as an individual level. It also has to be recognised that as stress problems are increasing in many levels of society and fields of work, the issue must be tackled at corresponding organisational levels. Professional associations, trade unions, political parties and other organisations that operate at a national level are other avenues for tackling the root causes of stress.

# Other issues emerging since the Education Reform Act

Under Local Management of Schools arrangements, not less than 75 per cent of the aggregated school's budget is allocated by a formula based on pupil numbers. Although each LEA devised its own scheme (subject to central government approval), control over most public educational expenditure has now effectively passed from the locally-elected councils and education committees into the hands of school governing bodies. As was predicted (Leonard, 1988), for LEAs responsible for areas with high levels of social disadvantage, this has created difficulties.

The costs related to educational disadvantage, including pupils with learning difficulties and special needs, are proving to be greater than is allowed for by the formula in schools with high levels of disadvantage, smaller classes, more specialist support and more pastoral care time per pupil than used to be considered advisable (Leonard, 1988). Today, the most disadvantaged pupils may be viewed as being of no benefit to the school's balance sheet. With class sizes rising for the sixth successive year (DfE, 1995), it is the schools that have been previously funded for social disadvantage which have been hit the hardest because of the operation of the formula. The publication of examination league tables is reinforcing marketing messages of 'success' and 'failure'. The 'failing' school is increasingly catering for the socially disadvantaged (Edwards and Whitty, 1994).

If the funding formula – driven mainly by pupil numbers – records 'success', so does the entrepreneurial market ethos. 'Successful' schools can also attract additional funds from their more affluent parents, and are more likely to be able to attract commercial sponsorship . The 'failing' school not only loses pupils, and therefore formula funding, it is also likely to have less ability to raise other forms of finance.

The inequality is further compounded by the clearly-signalled intention of central government to persuade schools to opt out of LEA control and become grant-maintained, by providing them with more funds:

> Having legislated to prevent local education authorities from redistributing funding between schools on the basis of pupils' social and educational needs, the government then imposed a redistributive formula of its own, geared to favour schools on the grounds of their acceptability to – and acceptance of – market-led educational policy. (Bourne et al., 1994, p.8).

Thus, the financial aspects of education have become increasingly significant in exacerbating teacher stress. A deteriorating teaching and learning environment is being experienced by many, as is a radical change in career expectations, as staff find that promotion, professional development and even the opportunity to move to another school are blocked, and an increasing number face the fear of redundancy. For those engaged in activities that may be regarded as 'peripheral' to delivery of the National Curriculum, such as special needs support, that fear can be very real indeed.

For the socially disadvantaged child, the education marketplace is proving to be an even greater disaster. Mary Warnock, commenting in 1991 on developments in the intervening years since the publication of the report produced by the Committee of Enquiry Into Special Educational Needs that she chaired, writes:

> In the market the underdog does not have his day. There is no place for him. So, educationally, there is no place for the dim, the disadvantaged, the disabled or the slow. We may be sorry for them and perhaps at Christmas give a little to a charity that helps them. But they are no longer entitled to the best. (Warnock, 1991, p.151)

With this perspective in mind, it is necessary to comment on the increase in school exclusions in recent years. The rising rate of exclusions recorded from the late 1980s onwards forced a government-initiated investigation to be established to monitor the incidence of permanent exclusions over the two-year period 1990–2. The National Exclusions Reporting System (NERS) uncovered 2,910 permanent exclusions in the 1990/1 school year. The figure for the following year had risen to 3,833 (Lloyd Bennett, 1993).

Alarming as these figures may be, they are likely to be just the visible 'tip of the iceberg' of exclusions. An NUT survey in 1992 found evidence of a 20 per cent increase in all exclusions over the previous year, which suggested a total of 25,000 pupils affected nationally (Bourne et al., 1994), and at least one researcher has suggested that recorded permanent exclusions account for less than 10 per cent of all exclusions (Stirling, 1993). Official statistics may be gross underestimates of the actual position, since they are based on the figures that schools and LEAs choose to divulge in an atmosphere of increasing sensitivity to the issue. Children may be 'informally' or 'unofficially' excluded from their school, and thus not adversely affect the school's position on any league table of exclusions.

If the NERS and other investigations confirm what is suspected about trends in the number or scale of exclusions, there is also growing evidence that excluded pupils are typically socially disadvantaged and are likely to have special educational needs. Garner notes that among excluded pupils, there is an over-representation of children who have special educational needs or are from minority (mainly African-Caribbean) groups (Garner, 1993). McManus comments:

> Surveys indicate that most excluded pupils are male, working-class teenagers whose lives are characterised by domestic deprivation and disorder, erratic parental discipline, and poor attainment and ability. (McManus, 1993, p.219)

In 1994, the Association of Metropolitan Authorities (AMA) published a report which suggests that the number of pupils identified as emotionally disturbed is rising, and that schools are increasingly likely to exclude them. The report (which also suggests that the increase in exclusions is often hidden) concludes that schools have become less tolerant of poorly-behaved pupils and are competing to recruit the brightest and least difficult children in response to the publication of league tables based on raw National Curriculum results (AMA, 1994).

For special educational needs co-ordinators and others with prime responsibility for the education of children with learning difficulties and special educational needs, the exclusion of a socially disadvantaged pupil frequently saps morale and promotes feelings of powerlessness and lack of professional worth. Heralding the total breakdown of a home–school relationship that such teachers will have worked hard to promote, a permanent exclusion may mean the undoing of years of painstaking work. The knowledge that the child will be experiencing trauma, a sense of rejection and alienation (Stirling, 1993) and, if being 'educated otherwise', will in all probability receive a very few hours of tuition each week (DfE, 1993) only adds to the sense of guilt and failure experienced by the teacher.

## Official responses to issues identified

One of the consequences following the growth in social disadvantage is an increase in disaffection and crime among the young (Hagan, 1994). Despite a number of government-initiated or funded projects, some of which have had very positive outcomes, the knee-jerk ministerial reaction to the growing problems created by their own legislation has been to blame the teachers. One example quoted by Garner (1994), was the remark of the Secretary of State for Health, who is reported to have told an audience: 'We must challenge the indifference of teachers and social workers and the do-gooders who don't' (p.104). Such sentiments, quickly echoed in the national press and on radio and television broadcasts, do nothing to raise teacher morale or reduce stress.

Another typical response has been to initiate an official report in response to a problem, in such a tone that it tends to further undermine teacher morale. For example, the Elton Committee was established: 'In view of the public concern about violence and indiscipline in schools and the problems faced by the teaching profession' (DES, 1989, p.54). Yet teachers of the socially disadvantaged need to look carefully at the recommendations of this report, many of which contain practical suggestions which can be used to build stronger links between teachers, pupils and parents, and contrary to ministerial pronouncements, view ineffective pupil management of behaviour not in terms of personal inadequacy or indifference but in terms of lack of skills training (DES, 1989).

The Elton Report accepts that there has been an increase in family stress, single-parent families and child poverty in recent years, and of particular relevance are the recommendations that local authorities should ensure 'that adequate provision for pre-school education for severely disadvantaged children is available in their area', and that all 'LEAs and schools should ensure that the special educational needs of pupils with emotional and behavioural difficulties are assessed and met' within six months. Similarly, the OFSTED publication *Access and Achievement in Urban Education* (OFSTED, 1993) and other research and reports contain many positive suggestions. What has to be both recognised and clearly stated, however, is that achievement in schools serving socially disadvantaged communities is being severely damaged by national educational policy changes. As Tim Brighouse, Chief Education Officer of Birmingham points out:

> a pecking order of schools who choose parents not vice versa and of consumerism, fed by league tables information and a charter of rights devoid of responsibility, are at the root of our present troubles. Unless someone tackles the issue of admission by legislation, the outcome ten years from now will be ever widening gaps between the educationally rich and the educationally poor. (Brighouse, 1995, p.8)

Central government policies are the primary cause of the increased levels of stress among teachers of the socially disadvantaged. Ultimately, changes in those policies will be needed to reduce that stress.

# References

AMA (1994) *Reviewing Special Educational Needs*, Luton: Local Government Management Board.

Bash, L., Coulby, D. and Jones, C. (1985) *Urban Schooling: Theory and Practice*, London: Holt, Rinehart and Winston.

Brighouse, T. (1990) 'And for our next act', *The Times Education Supplement*, 19 January.

Brighouse, T. (1995) quoted in 'A vision for urban schools', *Parents and Schools*, 81, Campaign for the Advancement of State Education.

Bourne, J., Bridges, L. and Searle, C. (1994) *Outcast England*, London: Institute of Race Relations.

Brown, P. (1990) 'The third wave: Education and the ideology of parentocracy', *British Journal of Sociology*, 11, 1, 65–85.

Central Advisory Council for Education (1967) *Children and their Primary Schools* (the Plowden Report), London: HMSO.

Central Statistical Office (1993) *Social Trends*, London: HMSO.

Coard, B. (1971) *How the West Indian Child is Made Educationally Sub-normal in British Schools*, London: New Beacon.

Cox, T. (1993) 'Coping with unhappy children who have educational disadvantages', in Varma, V. (ed.) *Coping with Unhappy Children*, London: Cassell.

Cox, T. and Jones, G. (1983) *Disadvantaged Eleven Year Olds*, Oxford: Pergamon Press.

Davie, R., Butler, N. and Goldstein, H. (1972) *From Birth to Seven*, London: Longman.

Day, C., Whitaker, P. and Johnston, D. (1990) *Managing Primary Schools in the 1990s*, London: Paul Chapman Publishing.

DES (1989) *Discipline in Schools* (The Elton Report), London: HMSO.

DfE (1993) *Pupils with Problems: Draft Circular No.3*, London: Department for Education.

DfE (1994) *The Code of Practice on the Identification and Assessment of Special Educational Needs*, London: HMSO.

DfE (1995) *Statistics of Education – Schools in England 1995*, London: HMSO.

Drew, D. and Gray, J. (1990) 'The fifth year examination achievements of young people of different social origins', *Education Research*, 32, 2, 107–17.

DSS (1992) *Households Below Average Income 1979–1988/9*, London: HMSO.

Dunham, J. (1981) 'Disruptive pupils and teacher stress', *Education Research*, 23, 3, 205–13.

Dunham, J. (1992) *Stress in Teaching* (2nd edn), London: Routledge.

Edwards, T. and Whitty, G. (1994) 'Education opportunity and efficiency', in Glyn, A. and Miliband, D. (eds) *Paying for Inequality*, London: IPPR/Rivers Oram.

Essen, J. and Wedge, P. (1982) *Children in Adversity*, London: Pan Books.

Garner, P. (1993) 'Leaving them out', *Education*, 2 July, 12.

Garner, P. (1994) 'It's all society's fault', in Sandow, S. (ed.) *Whose Special Need?*, London: Paul Chapman.

*General Household Survey* (1992) London: HMSO.

Glyn, A. and Miliband, D. (1994) *Paying for Inequality*, London: IPPR/Rivers Oram.

Goodman, A. and Webb, S. (1994) *For Richer for Poorer: The Changing Distribution of Income in the UK*, London: Institute of Fiscal Studies.

Grice, C. and Hanke, M. (1990) 'Suspending judgements: Teacher appraisal', *Education Today*, 40, 2, 42–4.

Hagan, J. (1994) 'Crime inequality and efficiency', in Glyn, A. and Miliband, D. (eds) *Paying for Inequality*, London: IPPR/Rivers Oram.

Harrison, P. (1990) 'Tackling the high cost of stress', *The Times Educational Supplement*, 28 December.

Harvey, K. (1989) 'Special needs services: An overview of the future', in Bowers, T. (ed.) *Managing Special Needs*, Milton Keynes: Open University Press.

Health and Safety Executive (1990) *Managing Occupational Stress: A Guide for Managers and Teachers in the School Sector*, London: HMSO.

Kelly, A. (1989) *The Curriculum: Theory and Practice*, London: Paul Chapman.

Leonard, M. (1988) *The 1988 Education Act: A Tactical Guide for Schools*, Oxford: Blackwell.

Lloyd Bennett, P. (1993) 'Stockpiling the unsaleable goods', *Education*, 13 August, 126–7.

LRD (Labour Research Department) (1994a) *Fact Service*, 56, 32.

LRD (Labour Research Department) (1994b) 'Why British lone parents lose out', *Labour Research*, May, 7–9.

Maclure, S. (1990) *A History of Education in London*, London: Allen Lane.

Marshall, G. and Swift, A. (1993) 'Social class and social justice', *British Journal of Sociology*, 44, 2, 187–211.

McMahon, A. (1989) 'School teacher appraisal schemes in England: The pilot scheme experience in Wilson', in Dunham, J. (ed.) *Assessment for Teacher Development*, London: Falmer Press.

McManus, M. (1993) 'Discipline in pupils excluded from school', in Varma, V. (ed.) *Management of Behaviour in Schools*, London: Longman.

Mortimore, P. and Blackstone, T. (1982) *Disadvantage and Education*, London: Heinemann.

Mortimore, P., Sammons, P., Stoll, L., Lewis, D. and Ecob, R. (1988) *School Matters*, London: Open Books.

OECD (1993) *Breadwinners or Childrearers: The Dilemma for Lone Mothers*, Paris, Organisation for Economic and Cultural Development.

OFSTED (1993) *Access and Achievement in Urban Education*, London: HMSO.

OFSTED (1994) *Handbook of Guidance for the Inspection of Schools*, London: HMSO.

Osborn, A. and Milbank, J. (1987) *The Effects of Early Education*, Oxford: Clarendon Press.

Pumfrey, P. and Ward, J. (1991) 'Term of birth and special education placement', *Research in Education*, 46, 61–72.

Rutter, M. and Madge, J. (1976) *Cycles of Disadvantage*, London: Heinemann.

Shipman, M. (1982) *Assessment in Primary and Middle Schools*, London: Croom Helm.

Smith, D. and Tomlinson, S. (1989) *The School Effect: A Study of Multi-racial Comprehensives*, London: Policy Studies Institute.

Stirling, M. (1991) 'Absent with leave', *Special Children*, November, 10–13.

Stirling, M. (1993) 'Second classes for a second class?' *Special Children*, May, 15–18.

Tomlinson, S. (1982) *Educational Subnormality: A Study in Decision Making*, London: Routledge and Kegan Paul.

Townsend, P. (1979) *Poverty in the UK: A Survey of Household Resources and Living Standards*, London: Verso.

Townsend, P. and Davidson, N. (1992) *Inequalities in Health*, Harmondsworth: Penguin.

Warnock, M. (1991) 'Equality fifteen years on', *Oxford Review of Education*, 17, 2, 145–53.

Wilkinson, R. (1994) 'Health redistribution and growth', in Glyn, A. and Miliband, D. (eds) *Paying for Inequality*, London: IPPR/Rivers Oram.

# 11 Physical and sexual abuse

*Neil Hall*

## Introduction

In every classroom, there will be children who have been abused. Only those people who wish to deny the reality and extent of child abuse suggest otherwise. Statistical evidence (e.g. the often quoted British population survey by Baker and Duncan, 1985) identified that at least 10 per cent of adults had been sexually abused by the age of 16. Other studies have produced even higher incidence rates, depending on the criteria used to define sexual abuse (Glaser and Frosh, 1993). Similar studies for physical abuse are rarer, although Hemenway et al. (1994) revealed that only 16 per cent of adults were not physically disciplined as children. While there are difficulties in defining what constitutes physical abuse (Hansen and Warner, 1992), there is also a problem in deciding whether physical punishment by parents constitutes abuse (Carey, 1994; Leach, 1993).

It has been hypothesised that the proportion of abused children with special needs is significantly greater than those who do not have special needs (Baladerian, 1991; Ammerman et al., 1988), suggesting that children with special educational needs are more vulnerable to being abused. The effect on staff in special education is that as they become more aware of the likelihood of the pupils having experienced some form of abuse, their anxieties increase, often for both personal and professional reasons. The role of teachers of abused children with special educational needs therefore additionally requires them to respond to a complex range of children's psychological and social needs beyond what has become an increasingly sophisticated analysis of children's special educational needs. An inevitable result for special needs teachers, recognised in other professional groups working with abused children (e.g. social workers, Hopkins, 1989; police officers, Scott, 1991), is the manifestation of a wide range of stress-related behaviour and illness.

169

The nature of teachers' responses to abused children appears only to be of recent interest to researchers (Mayes, et al., 1992; Wattam, 1990). Paradoxically, a teacher is the most likely adult in whom a significant proportion of abused children will invest their trust and faith and disclose their abuse, either directly or indirectly at least in mainstream schooling. There is no comparative understanding of children with special educational needs. How this process might come to affect teachers professionally and personally, in mainstream or special education settings, is virtually unknown. In a recently published symposium on stress, in the *British Journal of Educational Psychology* (consisting of seven articles), child abuse as a source of stress for teachers was not mentioned (see, for example, Pithers, 1995, and Chan, 1995). Nor is child abuse mentioned in the generally well-regarded texts on teacher stress, such as Dunham (1992).

Gulliford and Upton (1992) present information on the problems associated with particular impairments which some children with special educational needs experience. For teachers in special educational settings, stresses are undoubtedly more pervasive and unremitting, as the range of children's presenting behaviours and conditions is so extensive. As children and young people with special educational needs are proportionately more likely than any others in this age group to be the victims of physical and sexual abuse, the consequences and implications for adequately responding to these children within the special educational needs context are abundant. These children manifest widely differing psychological and behavioural characteristics. They obviously do not constitute a homogeneous group, and therefore, those who are physically and/or sexually abused are highly likely to vary in how they respond to the abuse, according to the nature of their special needs. Thus, there will be gross differences in their responses because of the varying abilities children have for communication – consider the differences likely to arise for children within and between the main categories of special need – speech and language difficulties; visual and hearing impairments; physical disabilities; multi-sensory impairments, and moderate and severe learning difficulties. The use of cognitive and linguistic skills varies enormously among children with special educational needs, and to such an extent that the means for facilitating and accessing these children's life experiences necessarily differ radically.

Hall (1992) has discussed some of the psychological and health-related problems of children with special educational needs as they relate to child abuse. An outline of a model is provided, based on certain features of children's behavioural and psychological responses to abuse – (1) their experience of stress; (2) their involvement in self-injury and stereotypical behaviour; (3) the manifestation of sexualised behaviour, and (4) children's experience of pain – which teachers in special schools can utilise to identify and understand aspects of their pupils' needs. Yet identifying children who have been physically and/or sexually abused differs fundamentally. Evidence for the former is chiefly sought through physical examination, usually to confirm the presence of non-accidental physical injuries. The range of such injuries is vast. Hansen and Warner (1992) suggest that physical abuse 'may include beating, squeezing, burning, lacerating, suffocating, binding, poisoning, exposing to excessive heat or cold, sensory overload (e.g. excessive light, sound, stench, aversive taste), and prevention of sleep' (p.124). With regard to children who are thought to have been sexually abused – most frequently occurring within the child's family or where the abuser is well known to the child – much greater reliance is placed upon their spoken evidence, and less on physical evidence (Glaser and Frosh, 1993). The implications for teachers are manifold.

The aims of this chapter are twofold: to inform teachers in special education about the ways in which working with children who have been, or are at risk of being, abused can be a potential source of stress; to consider ways in which teachers' stress can be reduced through awareness of policy and procedures, and by examining the facilitation of communication between special education teachers and abused children. There is, by design, little discussion in this chapter on the specific forms of abuse suffered by children. Thorough expositions on physical and sexual abuse are provided by Knutson (1995), Glaser and Frosh (1993), Ammerman and Hersen (1992), Briere (1992), Mayes et al. (1992) and Maher (1987), which provide a comprehensive understanding of the nature of child abuse, the psychological consequences of child maltreatment, and a discussion of issues and practice-related dilemmas for a range of child protection workers, a significant proportion specifically written for teachers.

# Special education and abused children: Reasons for teacher stress

For some teachers, the fear of what has happened or what could continue to happen to abused children negatively affects the way in which they interact with them and/or their parents. There is the anxiety that whatever they as teachers do, their actions could be harmful to the child – they might say or do something wrong. Being informed of child abuse can mean that the usual relationship a teacher has with a pupil is changed. This is likely whether physical or sexual abuse is involved, depending upon the severity and nature of the abuse, and can as easily result in overprotective behaviour as it can mean that the child becomes somewhat ignored. A wide range of highly effective interactions falls between these two positions, although the research literature has yet to identify these comprehensively. Powerful interpersonal demands are made on teachers in child abuse investigations and follow-up interventions, and these can seriously jeopardise a range of working relationships, not only with the abused child but sometimes with colleagues too. Complex emotional reactions are induced by the knowledge of physical and/or sexual abuse of children, probably none more so than when the abuse has happened to the very young or those of whatever age who have special needs.

Importantly, teachers often devote considerable amounts of time to developing positive relationships between families and school, and do not want to jeopardise these by unwarranted accusations of child abuse. Teachers also worry about maintaining a sense of confidentiality between pupils and themselves: they want to respect children's wishes to keep a secret, but know that it is their professional imperative to report any suspicions of child abuse to their superiors or designated local agencies. However, teachers have often stated that they lose a sense of control once the report of a suspected case of child abuse is passed on to their local social services department or police station, especially in terms of maintaining the relationship between the abused child and the teacher to whom the child disclosed. There are also anxieties about presenting information to case conferences or presenting evidence as a witness in a court hearing.

Miller (1990) argues that 'To beat a child, to humiliate him or sexually abuse him, is a crime because it damages a human being for life.' Her thesis is that abused children must encounter someone they know cares for them: significantly, her list is headed by 'a teacher'. This person must be able to offer them:

> the experience of being loved and cherished [so] that the child can ... discern cruelty as such, be aware of it, and resist it. Without this experience he has no way of knowing that there is anything in the world except cruelty; the child will automatically submit to it and, years later, when as an adult he accedes to power, will exert it as being perfectly normal behaviour. (p.193)

It should be noted that, somewhat controversially, Miller refuses to categorise child abuse as predominantly a male crime. She pursues the argument that the abuse of power over children is as possible by women as it is by men, whether in terms of physical abuse or sexual abuse, although it is clear that she is stating, in common with most other commentators, that the vast majority of sexual abuse is perpetrated by men. Her point is that any parent or professional fails to protect a child when they repress their childhood abuse, for it is likely that they will be unable to bear to be reminded of their own suffering by incidents in another's childhood, whether it is their own child or, for example, a pupil. Therefore, teachers who have a history of having been abused, by denying to themselves their pain and suffering, make it more likely that they will not want to become involved in working with abused children because of their anxiety about stirring up memories which they have actively or unconsciously attempted to keep hidden.

If research with other professional groups is relevant (e.g. Wilson, 1987), some teachers will certainly never have had the opportunity to disclose or process the events of their personal experience of abuse. The prospect of working with abused children, possibly having contact with an abuser, and being required to talk with colleagues and other professionals about the consequences for the child has been sufficient to induce in some teachers delayed symptoms of post-traumatic stress disorder, whereby they have been flooded with intrusive memories and a re-experiencing of painful affects associated with their own childhood abuse (see, for example, Briere, 1992). It is not atypical for a teacher to have been abused as a child without having received any positive support. No research has been undertaken to indicate the proportion of teachers to whom this applies, but professional experience from training and teaching in a range of topics relating to child abuse and child protection substantially supports this view.

Several writers suggest a significant incidence of child abuse experience (physical and/or sexual abuse) among professionals who work with children. For some teachers, their childhood experiences may already have had serious consequences for their personal development. Teachers abused as children will also vary in whether or not they maintain a secrecy about the abuse. Some teachers abused as children may find that they exert heavy demands upon themselves to be hyper-alert to the signs and symptoms of child abuse, as if to protect others in ways in which they were not protected themselves. Little is known from research about the behaviour, thinking and feelings of teachers who have been physically and/or sexually abused. A complex of factors will affect their personal and professional behaviour. These will all be dependent upon the nature and level of support the teachers, when they were children, received at the time of their disclosure, and during the period of their subsequent attempts to comprehend the abusive experiences. For example, a basic distinction can be made between those teachers who, in their own childhoods, not only experienced being abused but were also unidentified in their suffering. Such a group can be divided for comparison into:

1   those who, as children, learnt how to deny their abuse – this usually occurs because of the pressure exerted upon them by their perpetrators, and possibly others who were involved; Miller (1990) argues that this will always emanate from within the child's family;
2   those who were able to retain their active memories of the abuse, and who were subsequently able to comprehend what had happened to them.

# Reducing stress about special needs children who have been abused

Much anxiety in a majority of special needs teachers can be ameliorated or removed by schools implementing various training and development programmes (see Wonnacott, 1995, for an easy-to-read review of typical examples). The basic elements covered relate essentially to:

- increasing teachers' knowledge and awareness about the behaviour and needs of abused children;
- promoting personal self-protection strategies for children;
- informing teachers about the requirements of the local child protection procedures, such as reporting suspected abuse, recording children's behaviour, and providing reports for case conferences and for court hearings.

Whole-school approaches (see Braun, 1988) will necessarily need to involve parents, children and lay and professional members of the local community, to ensure that individual teachers are supported in their work with abused children.

However, Johnson (1994) reports that while many school-based primary prevention programmes have been developed and introduced to a range of schools during the past fifteen years, various research and evaluation studies (see, for example, the reviews by Binder and McNeil, 1987; Finklehor and Strapko, 1987; Wurtele, 1987; Daro, 1990) have not been able to demonstrate convincingly many long-lasting and positive outcomes for children. These programmes are almost all exclusively concerned with child sexual abuse. Trudell and Whatley (1988) estimated that up to 500 prevention programmes were developed in the USA during the early to mid-1980s. Johnson (1994) considers that, in 'focusing almost solely on student outcomes, [researchers] have made invisible the complex thinking and decision-making processes teachers use when attempting to operationalize these programmes' (p.262).

The manner in which teachers have translated established programmes – for example, to match the specific needs of their classroom or whole-school settings and the cognitive, social and emotional characteristics of their pupils – is relatively unexplored. Johnson's research, based on the Protective Behaviours programme (Flandreau West, 1984) which is widely used throughout Australia and the USA, sought to comprehend the ways in which teachers, when implementing different elements of the programme, modified the prescribed contents and approaches. Significantly, Johnson (1994) found that teachers were 'omitting those sections of the child protection programme that are considered essential in developing the knowledge, attitudes and skills children need to protect themselves' (p.265). He discussed his results in terms of:

- teachers' selective use of the programme (most teachers omitted sections dealing with unwanted sexual touching, domestic violence and networking);
- teacher personalisation of the issues (some teachers, albeit often after much agonised thinking and not inconsiderable personal turmoil, were able to justify the exclusion of some of the more sensitive areas because of their own needs, rather than the needs of the children who were to receive those particular inputs);
- the problem of denial (some teachers continued to question the nature and extent of child abuse as presented in the programme);
- teachers' emphasis on tertiary prevention (believing that programmes are more valuable for children who have been abused, rather than for preventing abuse before it occurs);
- lack of school support to implement the programme (no fundamental support for teachers being trained to use the programme, resulting in feelings of isolation and not knowing what should next be done with the training).

The problems for teachers who work with abused children are further compounded by the general lack of recognition of the seriousness of the consequences of child abuse. Some teachers are unlikely to have their anxieties heard sympathetically if they are working in an environment where the often profound suffering of abused children is unacknowledged and not established as an accepted consequence. Teachers who attempt to be proactive in their work with abused children require a whole-school approach to produce clearly stated policy and guidance on the range of issues relating to physical abuse and sexual abuse. These need to cover, as Maher (1987) suggests especially for work within schools, 'factors which are largely cultural and attitudinal and as such capable of change ... attitudes towards women ... violence ... parenthood ... relationships ... coping with money (or the lack of it) ... effects of unemployment and enforced "leisure" ... [and] ... attitudes within the community' (p.210). Without such statements, individual teachers can find themselves working in isolation, and thus, prone to the stresses which arise from working without support.

Countering the harmful consequences of child abuse is not a role for individual teachers. The emotional demands are simply too great, and in some measure, reflect the enormity of the problem for the child who has been abused. However, the first and most important point is for teachers to be aware that child protection work can never be construed as a singular activity. A multidisciplinary team must always, at some stage, be involved in the

identification of the needs of abused children, and every local area child protection committee is charged with responsibilities to ensure that this process
is enacted.

## Facilitating communication between teachers and special needs children who have been abused

Following on from the guidance contained within the *Memorandum of Good
Practice* (Home Office/Department of Health, 1992), Bentovim et al. (1995)
propose the need for what they refer to as 'a second stage facilitative assessment interview' in the context of facilitating interviews with children with
special needs who may have been sexually abused. Their suggestions are
made within a framework of considering the traumatic effects of sexual
abuse, and provide essential insights for teachers into the ways in which
children process trauma. These essentially relate to:

- the intrusion of unwanted memories;
- avoidance of thinking about, speaking about or remembering the
  abusive experience;
- arousal, fearfulness and tension, giving rise to sleeping, concentration
  and eating difficulties;
- hopelessness, helplessness or severe depression, possibly resulting in
  serious emotional and behavioural disorders (e.g. anorectic behaviour)
  and developmental difficulties (e.g. physical inability to walk or to
  talk).

At issue is the problem – long understood by many teachers – that some
children with special educational needs (notably those with autism) are often
unable to describe spontaneously what has happened to them. Some of these
children respond positively to the approach known as 'facilitated communication'. In the child abuse context, this method has given rise to considerable
media attention, for it has enabled the voices of previously unheard children
to be heard (see the special issue of *Child Abuse and Neglect*, 1994, Volume 6,
especially Heckler, 1994, and Starr, 1994, for a detailed discussion). Special
needs teachers are familiar with ways of facilitating their pupils' communication – to get them to go beyond the question and spontaneously add
details of their own. Special needs teachers are familiar with using toys, play
material and various media to facilitate communication in both young and
older children. Their interactions typically involve a range of materials and
approaches, including the judicious use of physical contact to promote
communication. There remains much that is controversial.

However, in relation to child abuse, special education teachers are in pre-eminent positions to enable children to communicate their suffering. Greater awareness of their positive roles should be a considerable source of stress reduction for teachers. Gradually, it is being recognised by specialist workers in child protection that special education teachers have been a long-ignored resource in this arena. Unfortunately, too little use is made of such teachers in child protection units, where their understanding of communication processes in children with special educational needs would be an invaluable resource. Special needs teachers can adopt a psychological approach and apply their detailed understanding of children's cognitive and emotional development to the wide range of behaviours and interactions which they encounter in their schools. If this is undertaken systematically within a context of what is known about the expression of children's aggressive behaviour (physical, verbal, and sexual) towards others and themselves, teachers will be well prepared to make sense of what is often a baffling array of atypical behaviours (Hall, 1996).

When people signal that they are actively listening in conversation, this is often done non-verbally (i.e. through eye contact, discrete movements of the head such as nodding or shaking to show agreement or disagreement and non-verbal utterances to maintain or foreclose). In the same way, it is necessary for teachers to make use of the everyday system with which they are most familiar when communicating with pupils who have differing special educational needs. Teachers should ensure that they understand any special words that may be used, or behaviours which might be manifested to describe aspects of the abuse. It is vital that teachers produce a written record of their observations as soon as possible, making sure that their opinions about what was meant by certain behaviours and/or statements are kept separate from their direct observations. These records should be dated and the times of events provided as and when appropriate to the children's behaviour. Bray (1989) highlights some of the difficulties inherent in such a task when she suggests that:

> Listening to children can surely only be one part of the jigsaw; believing that they may have the ability to express what has happened to them is undoubtedly another. Finding ways as adults to help them accomplish that task is yet another. Perhaps one of the most difficult tasks facing those of us who deal professionally with abused children is the challenge of making it possible for the child to communicate that information as directly as possible to the decision-making process. (pp.60–1)

# Conclusion

As with any other professional group, teachers do not want to make mistakes when reporting suspected child abuse. Their professional credibility is at stake, in that their whole sense of judgement about child behaviour and development, in which they have attained expertise, is potentially liable to close examination if an assessment of, or suspicion about, child abuse is made public. Generally, the education of teachers has yet to include adequate information about child abuse, and for teachers of children with special educational needs, even less information is available. The judgements of special needs teachers often have to be made in the absence of objective knowledge. This can be a source of considerable stress.

Teachers are obviously concerned to ensure that they do not 'fail to protect' their pupils, but their situation means that they are not usually in a position to work directly with a child's parents. This means that their judgements must be derived from what the children communicate to them, verbally or non-verbally, directly or indirectly. Teachers of children with special needs become used to developing specific strategies for communicating with their pupils. Such specialist skills have to be applied to make sense of what children are communicating to them, and are a means of reducing the possible stresses felt in the context of working with special needs children who have been abused.

However, from a search of the scientific literature, the role of child abuse in the development of special educational needs remains underresearched. It is probably for this reason that the possibility of child abuse, and the impact of abusive experiences on the behaviour and development of children, appears to be omitted from formal consideration in the assessment of special educational needs. All abused children have special needs, but for some of these children, the consequences include the development of special educational needs.

It is still rare for teacher training courses to provide more than one-off inputs on child abuse and child protection – strange for a profession with such a high profile in the identification and monitoring of abused children (Wattam, 1990). It is as essential for student teachers as for qualified and experienced teachers to know about the nature of child abuse and child protection procedures. Without a basic knowledge of either of these, teachers will be less likely to identify abused children, less likely to respond appropriately, and far more likely to experience stressful feelings as a consequence. To reduce the potential for stress, all teachers need to be aware, as a minimum, of the basic tenets of the relevant legislation. The Department of Health (DoH, 1989) has produced a very useful overview of the 1989 Children Act, the legislation most concerned with the protection of children, a copy of which should be in every school. Also, there is guidance for promoting good inter-agency co-operation in child protection work (Home Office et al., 1991), where the roles of schools and individual teachers are contextualised within the broader perspective of different agencies working together. The most recently produced government guidance (DfEE, 1995), considers procedures for identifying child abuse cases and liaising with other agencies.

For more local information, teachers need to refer to their area child protection committee's child protection procedures. Every local authority is obliged by statute to produce such a document, in which specific guidance is provided about the roles of all agencies in that particular area. Moreover, each local education authority is also required to provide a child protection policy and procedures for all the staff it employs. In these two local documents, often substantial in content, teachers will find a wealth of information about the role of the designated member of staff for child protection (a requirement for each school, so it is important to identify who this person is), signs and symptoms of different forms of abuse, action for school staff; etc. Furthermore, each of the teachers' unions also publishes guidance for members, copies of which should be readily available and displayed in each school, along with relevant forms on which to record concerns.

Finally, stress in the context of child abuse and children with special educational needs is inevitable. The challenges of both conditions make complex professional and personal demands on special needs teachers. Some of these are more anticipatory than others, especially in relation to children who have been abused. Teachers who experience serious emotional difficulty because of the nature of child abuse probably do so mostly because of their personal experiences of an abusive childhood. They can be particularly vulnerable to the manifestation of stress in their professional contexts. All teachers, however, require a co-ordinated range of supports when they work with children who have special needs and who have also been abused. To date, there appears to be little recognition of the structural and organisational elements of such a system, and of how the implementation of this work could ameliorate much of the stress arising within special education settings. The resources relating to child abuse and child protection, derived both from personal and professional initiatives by special needs teachers, warrant closer attention by educational researchers.

# References

Abrahams, N., Casey, K. and Daro, D. (1992) 'Teachers' knowledge, attitudes, and health beliefs about child abuse and its prevention', *Child Abuse and Neglect*, 16, 2, 229–38.

Ammerman, R.T. and Hersen, M. (eds) (1992) *Assessment of Family Violence: A Clinical and Legal Sourcebook*, New York: John Wiley.

Ammerman, R.T., Van Hasselt, V.B. and Hersen, M. (1988) 'Abuse and neglect in handicapped children: A critical review', *Journal of Family Violence*, 3, 53–72.

Baker, A.W. and Duncan, S.P. (1985) 'Child sexual abuse: A study of prevalence in Great Britain', *Child Abuse and Neglect*, 9, 4, 457–67.

Baladerian, N.J. (1991) 'Sexual abuse of people with developmental disabilities', *Sexuality and Disability*, 9, 323–35.

Bentovim, A., Bentovim, M., Vizard, E. and Wiseman, M. (1995) 'Facilitating interviews with children who may have been sexually abused', *Child Abuse Review*, 4, 4, 246–62.

Binder, R.L. and McNeil, D.E. (1987) 'Evaluation of a school-based sexual abuse prevention program: Cognitive and emotional effects', *Child Abuse and Neglect*, 11, 4, 497–506.

Braun, D. (1988) *Responding to Child Abuse: Action and Planning for Teachers and Other Professionals*, London: Bedford Square Press.

Bray, M. (1989) 'Communicating with children – communicating with the court', in Levy, A. (ed.), *Focus on Child Abuse: Medical, Legal and Social Work Perspectives*, Hawksmere.

Briere, J. (1992) *Child Abuse Trauma: Theory and Treatment of the Lasting Effects*, Newbury Park, CA: Sage Publications.

Carey, T.A. (1994) 'Spare the rod and spoil the child: Is this a sensible justification for the use of punishment in child rearing?', *Child Abuse and Neglect*, 18, 12, 1005–10.

Chan, D.W. (1995) 'Multidimensional assessment and causal modelling in teacher stress research: A commentary, *British Journal of Educational Psychology*, 65, 4, 381–5.

Daro, D. (1990) 'Prevention programmes', in Howells, K. and Hollin, C. (eds) *Clinical Approaches to Sex Offenders and their Victims*, London: John Wiley.

DfEE (1995) *Protecting Children from Abuse: The Role of the Education Service*, Circular no. 10/95, London: Department for Education and Employment.

DoH (1989) *An Introduction to The Children Act 1989*, London: HMSO.

Dunham, J. (1992) *Stress in Teaching* (2nd edn), London: Routledge.

Finklehor, D. and Strapko, N. (1987) 'Sexual abuse prevention education: A review of evaluation studies', in Willis, D. (ed.) *Child Abuse Prevention*, New York: John Wiley.

Flandreau West, P. (1984) *Protective Behaviours: An Anti-Victimisation Programme*, Madison, WI: Protective Behaviours Inc.

Glaser, D. and Frosh, S. (1993) *Child Sexual Abuse*, Basingstoke: Macmillan.

Gulliford, R. and Upton, G. (eds) (1992) *Special Educational Needs*, London: Routledge.

Hall, N. (1992) 'Psychological and health-related problems', in Gulliford, R. and Upton, G. (eds) *Special Educational Needs*, London: Routledge.

Hall, N. (1996) 'Eliciting children's views: The contribution of psychologists', in Davie, R., Upton, G. and Varma, V. (eds) *The Voice of the Child: A Handbook for Professionals*, London: Falmer Press.

Hansen, D.J. and Warner, J.E. (1992) 'Child physical abuse and neglect', in Ammerman, R.T. and Hersen, M. (eds) *Assessment of Family Violence: A Clinical and Legal Sourcebook*, New York: John Wiley.

Heckler, S. (1994) 'Facilitated communication: A response by child protection', *Child Abuse and Neglect*, 18, 6, 495–504.

Hemenway, D., Solnick, S. and Carter, J. (1994) 'Child-rearing violence', *Child Abuse and Neglect*, 18, 12, 1011–20.

Home Office/DoH (1992) *Memorandum of Good Practice on Video Recorded Interviews with Child Witnesses for Criminal Proceedings*, London: HMSO.

Home Office, DoH, DES, and Welsh Office (1991) *Working Together Under the Children Act 1989: A Guide to Arrangements for Inter-agency Co-operation for the Protection of Children from Abuse*, London: HMSO.

Hopkins, J. (1989) 'No words ... just tears: Stress and distress amongst staff working in child abuse cases', *Child Abuse Review*, 3, 2, 3–8.

Hopkins, J. (1992) 'Secondary abuse', in Bannister, A. (ed.) *From Hearing to Healing: Working with the Aftermath of Child Sexual Abuse*, Harlow: Longman.

Johnson, B. (1994) 'Teachers' role in the primary prevention of child abuse: Dilemmas and problems', *Child Abuse Review*, 3, 4, 259–71.

Knutson, J.F. (1995) 'Psychological characteristics of maltreated children: Putative risk factors and consequences', *Annual Review of Psychology*, 46, 401–431.

Leach, P. (1993) 'Should parents hit their children?', *The Psychologist*, 6, 5, 216–20.

Maher, P. (ed.) (1987) *Child Abuse: The Educational Perspective*, Oxford: Blackwell.

Mayes, G.M., Currie, E.F., Macleod, L., Gillies, J.B. and Warden, D.A. (1992) *Child Sexual Abuse: A Review of Literature and Educational Materials*, Edinburgh: Scottish Academic Press.

Miller, A. (1990) *Banished Knowledge: Facing Childhood Injuries*, London: Virago.

Pithers, R.T. (1995) 'Teacher stress research: Problems and progress', *British Journal of Educational Psychology*, 65, 4, 387–92.

Russell, P. (1996) 'Listening to children with disabilities and special educational needs', in Davie, R., Upton, G. and Varma, V. (eds) *The Voice of the Child: A Handbook for Professionals*, London: Falmer Press.

Scott, I. (1991) 'Police stress in child protection', *Child Abuse Review*, 5, 2, 13–16.

Starr, E. (1994) 'Commentary: Facilitated communication – a response by child protection', *Child Abuse and Neglect*, 18, 6, 515–28.

Trudell, B. and Whatley, M.H. (1988) 'School sexual abuse prevention: Unintended consequences and dilemmas', *Child Abuse and Neglect*, 12, 1, 103–14.

Wattam, C. (1990) *Teachers' Experiences with Children Who Have or May Have Been Sexually Abused*, London: NSPCC.

Wilson, M. (1987) 'Child sexual abuse histories among professionals', *Child Abuse Review*, 1, 7, 4–5.

Wonnacott, J. (1995) *Protecting Children in School: A Handbook for Developing Child Protection Training*, London: National Children's Bureau.

Wurtele, S. (1987) 'School based sexual abuse prevention programs: A review', *Child Abuse and Neglect*, 11, 4, 483–95.

# Part III

## Effective provision

# 12 Supporting teachers of children with special needs in ordinary schools

*Harry Daniels and Brahm Norwich*

## Introduction

In this chapter, we will discuss one way in which schools may make it possible for teachers to cope with the stresses that they may experience when working with children with special educational needs (SEN) in mainstream schools. The approach with which we are concerned does not focus directly on teacher stress, rather it makes it possible for teachers to seek and obtain support for their own problem-solving in school. In our evaluation studies, we have obtained evidence that teacher stress may be reduced as a consequence of this form of support (Daniels and Norwich, 1992, 1994). This chapter is therefore not about therapeutic services for teachers; it is about support for teachers that may have some therapeutic effects. It attempts to deal with some aspects of what Clandinin and Connelly (1987) refer to as the emotional quality of personal knowledge in teaching.

Many teachers in mainstream schools feel that they do not have sufficient training and support to meet many of the challenges presented by children with special educational needs in their classes. They tend to lack confidence in their ability to provide programmes of study which are appropriately differentiated. Many teachers find themselves working in school situations where they regularly teach large classes with little or no internal special needs support, and where external resources are rarely available. Facing the task of meeting a wide range of needs in isolation can lead to acute stress or disaffection. This can happen to capable teachers working in unfavourable circumstances.

Teacher support teams (TSTs) are school-based problem-solving groups of teachers which function to support pupils indirectly through teacher collaboration. TSTs are novel in that they are an example of a school-based development designed to give support and assistance to individual teachers.

185

They may be seen to complement existing forms of SEN work within schools and existing patterns of informal, mutual peer support where these exist. Staff can approach teams of their peers for collaborative support in understanding problems and designing appropriate forms of intervention related to learning and behaviour difficulties. These teams aim to enable staff to develop their confidence and competence in making provision for children with SEN in mainstream classes.

The TST development should be seen in the context of recent moves towards teaching more children with SEN in ordinary schools and the recognition of whole-school approaches to SEN (DES, 1989; NCC, 1989; ILEA, 1985; Galloway, 1985). In this respect, TSTs represent a practical embodiment of a school's commitment to, and policy for, SEN. They have special relevance to schools now with the requirement in the 1993 Education Act and its associated Code of Practice (DfE, 1994a) that schools specify and publish their SEN policies and practices. This is in the context of the increasing difficulties faced by schools following the 1988 Education Reform Act to provide for SEN (Daniels and Ware, 1990; Evans and Lunt, 1992; OFSTED, 1993; Visser and Upton, 1993).

# How do TSTs work?

TST is a system of support from a team of peers for class teachers experiencing teaching difficulties in relation to special educational needs. Individual teachers request support on a voluntary basis from a team.

- Typically, three teachers (the SEN co-ordinator, a senior teacher and another class teacher) serve as the core team, who call on outside support and advisory staff and parents when needed.
- Teams meet weekly or fortnightly with the teacher making a request for support: meetings last about 30 minutes each (usually during lunchtime or after school). A team member usually collects relevant information about the teacher's concern before the meeting.
- Typically, one case is dealt with per meeting, either a new request or a follow-up. Unless a case is closed, a follow-up date is always agreed, at which the situation will be reviewed.
- Teams keep a log of meetings and confidential notes about cases to enable follow-up work.
- Teachers involved in meetings need to have some time release from other responsibilities.
- The principle and practical aspects of TSTs need staff and headteacher support.

For TSTs to operate successfully, there needs to be a clear specification of the kinds of teaching problems which can be referred by teachers to the teams. It is also vital that responsibility for referral rests with class teachers, not the headteacher or TST teachers. One teacher needs to co-ordinate the work of the team using clear procedures for referral, conduct of meetings, analysis of the problems and design of interventions, implementation, records and follow-up of interventions. In practice, referrals are often concerned with behaviour problems, though many are also about learning difficulties. Not all referrals may be about individuals; some may be about groups or classes.

## Peer support in schools

Because TSTs develop structured approaches to collaborative problem-solving with an emphasis on follow-up and review, they differ from much of the informal peer support which is to be found in many schools. Teachers may often ask each other for advice. However, these exchanges typically take place in the context of busy staff rooms in a very short space of time, and rarely with any possibility of reviewing the effects of the advice. TSTs allocate a dedicated amount of time to a referring teacher, in a calm and peaceful setting in which issues may be discussed in confidence and without interruption. Crucially, they embody the problem-solving cycle, in that teachers are offered the opportunity to monitor and review the situation through follow-up meetings.

Peer support teams have been discussed in a variety of professional contexts. Quality circles (Karp, 1983) are used in industry and have been developed in professional educational psychology (Fox et al., 1990). In the area of mental health consultation, the work of Caplan (1970) has been influential and has been extensively applied, adapted and even mandated in some states of the USA (Ritter, 1978; Chalfant and Pysh, 1989; Graden et al., 1985a, 1985b). In the USA, a Department of Education task force (Will, 1986) recommended that schools establish support systems for teachers as a way of responding to concerns about overreferral rates, misclassification of students, rising costs and the need to maximise opportunities for all students in the least restrictive environment (Chalfant and Pysh, 1989). In the UK, there has been much work on in-class support which focuses on the work of individual support teachers and SEN co-ordinators (Dyson, 1990; Garnett, 1988; Hart, 1986) but little on support teams. The work of Hanko (1989, 1990) is the best-known example of a school consultation and group support approach. In her approach, school consultation is led by outside professionals in a way which mirrors some of the American work. She has offered this as an approach to meet the recommendations for teacher peer support systems which were made in the Elton Report (DES, 1989). Whereas Hanko acted as a group facilitator, Mead (1991) advocated task-oriented peer support groups (PSGs) to increase the reflective nature of work in schools and thereby reduce teacher stress and increase teacher effectiveness. PSGs were seen to provide forms of organisational structure that reinforced informal social support and to result in greater feelings of ownership and personal competence. Chisholm (1994) also reports an evaluation of peer support approaches which were 'directed by teachers themselves within their schools and subsequently self evaluated, according to their own criteria'. The Newcastle educational psychology service has also been involved in training teachers to act in a support capacity to their colleagues (Stringer et al., 1992).

## Teacher tolerance and active engagement

There is much prescription about managing schools which is relevant to SEN, and much prescription about teaching pupils with SEN, but few specific theories about the conditions which affect the tolerance, capability and engagement of class teachers and schools in doing so. Gerber and Semmel (1985) and Gerber (1988) have developed a theoretical position on the costs to class teachers of extending their range of tolerance, which takes account of the purpose of class teaching, structural constraints and teaching resources. They suggest that in the context of limited resources, tolerance conditions the relation between equity and excellence. In using the concept of teacher tolerance, we propose a number of theoretical assumptions. First, we suggest that pupils come to be seen by teachers as varying in their difficulty to teach and manage, and that teachers have a range of teaching tolerance for variations in attainment and social behaviour. Beyond the limits of this tolerance, pupils come to be seen as unresponsive to teaching, and this can come to lower the teacher's perception of her/his teaching competence and therefore her/his professional self-evaluation. This can lead to feelings of insecurity and anxiety, which in turn can result in less appropriate teaching and even further unresponsiveness from pupils. By this process, teachers come to see certain pupils as beyond their teaching tolerance.

The range of tolerance is not a generic characteristic, but specific to each class and teacher, being influenced by pupil, teacher and school factors, including teaching materials and equipment, and teachers' teaching competence and confidence. Tolerance is also influenced by structural aspects – the class size and the purpose of class teaching. Underlying the concept of tolerance is the dynamic that class teaching involves a dilemma regarding aims for teachers whether to (1) seek an increase in the average attainment of the class (to seek excellence), or (2) decrease the variation in class attainment (to seek equity). Aim 1 involves a strategy of concentrating teaching time on the average to above-average, because this is most likely to increase average class attainments. Aim 2 involves the contrary strategy of concentrating teaching time on the below-average, as this is most likely to reduce variation in class attainment. This dilemma arises because of pupil differences in learning abilities, and is significant because teaching resources, including time available for class teaching, are relatively fixed and scarce. It is assumed that teachers respond to this dilemma by achieving a balance between bidding for and seeking more teaching resources; opting for ability setting/grouping, or trying to transfer responsibility for difficult-to-teach pupils to others, such as support teachers, inside or outside their classes, or referring for statutory assessment and Statementing.

Part of the current integrationist climate is the expectation that teachers must increase their range of teaching tolerance for pupils with SEN. By making increased tolerance legitimate, it is often assumed that the range of tolerance can be readily increased. However, this has not been easy to achieve, particularly in the context of a national educational policy to increase average school attainment levels (Daniels and Ware, 1990) and without major increases in resources for schools. The effect is to weight the trade-off even more towards increasing average class attainment.

Ironically, those teachers with the most effective teaching strategies for low-achieving students might be those who report that they tolerate less maladaptive behaviour in their classrooms, and that they may actively resist placement of handicapped students in their classrooms (Gersten et al., 1988).

Studies undertaken in the USA suggest that there is a dilemma concerning quality of instruction and access to the mainstream classroom:

> The 'effective' teachers – those with high standards and low tolerance for deviant behaviour – are those most likely to seek help in dealing with these problems. Moreover, the most successful teachers are those who efficiently use their instructional time. Therefore, one reason for the type of resistance identified in this study may be the effective teacher's attempt to guard against inefficient use of academic instructional time, which could result in an overall decreased level off student performance. If the necessary technical assistance could be provided to implement teaching models that are effective for all students, it is likely that these skilled teachers with high standards would be the first to accept handicapped into their classrooms. (Gersten et al., 1988, p.437)

What is needed to increase teaching tolerance, given the social psychological, structural, functional and resource conditions, is an organisational strategy to extend and make good use of existing teaching resources. TSTs, by enabling teachers to support each other and share their teaching competence, can provide one way to increase the range of teaching tolerance and enhance active engagement in providing quality teaching for pupils with SEN.

We have proposed the following dimensions to contrast TSTs with other kinds of school-based teacher groups and teams, such as staff and department administrative meetings, in-service training groups, and curriculum and general planning groups, Statement review groups, outside consultant groups and whole-staff case discussions. These dimensions do not represent absolute differences, but are a matter of degree and emphasis:

1    quick response with follow-up versus delayed response with less follow-up;
2    analysis of particular concerns/cases versus general planning for groups;
3    non-directed/voluntary versus directed/involuntary;
4    teacher/teaching focus versus learner/learning focus.

Using the first pole of each dimension, TSTs can be characterised and contrasted with the above-mentioned school groups and support approaches as involving a quick response with follow-up based on the analysis of particular teaching concerns, where the focus is on the teacher who participates on a voluntary basis.

The way in which schools, both primary and secondary, approach pupils with SEN can be understood in terms of the processes of tolerance and active engagement at institutional and teacher levels. Active engagement and tolerance can be seen as complementary and interrelated processes, with 'active engagement' referring to the ways in which teachers and schools include and provide for the diversity of pupils, and 'tolerance' referring to the limits of the challenges within which schools and teachers can operate. Active engagement involves planned attempts to provide quality learning opportunities for children with SEN, to include them in the general planning and teaching of all children. It is expressed in both curriculum and behaviour management at a school level, the level and quality of internal and external support for SEN, and the differentiation of teaching and class management at teacher level. Tolerance, by contrast, involves enduring the challenges and unresponsiveness of pupils with SEN. At a school level, it is expressed through requests for external support, advice or exclusions, willingness to accept pupils with SEN, satisfaction with SEN policy and practices, and complaints to parents and LEAs. At a teacher level, it is expressed by attitudes to integration and inclusion, by views about the feasibility and desirability of making classroom and teaching adaptations and by personal teaching priorities. It is indicated by teachers' perceptions of: (1) how well they can cope with the range of teaching challenges, and (2) the teaching demands made by children in their class (see Table 12.1).

The potential advantages of TST may be described as follows:

- as a school resource for collegial assistance and support;
- as a forum for teachers to share expertise and understanding;
- as a way of enabling teachers to develop their approaches to children with special educational needs;

Table 12.1   **Theoretical framework of active engagement and tolerance**

|  | *Active engagement* | *Tolerance* |
|---|---|---|
| **School level** | Curriculum management | Referral activity |
|  | Behaviour management | Willingness to accept SEN pupils |
|  | Internal support activity | Support for SEN policy/practice |
|  | External links | Policy and practice for sanctions |
| **Teacher level** | Class organisation/pedagogy | Concepts/reasons for support |
|  | Class management | Attitudes to SEN pupils |
|  | Links with support | Personal teaching priorities |

- as a support for the implementation of stages 1–3 of the Code of Practice;
- as a system for schools to offer more effective provision for children with special educational needs in the context of Local Management of Schools.

In the context of devolved and perhaps dwindling resources for meeting SEN, questions of cost-effectiveness spur the need for the development of services which make the best use of what is available. TSTs offer the possibility of intervention that is distinctive by dint of the focus on teachers rather than children or school policy. They utilise the sadly underused resource of the potential support that consultation and collective problem-solving can offer teachers. They also provide a way in which a school may structure and organise its response to the Code of Practice. In so doing, they may well enhance and refine the role and effectiveness of the SEN co-ordinator. TSTs may support the formulation and review of IEPs as part of the practice of offering more general support to teachers. They may help schools to establish priorities in their negotiation for external support services. Issues raised in TSTs may also feed back into the institutional and SEN policy development planning process.

## Responses to TSTs in action

Eight primary schools in the south-east of England undertook to set up and run TSTs. The Economic and Social Research Council funded a study which aimed to evaluate the processes of setting up and maintaining TSTs in addition to the short-term effects and perceptions of their usefulness. Baseline assessments were compared with follow-up assessments in order to assess any changes which might have resulted from TSTs. The evaluation used a mixture of quantitative and qualitative methods which focused on several dimensions relevant to schools' approaches to SEN. These included aspects of the schools' curriculum, behaviour and support systems; the teachers' approaches to teaching, behaviour management and work with outside support systems; the training of TST members and the setting-up process; the actual working of the TSTs, and the case outcomes and perceptions of TST usefulness.

The evaluation showed that TSTs were set up and run in 6 of the 8 schools. In one of the other two schools, a TST was set up but no referrals were received. This could be attributed to the fact that the TST principle was communicated to colleagues by the senior teacher member of the team as concerning personal counselling rather than work-related support. Staff in this school felt that they were already well supported, so they questioned the value of a TST for them. The other school set up a TST but had difficulties in running meetings. The teachers were in favour of the system, but there were management and organisational difficulties in carrying through their commitment. This school was coping with a high degree of social disadvantage.

Most of the teachers in the other six schools were supportive of the TST arrangement. Referring teachers felt encouraged to request support, while only a minority of non-referring teachers felt unencouraged. The most common reason given by non-referring teachers for not requesting support was that they already had support from colleagues. Some reported that they did not have any teaching difficulties, and others mentioned being unwilling to consult particular colleagues who were in the TST.

TST meetings were between 30 and 45 minutes long and were usually held during lunchtime or after school. In a few schools, they were carried out during the last period of the timetable in the afternoon, with some teaching cover arranged. Typically, one case was dealt with per meeting, either a new request or a follow-up. There were, across the six schools, between six to seven TST meetings on average per term. Teams kept confidential notes about the cases (to enable follow-up work) and a log of meetings. Most of the referrals were about behaviour problems, though many were about learning difficulties. Not all referrals were about individuals; some were about groups or classes. Support included providing emotional support and encouragement, specific approaches to managing behaviour, teaching strategies, consulting others, such as the headteacher, the educational psychologist, and involving parents.

Teachers appear to be supportive of the TST concept and its practice. Teachers who have used TST state that it leads to increased confidence, and that the strategies and approaches offered by the teams were workable and useful. All but one of the referring teachers reported that they would be happy to request support again. Most teachers (95 per cent) felt that strategies and approaches offered by TST were fairly, or very, workable. All were able to use them, and all felt that they had been fairly, or very, useful. The majority (78 per cent) had also used them with other children. This was true despite the fact that the approaches, strategies or materials suggested were already familiar to the teachers. 'Nothing new, but of real value nevertheless' summarised a common attitude. TSTs were seen to help teachers access relevant aspects of their own teaching competence. They saw the TST as giving them the chance to air problems in a sympathetic setting, and that this enabled them to distance themselves from the problems and to re-examine what they were doing:

> The teacher support team were really good and they reflected back and they said 'Look for goodness, you've actually been wonderful with this child.' I got some pats on the back and also some practical suggestions of help which didn't mean extra work for me it just gave me some support with dealing with it. (Experienced ClassTeacher)

When teachers refer to a TST, they are helped to cope with a difficult situation. Their increased confidence may lead to a situation appearing more tolerable. This is particularly the case when they find a way of engaging with a problem which has previously seemed intractable:

> I think we have actually become more tolerant and we are developing our skills as a staff in dealing with that. We are getting together more and seeing that it's not just one person's problem but it is a problem that we share with the child and if we want our lives to be OK then we all have to have some input as well and help the child to make a valuable input as well. (Experienced Class Teacher)

> I've used it twice and I've found it very useful. Perhaps because I am an inexperienced teacher, I have only been teaching for a year, I don't have strategies to cope with things and I do feel that there is a great sense of ... I don't know when you go there it's not as if it's a major thing they just make you feel at ease about it really. The confidentiality as well, I know that it's not going to go any further and I do feel very relaxed about going in there. I do think it's working very well in the school because everyone is using it, everyone's booked up and they are all eager to get in there. It's working very well. (Inexperienced Class Teacher)

Referring teachers report significant benefits from finding that their perceptions of difficulty were validated and that the utility of their own intervention strategies were reaffirmed by TST teams. This was a significant source of encouragement:

> I felt that I was 'allowed' to feel as frustrated as I was feeling, that it was quite understandable.

> It was OK to have the feelings I did – and still is.

Although some of the suggested TST strategies were unfamiliar, most were not. The high level of satisfaction with advice indicates that TSTs acted to stimulate teachers to access a pedagogic competence that had already been acquired but was not available in their particular contexts. Non-referring teachers had distinct attitudes to TST. They either felt that it was not relevant to them, or that although it was not of immediate value, it might be of use in future:

> No, no I haven't had any contact at all with the TST at all in the time that it's been running. I think because I did feel that I was keeping on top of the class last year, I mean it drained me but I did feel able to cope and because of my network of contacts here I felt I was already receiving a lot of suggestions that I could put into practice. (Non-referring Class Teacher)

> I don't really mean to imply that it's a paper tiger, but I do think it could be just a sop. If they had hours allocated for support if you went to them or something, then I think it would be much more powerful and I might go along. (Non-referring Class Teacher)

Headteachers became supportive of the TST in action. The confidential nature of TST activities made it difficult for them to comment on their usefulness. However, headteachers perceived no negatives in having a TST in the school. Where benefits were cited, it was felt that TSTs led to a smoother-running school with a happier staff:

> I don't know what problems I would have had to deal with myself if the TST hadn't been there because I am sure that it has defused some situations that could have been worse had it not been there. (Headteacher)

> I've so far been wrong because I didn't want it, I voted against it, I was very sceptical about it for, I thought, very sound reasons. My colleagues on the whole were very much in favour of giving it a go and without doubt they've been proved right. (Headteacher)

TST members believe that they gain much from the TST experience: for example, the importance of listening, learning new teaching strategies and gaining confidence themselves. There was also a widespread view that TSTs positively affected the work of the SEN co-ordinators in that they increased awareness of SEN across the school.

# Setting up TSTs in schools

Evaluations show that setting up TSTs requires clear and detailed initial communications and negotiations between the schools and those with the development ideas and training resources. This depends upon the head-teachers and all the staff understanding what is involved, considering what the TST arrangement has to offer the school, and then deciding to commit the school and the resources to enable TSTs to work. In addition to these factors, evaluation indicates the importance of the whole staff and headteacher supporting the principle of TSTs. School staffs should therefore be given the choice to adopt the TST approach and to design it to fit the school's particular circumstances and needs.

Preparing a school for a TST should involve enabling participating teachers to:

- be familiar with the concepts and principles of school-based teacher support teams as providing peer support *and* meeting special educational needs;
- understand the function, risks and constraints of designing and running teacher support teams;
- through consultation with colleagues, design an appropriate teacher support team for their school;
- be aware of, and sensitive to, the needs and feelings of the teachers making requests for support;
- be proficient in

  - receiving requests for support;
  - conducting meetings;
  - liaising with parents and support services;
  - making sense of teaching problems;
  - devising appropriate forms of advice;
  - assessing outcomes in the classroom;
  - reviewing and evaluating the overall TST arrangement.

Above all, team members need to be involved in simulations of the processes of analysing and conceptualising problems, deciding on intervention goals, and planning and evaluating interventions. This involves consideration of issues common to many consultation settings, such as active listening. If they are to function successfully, TSTs need to be designed to fit the perceived needs of the schools by the TST team and their colleagues.

### How do arrangements work?

When a TST is being planned in a school, there are a number of issues which need to be resolved. The following list may serve as an *aide-mémoire*:

- Who is the target population?
- Who can refer to the team? Some schools may wish to extend the TST principle to all staff, including classroom assistants.
- Who serves on the team, and how are they to be identified?
- Who co-ordinates the team?
- Receiving referrals – how many referrals may be handled at one meeting?
- How will meetings be conducted, and how will their times be set?
- How can you make use of others – parents, psychologists, advisory and teacher support services?
- How can you co-ordinate and overlap with other support systems?
- How will you make recommendations and gain access to resources?
- How can you minimise the amount of recording in the design of recording sheets?
- How do you follow up recommendations?
- How will you support and encourage team use?
- How will you review and evaluate the team process – adapting team procedures?

TST members value the mutual support given by the regular meetings of networks of other schools running TSTs. The guidance given in the recent circular on the organisation of special provision provides strong support for the notion of such cross-school collaboration (DfE, 1994b).

# Conclusion

Our findings illustrate the pressing demands on schools and teachers of teaching the range of children in mainstream schools, and the extent to which schools organise their own internal support systems. Overall, schools and teachers were dissatisfied with the level of internal support, and wanted more external support services.

As noted above, setting up effective TSTs depends on clear and detailed initial communications and negotiations between the schools and those with the development ideas and training resources. This involves the head-teachers and the whole staff in understanding what is involved, considering what the TST arrangement has to offer the school, and then deciding to commit the school and the resources to enable TSTs to work. Despite initial reservations about finding time for TSTs to meet with referring teachers, this did not turn out to be a problem once the time was committed. Our study also showed the importance of the training approach which not only enabled TST members to simulate giving and receiving support, but also to plan the process of setting up their TSTs with their school colleagues. Support teams were designed to fit the perceived needs of the schools by the TST team and their colleagues.

When teachers refer to a TST, they are helped to cope with a difficult situation. Their increased confidence may lead to a situation appearing more tolerable. This is particularly the case when they find a way of engaging with a problem which has previously seemed intractable. Referring teachers found that their perceptions of difficulty were validated and enhanced, and that the utility of their own intervention strategies was reaffirmed. This was a significant source of encouragement. Structured follow-up which permitted extended, systematic discussion was also highly valued. This form of follow-up distinguishes TST from informal peer support, which TST was seen to complement.

Given appropriate conditions within the school, TSTs can make a significant difference to the quality of teaching and learning. Schools may become more actively engaged as organisations by not treating support as being provided mainly by individual co-ordinators or support teachers to individual teachers. Difficulties may be dealt with more collectively and collaboratively. TSTs also enable individual teachers to become more actively engaged with SENs in their class teaching through the systematic approach used by TSTs in analysing difficulties, making positive action suggestions and following up referrals. TSTs may make it possible for schools to be more actively engaged with SEN, in that better use may be made of staff resources, and individual teachers may have opportunities to both rediscover and develop their own teaching knowledge and approaches. As such, the operation of TSTs has some contribution to make in alleviating some of the stresses of teaching.

# Acknowledgements

We wish to acknowledge the support of the Economic and Social Research Council in funding the project on which this chapter is based, *Evaluating Teacher Support Teams: A Strategy for Special Needs in Ordinary Schools* (award no.R-000-23-3859).

# References

Caplan, G. (1970) *Theory and Practice of Mental Health Consultation*, New York: Basic Books.

Chalfant, J.C. and Pysh, M. (1989) 'Teacher assistance teams: Five descriptive studies on 96 teams', *Remedial and Special Education*, 10, 6, 49–58.

Chisholm, B. (1994) 'Promoting peer support among teachers' in Gray, P., Miller, A. and Noakes, J. (eds) *Challenging Behaviour in Schools*, London: Routledge.

Clandinin, D.J. and Connelly, F.M. (1987) 'Teachers' personal knowledge: What counts as personal in studies of the personal', *Journal of Curriculum Studies*, 19, 6, 487–500.

Daniels, H. and Norwich, B. (1992) *Teacher Support Teams: An Interim Evaluation Report*, London: Institute of Education, London University.

Daniels, H. and Norwich, B. (1994) *Evaluating Teacher Support Teams: A Strategy for Special Needs in Ordinary Schools*, final report to ESRC (award no.R-000-23-3859).

Daniels, H. and Ware, J. (1990) *Special Educational Needs and the National Curriculum: The Impact of the Education Reform Act*, (Bedford Way Series) London: Kogan Page.

DES (1978) *Special Educational Needs* (The Warnock Report), London: HMSO.

DES (1989) *Discipline in Schools* (The Elton Report), London: HMSO.

DfE (1994a) *The Code of Practice on the Identification and Assessment of Special Educational Needs*, London: HMSO.

DfE (1994b) *The Organisation of Special Education Provision*, circular 6/94, London: HMSO.

Dyson, A. (1990) 'Effective learning consultancy: A future role for special needs co-ordinators', *Support for Learning*, 5, 3, 116–27.

Evans, J. and Lunt, I. (1992) *Developments in Special Education under LMS*, London: Institute of Education, London University.

Fox, M., Pratt, G., and Roberts, S. (1990) 'Developing the educational psychologist's work in the secondary school: A process model for change', *Educational Psychology in Practice*, 6, 3, 163–9.

Galloway, D. (1985) *Schools, Pupils and Special Educational Needs*, London: Croom Helm.

Garnett, J. (1988) 'Support teaching: Taking a closer look', *British Journal of Special Education*, 15, 1, 15–18.

Gerber, M.M. (1988) 'Tolerance and technology of instruction: Implication for special education reform', *Exceptional Children*, 54, 4, 309–14.

Gerber, M.M. and Semmel, M.I. (1985) 'The micro-economics of referral and re-integration: A paradigm for evaluation of special education', *Studies in Educational Evaluation*, 11, 13–29.

Gersten, R., Walker, H. and Darch, C. (1988) 'Relationship between teacher's effectiveness and their tolerance for handicapped students', *Exceptional Children*, 54, 5, 433–8.

Graden, J.L., Casey, A. and Christenson, S.L. (1985a) 'Implementing a pre-referral intervention system, Part 1: The model', *Exceptional Children*, 51, 377–84.

Graden, J.L., Casey, A. and Christenson, S.L. (1985b) 'Implementing a pre-referral intervention system, Part 2: The data', *Exceptional Children*, 51, 487–96.

Hanko, G. (1989) 'After Elton – how to manage disruption', *British Journal of Special Education*, 16, 4, 140–3.

Hanko, G. (1990) *Special Needs in Ordinary Classrooms, Supporting Teachers*, London: Blackwell.

Hart, S. (1986)' Evaluating support teaching', *Gnosis*, 9, 26–32.

ILEA (1985) *Equal Opportunities for All?* (The Fish Report), London: Inner London Education Authority.

Karp, H.B. (1983) *A Look at Quality Circles – 1983 Annual for Facilitators, Trainers and Consultants*, Baltimore: University Associates.

Mead, C. (1991) *A City-Wide Evaluation of PSG Training*, Birmingham: Birmingham Local Education Authority.

NCC (1989) *Circular Number 5*, London: National Curriculum Council.

OFSTED (1993) *Education for Disaffected Pupils, 1990–92*, London: Department for Education.

Ritter, D.R. (1978) 'Effects of school consultation program on referral patterns of teachers', *Psychology in the Schools*, 15, 2, 239–43.

Stringer, P., Stow, L., Hibbert, K., Powell, J. and Louw, E. (1992) 'Establishing staff consultation groups in schools', *Educational Psychology in Practice*, 8, 2, 87–96.

Visser, J. and Upton, G. (1993) *Special Education in Britain after Warnock*, London: David Fulton.

Will, M. (1986) *Educating Students with Learning Problems: A Shared Responsibility*, Washington, DC: US Department of Education, Office of Special Education and Rehabilitative Services.

# 13 Providing support in the special school

*Rob Ashdown*

## Why consider stress management?

It may be asked whether there is a need for any school to develop a highly-organised approach to stress management. There are probably a variety of reasons why many schools do not have specific stress reduction programmes and support systems: for instance, some people might have found that the informal support given by colleagues has been sufficient in the past; others may not accept that the levels of stress are so very great; others may cope with the pressures so well themselves that they cannot recognise the need, and others may not wish to admit that they are suffering from stress, perhaps out of fear that they will be perceived to be weak or incompetent. Certainly, there have always been pressures inherent in teaching in special schools, but it will be argued here that they now significantly outweigh the ability of individual staff members to cope with them. Too often, the result can be that staff experience severe stress, and either become incapable of doing their job well, or become sick, or leave their job as a means of self-preservation. The human cost can be high, and there can be major disruption to the education of pupils, not to mention the crippling financial costs to schools of covering long-term absences through sickness brought on by stress. For these reasons, approaches to stress management must be given serious consideration.

Of course, schools do have in place strategies which can help to alleviate pressures. There is normally a pastoral aspect to a school's policy on staff development and opportunities for in-service training (INSET). Also, each school will have its particular mechanisms for consultation with staff about issues which cause concern. The school development plan has a critical importance too. In fact, one of the supposed advantages of the development plan is that it can help to relieve the stress on staff caused by the pace of change; staff come to exercise greater control over change, rather than feeling controlled by it (Hargreaves et al., 1989). A school development plan should address the issues which are creating pressures, including inadequate levels of staffing, staff development, school organisation, curriculum development, resources development, and so on. The result should be the identification of specific objectives and strategies and resources, including relevant INSET, needed to achieve them. Therefore, it is probably the case that the development of systematic approaches to stress reduction will largely capitalise on existing strategies, rather than demanding radical changes in school organisation. The emphasis of any stress reduction programme is likely to be on raising consciousness about the nature of stress and its causes, and identifying ways in which staff can support one another most appropriately.

In this context, it is worth noting the economic and political context which contributes to the creation of pressures in schools. Pupils in special schools require expensive specialist equipment and materials as well as trained staff with appropriate skills and knowledge. The need for these physical and human resources is increasing due to the development of a pupil population with more complex learning difficulties in special schools at the very time when central government is seeking to channel money away from special schools into ordinary schools, to meet special educational needs in the mainstream. Thus, there are no absolute guarantees about the adequacy of future funding and central support for staff development programmes for special schools. Unfortunately, there is no mandatory qualification required for working in many special schools in England and Wales, and there is a looming prospect of a lack of suitably-trained staff with the demise of specialised initial training and reduced opportunities for in-service training courses (Miller and Porter, 1994). There are many models for school-based induction courses and well-organised INSET (see, for example, Gadsby, 1991), but individual schools cannot provide effective specialist training without some external support from the institutions and organisations which have a responsibility for the training of staff. The staff of special schools need to campaign systematically to secure better training opportunities and better resources as part of the proper entitlement of their pupils. To achieve this end, they will have to involve parents, governors and advocacy groups, who have proved in the past that they can be powerful allies and major forces for bringing about change.

# What are the pressures?

Particular pressures have always been experienced by staff in special schools. There are unusual pressures involved in the day-to-day teaching of pupils who tend to have very complex learning difficulties, and often, additional physical, sensory and/or psychological disabilities. In fact, as was noted above, new pressures are being created by the fact that the proportion of such pupils in all types of special schools seems to be increasing dramatically. Although classes may be smaller than those in mainstream schools, the wide range of needs and degrees of disability in classes demand exceptional organisational skills (for guidelines, see Lacey, 1991). Designing, implementing and monitoring individualised education plans means that teachers must have in-depth knowledge of each individual pupil's needs; the conditions necessary for them to learn both in one-to-one teaching situations and groups; the relevant aspects of patterns of normal child development and learning; aspects of abnormal development; the effects of medical conditions; ways of conducting task analyses of teaching objectives; special teaching methods; special assessment techniques, and so on. Acquiring these skills and this knowledge requires good support for staff from their line managers (e.g. through mentoring and appraisal), together with an effective programme of staff induction and subsequent INSET.

Staff in special schools have to work in much closer proximity to one another than most colleagues in mainstream schools. In many classrooms in special schools, there may be two or more adults working in the same room with the same group of pupils. Team teaching can impose strains on team members, especially when staff may have different views about pupils' needs and appropriate teaching strategies. The effective use of special support assistants (SSAs) demands special skills, and teachers are not usually trained in the harmonious management of SSAs. All too often, teachers are left to learn from experience the value of taking pains to involve SSAs in designing, implementing and evaluating educational programmes as much as possible. Similarly, teachers have to be prepared to accommodate the ideas of other professionals and parents, who may have divergent views on targets and methods. These pressures may be alleviated by team-building activities, access to senior staff for guidance, and specific INSET on aspects of personnel management.

The Department for Education (as it then was) indicated that it would like all new building developments in special schools in England and Wales to conform to the guidelines on accommodation contained in a recent building bulletin (DfE, 1992). These guidelines reflect teachers' aspirations and modern educational ideas about the equipment and conditions required for teaching a pupil population with increasingly more complex learning difficulties and multiple disabilities. Unfortunately, staff in many special schools have to teach in environments which do not meet the DfE's recommendations for size of teaching spaces or specialist facilities. These inadequacies cause many problems. The need to make some physical improvements may be addressed by the managers responsible for each school using the disposable income available to the school. However, in many cases, the implementation of these new recommendations may entail a substantial input of capital and detailed development plans. With the limited funds available, the private sector-organisations and the local education authorities (LEAs) in England and Wales which are responsible for special schools are not able to implement large-scale schemes as soon as staff would like them to happen.

Pupils with complex learning difficulties can be disruptive. It is not that they *intend* to create chaos, but their learning difficulties can be such that they just do not realise the frustration they engender by being noisy, upsetting equipment, interfering with planned lessons, etc. In addition, a proportion of the pupils in every special school present severely challenging behaviours which can pose risks to other pupils and be physically and mentally exhausting for staff. Some of these pupils may require highly-specific behaviour management plans, which, in turn, require careful preparation, implementation and oversight in consultation with senior staff, external experts and parents. These issues require a co-ordinated response within each school, with an emphasis on developing planning and evaluating procedures, support systems and training for staff.

Some pupils have physical disabilities or medical conditions which cause pain and distress to them at times. Staff may not be able to prevent or ease such pain or distress. Some pupils will die prematurely, either because of the effects of the physical impairments with which they were born or because they have degenerative conditions which result in progressive deterioration of their physical health. Counselling for staff, perhaps by external experts, and preparation for the death of a pupil have to be addressed by schools.

One of the rewards of teaching is seeing pupils making progress, and knowing that this is due to your teaching. Unfortunately, for a variety of reasons, many pupils in special schools make very limited progress, and some may even regress in various ways over time. This generates a demand on staff to be inventive in devising activities which are intrinsically interesting for the pupils and which provide repeated opportunities for them to learn skills and/or experience similar activities at the same kind of level for a long time, perhaps years. Again, guidance from senior staff, subject specialists and external experts is necessary. Specific INSET is required, with an emphasis upon ideas for teaching activities, task analyses of teaching objectives, careful planning of teaching methods, and assessment methods which are sensitive to minimal progress.

Not surprisingly, staff may find themselves in the position of having to counsel distressed parents so that they can find their own solutions to the pressures of having a handicapped child in the family. The problem for most staff is that they may never have been given the opportunity to develop the skills needed for this kind of work with parents, or perhaps worse, they may not realise the limitations to what they can offer. In both cases, the outcome can create undue pressures for the staff unless there is some recognised system for supporting them by involving senior staff in schools and external agencies with special skills and resources (e.g. clinical psychologists, respite care providers, community nurses, etc.). Again, specific INSET on working with parents is helpful.

As well as these pressures, which have always been experienced by staff in special schools, there are a number of new pressures. One of these has already been mentioned: special school populations are changing, and now include a high proportion of disruptive pupils and pupils with complex learning difficulties, often with associated medical conditions. Therefore, staff have to be prepared to adapt their teaching to suit the ever-changing needs of the pupils in their assigned class. They have to be innovative and remain open to new ideas about teaching, assimilating them into current practice even when major changes are demanded. Guidance and support for senior staff and INSET must be available, with an emphasis upon new teaching methods and approaches to classroom organisation which are more appropriate to the changing population.

An entirely new set of pressures has been generated by the push for accountability of teachers that has been a feature of many central government initiatives. The introduction of the National Curriculum in England and Wales in 1988 created special problems because it was not formulated with pupils with special educational needs in mind. Even the 1995 revision of the National Curriculum has not met all of the concerns of teachers. Byers (1994) and Ashdown (1994) complain that there are still problems in ensuring meaningful access to all subjects, giving space to important personal, social and health education activities (which are not even mentioned in the statutory orders), planning a broad, balanced and relevant curriculum, and documenting pupil progress. Again, the onus is upon schools to show in their development plans what are the needs and priorities for future curriculum development, and their strategies for achieving these objectives.

Local Management of Special Schools (LMSS) has been extended to publicly-funded special schools in England and Wales. Delegated powers may have given special schools more flexibility in use of their disposable income, but LMSS has brought additional burdens, especially for administrative staff and senior teachers. With LMSS has come the need to balance the budget of the special school, and during the transitional years following the introduction of LMSS, many special schools have been forced to make staff redundant in order to meet this requirement. Staff have to recognise that nobody's job is secure any more, especially in a context of falling rolls, since fewer pupils mean less money. Such pressures mean that schools must plan carefully for the perceived changes in funding, and they must have very clear personnel policies, especially on redundancy and redeployment. Of course, private and charitable organisations involved in this field have always had to plan development in their special schools most carefully, according to the resources and income available. A major issue for these schools is convincing LEAs to buy their services. LEAs usually aim to place pupils in schools which they maintain, and a number of LEAs are seeking to develop specialist facilities and services lacking in the publicly-funded schools. Inevitably, this trend, coupled with escalating costs, has implications for the job security, work conditions and development opportunities of the staff in private special schools.

Another example of central government prescription in England and Wales is *The Code of Practice on the Identification and Assessment of Special Educational Needs* (DfE, 1994), which introduced new responsibilities regarding the preparation of educational advice by teachers for formal assessment procedures, and the conduct of annual reviews of each pupil's needs and the appropriateness of provision. Although laudable, these changes have increased further the burdens on teachers and senior staff in schools. Special schools must produce policies describing how they meet their pupils' special educational needs, and staff need specific INSET to enable them to meet their responsibilities.

The degree to which these pressures have an impact on staff in special schools depends very much on local circumstances in each school, such as falling rolls, rising rolls, experience of staff, level of staff turnover, quality of school management, strength of teaching teams, quality of external support, and so on. A critical element is the amount of time and human resources which schools can make available to investigate and find their own solutions to these various issues. Headteachers have to be prepared to 'hustle' to get whatever additional support they can from external sources to support new developments. They have to consult with staff and plan most carefully with the responsible authorities to produce a budget which makes allowance for this kind of activity. Headteachers of private special schools have always had to do this, and it is increasingly necessary for headteachers of publicly-funded schools to follow suit, due to the steady dwindling of the funding which is available through grants to LEAs from central government for specific developments.

# Coping strategies

One of the better sources for ideas on coping strategies is Dunham's (1992) book, which contains much anecdotal information from teachers, mainly from mainstream schools and colleges, about the strategies which they adopt to counter perceived pressures. This material is largely collated from verbal and written reports which teachers made for courses on stress management run by Dunham. His book must be recommended reading for anybody concerned with developing stress reduction programmes for staff.

Dunham defines 'coping strategies' as the means by which we change a situation which is stressful. We can do this by altering the nature of the situation itself and/or our perceptions of it. Also, when the pressures begin to outweigh our normal coping strategies, we find other ways of dealing with our thoughts, sensations, emotions and bodily reactions. Stress occurs when the pressures are so great that the coping strategies begin to fail, and an important approach to the management of stress is to plan ways of supporting one another, so that our existing coping strategies may be enhanced or new ones developed. Dunham's book is full of examples of the wide range of skills, techniques, knowledge, experience, relationships, thoughts and activities which teachers draw on as resources for coping. He classifies these as personal, interpersonal, community and organisational resources:

- 'Personal resources' are the individual's own attitudes and methods for coming to terms with stressful situations, including their idiosyncratic ways of using out-of-school activities to reduce feelings of tension, anger and agitation.
- 'Interpersonal resources' are spouses, partners and friends who are unconnected with school.
- 'Community resources' are the various activities which can have an importance beyond mere relaxation or pleasure. They can enable individuals to assume lifestyles which are entirely different from those which have to be followed in their professional life.
- 'Organisational resources' come from colleagues in school with whom they are able to discuss their problems, worries and feelings. They also include supportive senior management teams, appropriate INSET and induction courses, and help from external advisers or consultants.

Significantly, Dunham notes that the reports from teachers on his courses mention the use of organisational resources considerably less than use of other resources. When they do, references to good relationships with colleagues are more likely to be described as a positive factor than anything else. The overall impression from Dunham's book is that not enough is done by schools and the responsible authorities to develop stress management programmes, and far too much reliance is placed upon individuals or small groups of staff to develop their own informal networks for support. Colleagues may be able to provide sympathy and understanding, but what is required is a more positive approach from schools and their LEAs or organisations to ensure that appropriate professional support is available.

# What can individuals do to control stress?

In his book, Dunham identifies six ground rules for learning how to reduce stress:

1   Accept the possibility of the existence of stress in your colleagues and yourself.
2   Learn to understand what stress is.
3   Begin to tackle the problems by identifying the pressures from change, role conflict, poor working conditions and pupil behaviour in your school.
4   Learn to recognise your reactions to pressure, for example, in your behaviour and relationships, emotions, thinking and the reactions in your body.
5   Identify your coping strategies at work and outside work.
6   Develop stress-reduction training programmes at the individual department/pastoral team/whole-school levels which will enable you to develop a wide range of personal, interpersonal, organisational and community resources which you can use to deal with your pressures and reactions. (Dunham, 1992, p.123)

There has already been much emphasis in this chapter on schools making their own plans to provide specific INSET opportunities. The school's staff development programme should be flexible enough to offer the opportunity to individuals or groups of staff to identify these issues and secure appropriate INSET. People should have opportunities to learn to recognise stress. Some staff may be 'workaholics' or have unrealistic expectations about their capabilities, and they particularly need to learn to control what amounts to self-induced stress. They have to learn to examine and modify their attitudes to work, to adopt strategies for time management and make changes in their lifestyle that allow time for personal space, relaxation, hobbies and enjoyable experiences unconnected with school life. Dunham (1992) describes various types of stress reduction packages involving relaxation exercises, meditation, physical exercise, massage and so on, which could benefit individuals. Of course, the popular psychology section of any good book shop or library is likely to have a number of books on stress management which will contribute their own ideas (e.g. Burnard, 1991). INSET opportunities should also allow staff to develop what Honey (1988) calls 'people skills' – a broad spectrum of behaviour that can help establish and maintain good professional relationships. Other legitimate topics for INSET would be time management and assertiveness training. In discussions in each school, it should be mooted whether participation in these INSET experiences should be voluntary, but they should be open to all, since they could lead to individual staff or groups of interested staff developing effective personal and interpersonal resources.

# The pressures on staff with specific responsibilities

The demands which are made on schools have made it necessary for head-teachers to delegate certain management responsibilities to other teachers. Many teachers have 'co-ordinator' roles (e.g. child protection co-ordinator, subject co-ordinator, whole-school curriculum co-ordinator and staff development co-ordinator), and the task of bringing about changes in whole-school practices is often given to these co-ordinators. In this context, it is important to consider how headteachers can plan to minimise the pressures on staff who are expected to introduce some innovation in a school. Changing established practices in a complex organisation like a school involves far more than merely identifying a 'change agent' (e.g. a newly-appointed staff member with appropriate qualifications, or an existing member who has been given appropriate training) and then sending him or her out with a mission to fire everyone else in school with enthusiasm for the change. In an instructive article, Georgiades and Phillimore (1985) dismiss as disingenuous the idea that this type of approach will succeed in bringing about desired changes. They call this view the 'myth of the hero-innovator'. The fact of the matter is that organisations such as schools will rapidly destroy hero-innovators. The change agent is far more likely to encounter inertia, hostility and apathy instead of co-operation, and such experiences are likely to induce a sense of pessimism, isolation and failure.

Teachers with special responsibilities must not be put in an untenable position. What is required is thorough planning by the headteacher in conjunction with the change agent. There must be a realistic timescale for achieving changes, because an understandable desire for haste to meet legal or other requirements may produce support for the changes which is at best half-hearted and grudging. The headteacher must choose carefully how to deploy the limited economic and human resources which are available to maximise the impact. Also, it will be necessary to have ways of maintaining morale among the change agents if they come up against problems. Georgiades and Phillimore (1985) recommend six guidelines for planners of change who wish to establish a supportive culture for achieving changes. These are summarised here, as follows:

1 Work with the forces within school which are supportive of change, rather than working against those who are defensive and resistant to change.
2 Develop a 'critical mass' for each change project using self-sustaining teams, and never allow individual change agents to be isolated.
3 Work with the people or groups who have the will and personal resources to improve, and avoid being pressured into working with

people or groups who are barely able to cope with the existing situation, let alone the increased demands that the initial introduction of changes will bring.

4    Work with individuals and groups who have as much freedom and discretion in managing their own operations and resources as possible.

5    Try to obtain appropriate and realistic involvement by key staff.

6    Make arrangements for the agents of change to work in small groups or pairs for mutual learning and support, and provide frequent opportunities for them to meet and discuss their own anxieties and doubts about the kind of work they are doing.

This set of rules highlights the importance of developing teams which will bring about changes – for example, a specific class team to achieve changes in a particular part of a school, or a team of teachers with responsibility for specific aspects of curriculum development. Staff should not be left to work in isolation in stressful circumstances unless they are highly experienced. Also, the above rules stress the importance of working initially with the people within school who would be supportive of change. Ultimately, the headteacher will have to address the difficult problem of bringing into line those people who are weak or ineffective, or who are defensive and resistant to change. However, these are not the people on whom to waste energies unduly when setting up the momentum for change.

# Developing a supportive culture

The ultimate aim must be to develop a supportive culture within the school, where stress is not seen as a reflection of personal weakness, and people are encouraged to support colleagues and to talk about their feelings and the effects of stress. Little things help, like organising out-of-school activities for staff which provide opportunities to socialise, giving 'perks' like free school lunches for performing specific duties, sending cards or flowers to staff when they are ill, providing non-contact time to develop aspects of the curriculum, and so on.

Team-building activities and giving opportunities for staff to meet and plan together as teams are essential. However, there is still a need for a recognisable support system whereby individual staff can discuss concerns with other staff. This should allow for frank discussion, but there must be complete confidentiality. Some kind of staff-pairing could be helpful, where individual staff are linked formally with somebody in a similar position rather than with a line manager.

In addition, teacher appraisal could come to play a significant role, if schools are prepared to extend it to other staff groups and to put sufficient resources into the process using the school's own disposable income. In addition, regular meetings between line managers and individual staff members should occur, probably with associated observations of the classroom conditions by the line manager. The result of meetings with line managers should be that aspects of the staff member's work have been discussed (in relation to a clear job description), and that there is agreement about the evaluation, the objectives which must be achieved by the next review, and the INSET and resources which should be made available to enable the person to achieve them.

Guidelines for managers and teachers about strategies for managing occupational stress have been prepared by the Education Service Advisory Committee of the Health and Safety Commission (Health and Safety Executive, 1990). Of course, LEAs and the various private and/or charitable organisations maintaining special schools may have their own guidance for staff in schools, or identifiable sources for expert advice. In addition, the ground rules for stress reduction given by Dunham (1992), cited above, provide a convenient framework for a school-based approach to developing a positive stress-management programme.

Dunham suggests that the starting point might be a whole-school training day. There would have to be a great deal of preparation and planning for the training day, beginning several months beforehand. For instance, a working party of representative staff might identify, perhaps by questionnaire or interview, the pressures that staff are experiencing, how they are reacting to them, and the areas of concern for discussion. This would provide the information for the group to decide objectives and activities for the day. Important objectives must be that the training day should facilitate the subsequent development of stress-reduction policies in school, and that there are follow-up checks to evaluate progress towards identified objectives. The training day could also lead to the formation of further working groups of staff who are briefed to examine particular issues and produce guidelines for dissemination to all staff. Setting up this kind of programme demands a high level of commitment from staff at all levels, since it will inevitably bring into the open all sorts of problems which may never have been publicly voiced before. The training day itself will require careful management by the main facilitator in order to establish ground rules for discussion and to guide activities effectively. This person might be an external consultant rather than a member of senior staff in the school, but he or she must be made aware of any school-centred issues which have a bearing (e.g. many pressures may stem from non-negotiable aspects of the job, or senior staff may be trying to bring about particular improvements).

# Care and control issues

In England and Wales, national concern about instances of child abuse and inappropriate childcare practices have led to the development of formal child protection procedures and the 1989 Children Act enshrines the rights of children as individuals to proper treatment by adults. Also, as noted above, special schools are experiencing an increase in disruptive pupils, who may require external controls by staff, and increasingly disabled children, with whom staff must have physical contact to carry out care procedures and teaching. These developments have combined to create intense pressure to examine school policies and procedures for the care and control of pupils.

Pupils in special schools are not unique in presenting severely challenging behaviours. However, there is a correlation between the increasing severity of learning difficulties found in special schools and the prevalence, duration and intensity of challenging behaviours (Clements, 1987). The nature of these challenging behaviours is well documented (see, for example, Harris et al., 1993).

Working with pupils who behave in these kinds of ways can evoke a wide range of emotional responses, such as pity, hate, anger and despair. Teaching is not easy, progress is slow, and the skills of staff are tested at every step of the process in their dealings with pupils and with their families. Staff have to learn and use a variety of sophisticated teaching skills: they have to be able to analyse the conditions which have helped to establish and maintain challenging behaviours in the case of each individual; they have to be prepared to make alterations to aspects of classroom settings if such an analysis suggests that environmental changes may be required, and they have to be committed to careful analyses of the demands made on pupils, designing sophisticated interventions, ensuring consistency of approach and keeping systematic records at all steps.

To complicate matters, different adults will have their own idiosyncratic responses to the same set of problems, and these differences in interpretation of the meaning and management of challenging behaviour can exacerbate the problems if they are not settled. Crucially, there must be agreement on the details of any behaviour management plan, especially one which involves complex and controversial procedures. There is a requirement for a team effort, where everyone responds in the same way, giving a consistent message to the pupil, and the plan must have the full consent and support of parents and line managers.

There are major issues here which each school must address, but few schools seem to do so in a systematic way (Harris et al., 1993). Behaviour management plans need adequate staffing levels, and schools should have an agreed system for working out management plans, keeping records and reviewing plans regularly. Staff require much INSET and support to assimi-late these new ideas and to seek to apply them. Senior staff must be prepared to seek out information so that they can make adequate plans to develop policies and strategies. Fortunately, effective models for policies, procedures and approaches to staff development are available (e.g. Zarkowska and Clements, 1994).

Staff are regularly placed in positions where physical restraint is required, and the teachers' unions have expressed concerns that this exposes staff to potential allegations of abuse. The staff of schools in England and Wales and the responsible authorities must consider the implications of the Joint Department for Education/Department of Health circular, *The Education of Children with Emotional and Behavioural Difficulties*, which has a section on con-trol, restrictions and sanctions (DfE/DoH, 1994, paras 108–17) and the 1989 Children Act. Lyon (1994) has produced a guide for parents and carers about the legal issues arising from the care and control of pupils with learning dis-abilities who also present challenging behaviour. This provides an explana-tion of the law in England and Wales, and how professionals working within the legal system might interpret and react to complaints about individual staff or school practices. It describes the lawful excuses that schools may have if ever they are required to justify school policies and management plans. Lyon also points out that the cardinal principle from the 1989 Children Act is that courts must determine any question with respect to the upbring-ing of a child by treating the child's welfare as the paramount consideration. Therefore, at every stage and in every situation, school staff should be able to show that what they have done has been done in the interests of the pupil. Lyon states that this principle means that steps should always be taken to minimise the possible onset of challenging behaviour in the first instance. When severely challenging behaviour manifests itself, the principle dictates that all possible responses must be considered, and that the least restrictive and detrimental alternative should be employed. Even then, this method of control should be used for the shortest possible time.

Care and medical procedures create a need for close physical contact between staff and children in caring for pupils with physical, sensory or learning disabilities. Therefore, for the sake of both pupils and staff, clear guidelines are required on the administration of invasive medication and care (e.g. the administration of rectal valium, tube feeding, catheterisation, stoma management, etc.) and the conduct of some aspects of personal hygiene programmes (e.g. dressing, bathing and cleaning of adult-depen-dent pupils, and teaching independent toileting, bathing or showering pro-grammes). Physical contact may be a feature of communication development work and other basic-skills teaching. Similarly, there should be policies on the conduct of physiotherapy, massage, hydrotherapy, aromatherapy and other programmes involving close physical contact. Some aspects of health and sex education require policies based on a consensus of staff, parents and responsible authorities. The fear of unfounded allegations should never deter proper physical contact, but schools have to ensure that staff follow agreed procedures and that policies are communicated to pupils, parents and others as appropriate. It may be necessary to develop individualised care and education plans in consultation with staff, parents, pupils and other key people.

## Concluding remarks

Tilstone (1991) argues that central government and society have a responsibility for the morale of staff, who want better salaries and better resources, together with recognition of their value as professionals rather than mere employees. The policies and procedures of LEAs and private sector organisations can also do much to improve staff morale. At the school level, the headteacher can have a pivotal role in alleviating pressures. Headteachers must have a sympathetic understanding of the pressures faced by their staff, have ideas about ways of managing these, and must direct resources where they are most needed. Baker (1990) argues that headteachers all too often remain passive in the face of the changes which occur, and that when they respond, they do so in ways which are reactive rather than proactive. He believes that they have the power to be the architects of change rather than the victims of events. However, this is not to argue that the headteacher holds the solution to everybody's problems. Headteachers are fallible humans too, and may not receive sufficient INSET and support themselves. Also, there are inescapable pressures in special education which render it unrealistic to expect that the solution lies simply in channelling more resources (or INSET) in their direction.

Thus, staff must be encouraged to recognise that the responsibility for finding solutions does not lie solely in the hands of others. Staff have ownership of these problems too, and should accept some responsibility for doing something about them. Stress management programmes in schools should involve counselling staff to help them to find solutions which suit them and enable them to do a difficult job to the best of their ability. The staff of a school have the potential to be their own greatest resource for coping with stress, and it is in everyone's interest that they are given the opportunity to devote sufficient thought and time to this process.

## References

Ashdown, R. (1994) 'Planning for their future', *British Journal of Special Education*, 3, 110–12.

Baker, D. (1990) 'Headteacher: Architect of change or victim of events', in Baker, D. and Bovair, K. (eds) *Making the Special Schools Ordinary?*, Vol.1, London: Falmer Press.

Burnard, P. (1991) *Coping with Stress in the Health Professions: A Practical Guide*, London: Chapman and Hall.

Byers, R. (1994) 'The Dearing Review of the National Curriculum', *British Journal of Special Education*, 3, 92–6.

Clements, J. (1987) *Severe Learning Disability and Psychological Handicap*, Chichester: John Wiley.

DfE (1992) *Designing for Pupils with Special Educational Needs: Special Schools*, Architects and Buildings Branch, Building Bulletin 77, London: HMSO.

DfE (1994) *The Code of Practice on the Identification and Assessment of Special Educational Needs*, London: HMSO.

DfE/DoH (1994) *The Education of Children with Emotional and Behavioural Difficulties*, DfE Circular No.9/94, London: Department for Education.

Dunham, J. (1992) *Stress in Teaching* (2nd edn), London: Routledge.

Gadsby, A. (1991) 'Training for change: School-based INSET', in Ashdown, R., Carpenter, B. and Bovair, K. (eds) *The Curriculum Challenge: Access to the National Curriculum for Pupils with Learning Difficulties*, London: Falmer Press.

Georgiades, N. and Phillimore, L. (1985) 'The myth of the hero-innovator and alternative strategies for organisational change', in Kiernan, C. and Woodford, P. (eds) *Behaviour Modification with the Severely Retarded*, Amsterdam: Associated Scientific Publishers and the Institute for Research into Multiple and Mental Handicap.

Hargreaves, D., Hopkins, D., Leask, M., Connolly, J. and Robinson, P. (1989) *Planning for School Development: Advice to Governors, Headteachers and Teachers*, London: HMSO.

Harris, J., Cook, M. and Upton, G. (1993) 'Challenging behaviour in the classroom', in Harris, J. (ed.) *Innovations in Educating Children with Severe Learning Difficulties*, Chorley: Lisieux Hall Publications.

Health and Safety Executive (1990) *Managing Occupational Stress: A Guide for Managers and Teachers in the School Sector*, London: HMSO.

Honey, P. (1988) *Improve Your People Skills*, Wimbledon: Institute of Personnel Management.

Lacey, P. (1991) 'Managing the classroom environment', in Tilstone, C. (ed.) *Teaching Pupils with Severe Learning Difficulties: Practical Approaches*, London: David Fulton.

Lyon, C. (1994) *Legal Issues Arising from the Care and Control of Children with Learning Disabilities Who Also Present Severe Challenging Behaviour: A Guide For Parents and Carers*, London: The Mental Health Foundation.

Miller, O. and Porter, J. (1994) 'Teacher training: Settling the bill', *British Journal of Special Education*, 1, 7–8.

Tilstone, C. (1991) 'The class teacher and stress', in Tilstone, C. (ed.) *Teaching Pupils with Severe Learning Difficulties: Practical Approaches*, London: David Fulton.

Zarkowska, E. and Clements, J. (1994) *Problem Behaviour and People with Severe Learning Disabilities* (2nd edn), London: Chapman and Hall.

# Index